A
Questionable
Life

A
Questionable
Life

{ Luke Lively }

BEAUFORT
BOOKS

Library of Congress Cataloging-in-Publication Data

Lively, Luke.
A questionable life / Luke Lively.
p. cm.
ISBN 978-0-8253-0521-4 (hardcover : alk. paper) 1. Success in business.
2. Family. 3. Fables. I. Title.
HF5386.L752 2009
650.1--dc22
2009013504

Published in the United States by Beaufort Books, New York
www.beaufortbooks.com

Distributed by Midpoint Trade Books
www.midpointtrade.com

Dedicated to my mother, Wanda June Lively

ACKNOWLEDGMENTS

I want to thank my family (Teresa, Sarah, Bailey, Derek, Faith, Samuel Luke, Joe, Brandon) for their support and encouragement in this project. I also extend my gratitude to Teresa Cvetnich and Jim Ley for their super motivation. A major thanks to Trish Hoard and Sarah Vanover, two excellent editors. For believing in this book, I appreciate the trust and friendship offered by Eric, Margot, and Erin at Beaufort. And, for inspiring me through the years, the many people I have worked with and shared part of my life. Everything happens for a reason—and you played a part in making this dream a reality. Thank you!

{ Contents }

A
Questionable
Life

{
You'll be remembered
for what you gave
in life—not what
you took.
}

— BENJAMIN FRANKLIN PRICE

PROLOGUE:

How Will I Be Remembered?

"HOW WILL I BE REMEMBERED?"

I repeated the question silently to refocus my thoughts. The question, just like the surroundings, made me uncomfortable. I did not like cemeteries.

To ease my anxiety, I thought back to the first time I was asked that question. It was a little over two years ago. I was deep in the Blue Ridge Mountains of Virginia hiking with a man I barely knew. We were taking a break from our ascent of a rugged mountain. I was sitting on a massive rock perilously close to the edge of a steep cliff. Peering down from my seat atop the boulder, through a veil of rising fog, I could see a river rushing through jagged rocks, creating a torrent of white water hundreds of feet below. Since I am afraid of heights, my bird's-eye view of the gorge was more unsettling than awe inspiring. I could have never been mistaken for an outdoorsman—I had rarely ventured out of Philadelphia. It was my first real hike. The climb up the severe slope of the mountain had practically drained me of my already limited supply of energy. And if struggling with the unnatural conditions was not enough, I felt that the question the hiker asked was intrusive.

"What do you want to be remembered for, Jack?"

"I want to be remembered for living a successful life," I responded.

{A QUESTIONABLE LIFE}   I

I had met Benny Price only two days before the nature trek. At the time I didn't realize it, but this was one of many questions he would ask that helped to change my life.

"Well, what makes a person successful?" he asked.

I paused and thought about my definition of success. That should be easy to answer. In virtually every way the world measures success I was successful. At forty-five years old, my resume reflected a career chock-full of achievements worthy of someone twenty years my senior. I had reached some lofty career goals at a very early age practicing a fanatical work ethic. While I climbed the ladder of success, I had received minimal support from others. I did it on my own. I made mistakes, but who doesn't in the pursuit of their desires? To quote Frank Sinatra, "I did it my way." Wanting to hum the melody and feeling a deep self-appreciation for all of my ladder-climbing accomplishments, I responded, "I would define a successful person as someone who has attained all of their goals."

"*All* of their goals?" Benny asked without a pause.

"Yes, all of them. Otherwise the person would've failed," I answered without thinking.

"Have you reached all of your goals, Jack?" he asked, personalizing the question.

I almost laughed out loud. I had virtually everything I had coveted. To almost any objective onlooker, I appeared to have it all. But as I started to answer the senior backpacker's query, my usual state of supreme confidence was somehow shaken. I was sensing the pangs of self-doubt—something was still missing from my record of accomplishments. Smiling, I answered, "No, I haven't achieved all of my goals—yet."

"So that would make you a failure."

This angered me. How could a near-stranger imply I was a failure? I leaned forward and swatted a gnat from in front of my face trying to disguise my irritation. In that pause I realized I had defined myself as a failure in my response. Wanting to understand my inner conflict, I asked myself, *What's missing when I have it all?* The answer hit me as hard as the rock I was perched on. I wasn't satisfied; I didn't have it all.

I wanted more. More money, more power, and more prestige.

How could I be a success when there was so much more I coveted and could achieve and acquire? Until I literally had it all, I would feel like I was a failure, something I was not ready to admit to Benny or anyone else.

"No, I'm not a failure," I said sharply, sitting straight up on the uneven surface of the boulder to reinforce my retort. "I've achieved a lot in my life. You've seen my resume."

"But you can't post your resume on a tombstone," he said, allowing a smile as he turned away to look down into the deep gorge. "When will *you* believe you're successful?"

In my thoughts I could see my tombstone emblazoned with the words SUCCESSFUL FAILURE, with tattered pages of my resume posted on it. The thought was comical, a grave marker for the humor section of *Reader's Digest,* but that was how I honestly felt. Sneaking a glance, I was glad to see his attention was turned away from me toward the gorge. There was no way I could hide the internal turmoil etched on my face. Still struggling after realizing I was a failure, I countered with a conclusive tone to end the cross-examination. "I'm still working on getting everything I want out of life. You'll be the first to know when I do."

What the old guy was ignoring was the life behind my impressive resume. Or maybe he did see. I'd dedicated my life to the inflexible pursuit of success by any means. To keep focused on my ruthless quest, I had placed blinders on my thoughts, beliefs, and feelings. My tsunami of cravings didn't require a conscience, only direction. Just like the churning white water in the river far below, the rapid current of the life I had created released waves of want that rolled over any impediments that stood in the way, drowning anyone not prepared to try my course. The only place safe for others in my life was behind me. Otherwise, they would be washed away. I had one speed and direction—full greed ahead!

But were any of my self-gratifying, greed-induced accomplishments worthy enough to be affectionately recalled? While I did not like it, the answer was clear. Despite all of my efforts, I had failed to achieve anything worth remembering.

As I waited to see if his interrogation had finally ended, I realized that being memorable had not been something I sought in life. That would be up to the opinion of others, which meant nothing to me. I was more concerned about my welfare, not what anyone else thought of my actions. The gift of life was a pursuit of wealth I didn't have to share. It was a choice I had made many years earlier.

Breaking the brief silence Benny looked at me and said with sincere concern, "Jack, be careful what you want—you just might get it."

• • •

How do I want to be remembered? Over two years had passed since that hike, but the question remained open, awaiting an honest response. I was now standing under the cover of a cold, gray Virginia sky, preparing to finally answer the hiker's question—knowing he would not hear my reply. As I bowed my head removing his casket from my line of sight, I recalled what he said to me in our final few moments together. "You'll be remembered for what you gave in life—not what you took."

I slowly raised my head to see the wooden box holding his remains. I understood how his guidance and friendship had changed me. My answer bore little resemblance to my earlier reply. *I want to be remembered for the way I am now, not the way I was.*

It is possible to change for the better, I thought, glancing up into the gloomy sky. I'm living proof. If Jack Oliver can change, anyone can.

But could others see how I had changed? Benjamin Franklin Price would no longer bear witness to the dramatic change. Only a few standing in the crowd knew the old me. So, while they could attest to my transformation, the people I loved, my family, were far away, unwilling to see the remarkable changes I had made in my life. I had to accept that their memories of me would never change. I had taken too long.

As I returned my gaze toward Benny's casket, another question came to mind.

1. How Did I Get Here?

"How did I get here?"

The graveside rites had commenced. In a few moments, I would eulogize my best friend. Our time together had been relatively brief, but time was not important. He had saved my life.

As I stood in the light drizzle and chill of the March morning with over three hundred of his family and friends huddled closely around the grave site, I recalled a gift he had given to me. The gift was something he created, making it all the more valuable, especially now that he was gone. At first glance it did not look like anything special—a few printed words and a photo tucked into a wooden frame. You can buy something similar at card shops. But his gift had a special purpose. The words are printed in green ink on a pale parchment background surrounded by a dark olive border. The green text appears to grow out of the paper like early spring grass fighting to survive. The small size of the print requires you to look closely, echoing the way he had reminded me to look at all words. I am sure he intended it that way.

Above the text is a photo he took of a sunrise ascending above the fog-covered mountains of southwest Virginia. You can almost feel the rays of the new dawn's light touching your face as the thick mist slowly rises and fades into the brightening sun. The gift sits on my desk occupying an exclusive place by several pictures of my children. The grouping of photos and Benny's gift serve as a reminder of why I am here.

"You're here not by chance but by God's choosing," begins the text. He especially loved the title, "Just Think." I had heard him use that phrase to open many a sentence in our conversations over the past two years. "Just think" wasn't just a habitual expression. He meant it. I recalled what he said when he gave me the gift.

"Just think, Jack, the first step in making us who we are is a thought," he said, his eyes twinkling while the right corner of his lip curled slightly upward into a half-smile. "We know the difference between right thoughts and wrong thoughts. It doesn't take a genius—just being honest with the person who looks back at you from the mirror."

The man in the mirror I saw this morning had changed. However, at this moment, looking at his casket poised above the grave, my thoughts were scattered. They did not feel right or wrong. The last time I saw him was at his cabin ten days ago. Now he was gone. I missed him.

The light rain continued to fall through the leafless trees, hitting the rugged mountain soil, and provided a calming, natural melody for all of us gathered in the cemetery. My mind swirled with the memories of the many life experiences he had shared with me. Turning the complex to simple was his gift.

"Thinking should be a simple process, but we create complexity in our thoughts, confusing how we see the world around us. Our imagination distorts our vision. What we see isn't real, but an image of what we *think* we see. The result is that we tell the most harmful lie we can ever tell—a lie to ourselves," Benny said.

I had always thought complexity was the way to go in life. I never wanted to be accused of being simple minded. I believed thinking was a private matter, not something to be openly discussed with others. I had asked him, "Isn't what you say or do more important than what you think?"

"What determines your words and deeds, Jack? Your thoughts! The quality of your thoughts determines the quality of your life. What you think changes the world," he responded. "Think confused, live confused."

A shift in the wind blew the light drizzle into my face, bringing me back to the service. The sky continued to darken, lowering a forbidding gray shroud over the Virginia hilltop. The sadness was almost unbearable. With my head bowed and eyes shut as the minister began to speak, I could not imagine how I would fill the void Benny's death had created. I recalled him questioning me about life and death the last time I saw him alive.

"Death shouldn't be a surprise—it's inevitable. Death is a natural part of life. Why should we fear it?"

"Because what happens after we die is unknown," I responded.

"Why fear the unknown? Life is change, and what happens to us from one second to the next is unknown. If you're afraid of the unknown you're afraid to live. Death is a known step in our life—it's part of the process of living." He sat upright—relaxed—speaking in a voice void of any anxiety. Despite the ravages of a disease that allowed no survivors, Benny did not appear to be a person resigned to the inevitable.

"We don't get a second chance with death," I said, unable to hide my fear of the unknown. "It's conclusive, and that's frightening to me."

"Nothing happens by chance. Don't be frightened, Jack. Death is not an end, but a beginning."

"I wish I was brave enough to think like that," I said.

"It doesn't take courage to die—it takes courage to live. Every second is a new beginning, even when it's your last. I know I'm nearing the finish line," he said smiling.

"You're going to be okay," I said, attempting to reassure myself as much as him.

"Death can be our greatest teacher if we accept life is impermanent."

"What can you learn from dying?" I asked, puzzled at the idea.

"You learn the value of life! Value every moment as if it were your last, Jack. Then you won't be afraid of dying—you'll live a fearless life with no regrets."

My attention turned back to the graveside as I heard the minister say, "He lived a courageous life." As he read a summary of the many contributions my friend had made to the world, I suddenly grasped where Benny's resolve to live so effectively came from—it was in the discipline of his thoughts. While I had contemplated some of the great philosophic questions like *Who am I?* and *What is my purpose?* on rare occasions in brief moments of self-doubt, he had *lived* those questions moment by moment, day to day, seeking the answers. He had the courage to question his life and live responsibly without fear. Questioning your life demanded courage.

The more I recalled our time together I realized almost every memory I had of Benny involved a question. "Questions are more important than answers. How can you find answers if you don't ask questions? Ask the right questions, and you'll discover the right answers. *Questions lead!*"

A life built on questions wouldn't have made sense to me two years ago. He called this practice of self-interrogation the integral part of his "questionable life."

"I'm the first person who should question my life," he said. "My life is my life. What I think, say, or do is my responsibility. How will I know if I'm on the right path unless I constantly and honestly question my life?"

I felt the chill of the northwesterly breeze filtering up the steep hill over monuments and grave markers as the minister read, "Lord, make me an instrument of your peace." The prayer by Saint Francis of Assisi was one of Benny's favorite readings. Hearing the words *love, pardon, faith, hope, light,* and *joy* reminded me of how I had changed. "*For it is in the giving that we receive*" the minister read. The sins of my past still haunted me. For most of my life I had been guided by asking, *What can I take?* when I should have asked, *What can I give?*

Benny's questions had redirected my own questionable life. But I had regrets for the many wasted years. I wondered if I could ever overcome my guilt for all those misguided years of my past.

I could hear Benny saying to me, "Everything in life has a reason and a purpose. Living isn't a game of chance. Your life is yours to live, not wager."

I had gambled with my life and nearly lost it. By telling me his life experiences, Benny had enlightened me. And learning had been painful. Being disciplined by the things life throws at you was not what I would have chosen as a method of learning.

"Pain teaches," Benny had said in that initial hike in what now felt like a lifetime ago. He was right—I had to learn the hard way. *But that's life,* I thought as I heard the minister nearing the conclusion of his remarks.

My mind was in the past. Struggling to stay in the present, I took a deep breath, and as I slowly exhaled I remembered what he had said about the delicate balance between intention and attention.

"The learning is in the journey. If you focus on what you want, you'll miss what you have. The here and now is where we live. Live for the journey not the destination."

The minister concluded with a brief prayer. My heart was pounding. I took another deep breath and looked down at the notes I had written on an index card. As I lifted my head at the end of the prayer, I looked at Benny's wife, Ann. She smiled a warm, half-smile. I looked to her side and saw our friend, John Helms. He made eye contact, nodding his head as if to say, "I'm here with you, Jack."

How did I get here? again leapt from the whirlwind of my thoughts. Every ending is a new beginning, Benny had said. I immediately felt at peace in the moment. This wasn't an end, but a beginning. This moment was "to be." It wasn't by chance—there was a purpose. I had been led here to find the real me. With the help of others I had changed.

The musical director stepped forward a few feet away from me. I would speak afterward. As she sang the words "On a hill faraway," my thoughts returned to what had brought me here.

My quest had been launched with a simple question—a question that had changed my life.

2. What Should I Do?

"WHAT SHOULD I DO?" I asked my friend John Helms.

It was a question I rarely asked—I always knew what to do. I had a plan. But this was different. Things had changed. My life was in turmoil.

For the past year I had struggled working for a new employer, Merchants Bank. Merchants, one of the largest banks in the country, had acquired my previous employer, Philadelphia Trust and Guaranty (or PT&G as everyone referred to it in Philly). I had been a dedicated employee for twenty-seven years at PT&G and had risen from an entry-level job to the second-highest position in the bank. The acquisition of Philly's largest bank and one of the oldest banks in the country by a bank with headquarters in Charlotte, North Carolina, was unexpected—so was the aftermath. John had called to try to help me.

"Jack, I know you're miserable. I can hear it in your voice. Do you want a change?" he asked.

John was one of the few people in my life I trusted. I had met him at Wharton, one of the top business schools, where we were both pursuing MBAs. He stood out from the crowd. As a self-acknowledged redneck from the Deep South, he "came up North to learn like a Yankee" as he was fond of saying. His thick southern accent cultivated in his hometown of Little Rock had gained him instant notoriety. At first semiridiculed for his slow, deliberate enunciation of words, he quickly gained everyone's respect with his remarkable intellect. He was as close to a genius as anyone I had ever met. To help his cause, he looked like John F. Kennedy Jr.

"Yes, I would like a change," I said. "But a good change—not just any change."

"Well, Jack ole boy, opportunity is knockin' on your door," he said. "You'll thank me for playing employment consultant someday. I know all about Merchants Bank and what you're goin' through."

"Yeah, right!" I said laughing. "You're the guy who was belly-aching about your bank being bought by Merchants four years ago if I remember correctly. If you would have stayed put, we would've been working together."

"I'm not so sure even a bank as big as Merchants could handle the two of us. But I did the right thing and left," he said. Using his imitation of a southern evangelist, he nearly shouted into the phone, "I didn't stay around and mope about it. Your boy, John, took a leap of faith and found solid ground. Hallelujah! Just like me, you need a change my boy—you need a change!"

"A change would be nice, but I don't have a lot of options right now," I said. The idea of a change was something I had had on my mind since the Merchant takeover, but I didn't like change, and how could I jump ship? I was entrenched in Philly and had made a commitment to stay until the end of the new employment contract I had entered into with Merchants. I couldn't do what our CEO had done—leave with millions in severance pay and stock options. He had a golden parachute—I had, at best, a life preserver. If I stayed till the end of my two-year contract, I had a quarter-of-a-million-dollar bonus waiting for me. Another twelve months and the bonus money was mine.

"Change is good," John said, calming his evangelistic swagger to a more normal tone of voice. "Look at me. I've done pretty well with mine." John had left Merchants after they acquired his bank to join a much smaller bank as CEO. He seemed to be enjoying life more than ever. "Listen, Jack, my friend Benny needs someone just like you. You'd be a great fit. Get away from it all and move to the beautiful countryside in Virginia. It's not Philly, thank God!"

"Benny? Virginia? You didn't have to move from Philly to some hick town in Virginia to change jobs, did you?"

"No, I didn't," he said with a serious tone. "But you should consider it."

"Okay, explain how this is an opportunity? Why would Benny, the banker and writer, need my help?" I asked. John had told me about his friend before. His full name was Benjamin Franklin Price, CEO of Citizens Bank of Virginia. He was at least seventy years old. Citizens Bank was one of the top-performing midsize banks in the country, based in Roanoke, Virginia. Benny had been the guiding force in organizing the business. He was renowned in the industry for his storytelling abilities and gift of gab. He had written a book, *Bank on It!*, about his leadership style and how to deal with change—something bankers were being exposed to now that mergers were commonplace. I had read his book at John's urging several years earlier and reread it after Merchants came to Philly. It was a good read, even though I wasn't fond of self-help books. John's close friendship with the elderly banker had evolved through banking association meetings and hiking excursions on the Appalachian Trail. I always kidded John that Benny had adopted him.

"Opportunity abounds. First, he is a great guy—you'd like him a lot. He is the wisest man I've ever met—hell, he's smarter than me. Seriously, he helped me, Jack. I was going through a rough time. You know how bad things were for me. Just talking to the man helped. I know you'll learn a lot from him. Second, you need to get out of cold, nasty Philly for some healthy mountain life in Virginia. Third, this is right up your alley. This is what you've always wanted. He wants a successor. You've always wanted to run a bank. His bank is one of the best. Just because it's below the Mason-Dixon Line don't make it less than what you're accustomed to, Mr. Yankee," John said, laughing.

"Why would he want *me*?" I asked.

"Well ol' buddy, he didn't—he wanted me. But I told him I was stuck here in Little Rock between exes and trying to keep all of the Arkansas southern belles happy. But I told him I knew the perfect guy who fit the bill for exactly what he wants. You're the guy," he replied. "Virginia isn't that far from civilization."

"Thanks, John, but what's this guy Benny want in someone

like you or me?" I asked. As I listened, I kept thinking, *Benny*, what a name for a banker. He would get some real ribbing if he were in Philly. I had a feeling the man was a relic, a dinosaur, a throwback to a different generation.

John summarized the situation: "Well, Benny is battling a takeover attempt by a large bank. I don't know who the bank is that's trying to buy them—it's probably more than one—you know how sharks gather. He's in a war with some directors at the bank. They want to sell, and Benny doesn't want to. Even though it's a great bank, the directors are getting old and greedy. Benny is past retirement age and doesn't have a successor. He wants someone to join him while he's there, to provide some succession management that would keep the bank independent."

"How in the world could a Philly banker make it in the rural Virginia market? They would probably want to shoot me," I said, picturing a lynch mob standing outside the bank's offices.

"Yeah, if you acted like a Yankee they would," he said. We both laughed. "We'll need to put you through Redneck 101 if you join Benny. But seriously, after talkin' with him, I believe this is in your swing zone. You would be heading up a medium-size bank with incredible profits that wants to stay independent and grow. That's what you want, isn't it?" John was baiting me for a response. "This isn't just a dinky little bank—it's about the size of PT&G when you guys were bought."

"I can't imagine me in Virginia," I said.

"I can't imagine you staying where you're at and surviving another year, my friend," John said. "Just give Benny a call, and let fate work its magical wonders."

"Fate? You still believe in that crap?" I asked.

"Fate makes the world go 'round, Jack," he said. "Now, why don't you give in to my outstandin' persuasive sales efforts and just talk to him?"

"Okay—I'll talk to him," I said. "Just to have the chance to speak with the guy who adopted you. But I don't see me moving to Virginia—ever."

John sounded happy to hear I would make the call. At least I made someone happy. "Let me give you his direct line. He's expecting your call."

"Expecting my call? That was assuming a lot. How did you know I would even call him?" I asked.

"I knew you would. You need a change and I'm glad to help two friends, you and Benny, get together," John responded. "Call him now, you'll enjoy talking with him—then you can see if you're interested. Talkin' can't hurt."

"That hasn't always been true for me," I said.

• • •

After hanging up, I kept looking at the number he had given me. Something about this idea made me feel some hope. At least it was an option. Swiveling my chair to look out my window at the Philly skyline, I thought of the many times I had gazed out at the surrounding high-rises believing that my career was progressing skyward as planned. Now, for the first time in my life, I didn't have a plan in place. My ladder of success had reached a cloud of uncertainty. I was simply surviving—going through the everyday motions Merchants was putting me through. While Virginia probably wasn't the place for me, at least it represented an option. My two-year contract only had a year left. Then I'd be without a job.

I pulled my cell phone from my briefcase. I didn't want to call from my office and felt guilty spending even a couple of minutes on Merchant's time talking about another job, but Benny was expecting my call. As I dialed the number, the thought crossed my mind that I had fired people for doing the same thing I was doing.

"Good morning, this is Benny Price. How can I help you?" The voice had a rich sound with almost no accent, unlike John's definitive drawl.

"Good morning, Mr. Price," I responded. "This is Jack Oliver. John Helms asked me to give you a call."

"Jack, I'm so glad you called. John speaks in the highest regard about you," he said. "And please—call me Benny."

"Okay, Benny. I've heard a lot about you," I nervously exchanged. "I read your book, *Bank on It!*. It was very interesting. Actually I read it twice."

"Thanks for using your valuable time to read an old man's

mumblings set to print," he said, laughing. "I hope you gained at least some benefit from reading it."

"I did," I said. I hadn't really thought about the book's value to me over the past year until I spoke the words. "The book has a lot of passages that meshed with my situation."

"Change is always interesting," he said, "but that's life."

My change had been more than interesting, but I wasn't going to discuss it with a stranger. "John says you may need some help. I doubt if I am the one you're looking for—Virginia is a long way from Philly."

"Not really. One of my heroes is my namesake, Benjamin Franklin. I know a lot about your great city," Benny responded. "I've visited Philadelphia several times. I want to visit again before I get too old to enjoy walking the streets and visiting all the sights."

"Tell me what you're looking for, if you don't mind," I said, feeling the pressure to dispose of the conversation quickly.

"Well, I know you're probably at work making talking difficult," he said, appearing to read my mind. "I know from talking with John that you're a very ethical person. I'm sure you're probably nervous speaking to me while you're earning money from your employer. So, if it's all right with you, let's talk this evening. Will that work for you?" Benny asked.

"That would be fine," I responded, feeling less than compelled to talk further about the job.

He gave me his home phone number and told me to call around seven o'clock that evening. He laughed and said, "We go to bed with the chickens and get up with them." While I did not understand exactly what he meant, I was sure he didn't have chickens in his house—or at least I hoped he didn't.

After hanging up the phone I thought, *Jack, you're dealing with a different world.* I wasn't wrong.

3. What Is Stopping You?

"WHAT IS STOPPING YOU?" I asked Naomi.

After my conversation with Benny, I left my office and drove to our Fifth Street branch bank to speak with Naomi Preston, the office manager. Less than a year ago she had been one of the most productive office managers in PT&G, but since the Merchants takeover her performance was languishing at the bottom—a nightmare for a former high performer. I could relate. I wanted to find out what was holding her back. Adding to my curiosity was the pressure from my new supervisor: "Get her performance up or get her out!"

"I just don't believe in myself anymore," Naomi said. "Mr. Oliver, I feel like all I do is put out fires. My job isn't fun anymore—it's torture."

"I understand, we're all going through change," I said. "But we have to move on and keep doing our best."

"My best isn't good enough anymore," she said, now with tears forming in her eyes. "I liked things the way they used to be." I knew this was a problem for over five thousand people in greater Philadelphia. We were the former employees of PT&G—but now we were employees of Merchants Bank. It was like changing from a horse to a zebra—the change was evident to everyone. I couldn't find anyone from PT&G who said they liked the change to Merchants. Not one.

Our customers were noticing the difference and voting with their feet by leaving us for competitors. Once the dominant bank, we had lost our top spot in market share in less than one year. But, good or bad, I had a job to do.

"Naomi, if you can't get yourself together you know what will happen," I said firmly, reminding her of the guillotine awaiting underperformers. "Now, quit whining and get fired up the way you used to be." As I spoke I did my best to mask my own doubts.

Driving away from the office, I started to think about my conversation with Benny and my agreement to call him later. I was torn. Why should I even talk to him? *It's a waste of time,* I said to myself. The phrase reminded me of the person who had said it so many times before.

I sounded like my father.

• • •

"Why are you wasting your time?"

The question was one of my old man's favorites. Coming home unusually early with the smell of alcohol accompanying his entrance, Joseph Oliver was on the verge of launching into a familiar diatribe about how my mother spent her time. But this time was different—and worse.

"You spend hours wasting your time," he said to her, raising his voice with each word. "Why can't you find something to do that pays?"

Unlike my father, who never showed a passion for anything other than complaining, drinking, or gambling, my mother had a fervent desire to serve others. Limited by time and financial restrictions imposed by my father, she had found a way to give something to others—quilting. Carolyn Oliver could do almost anything with simple cloth, thread, and a needle. But she never made any money from her efforts, which aggravated my father's frustrations. She gave the quilts away, typically to new mothers who attended Sacred Heart Catholic Church where we were members (but rarely attended). These were no average quilts. With incredible care my mother created near works of art. No two were alike. She always put the child's name at the bottom right-hand corner. Her name never appeared anywhere.

"How can you give something away like that? You could sell it and make some money," he said, resuming his verbal barrage, scorning my mother's efforts to help others without charging a fee.

Time was obviously not the issue—it was money. My father's tirades always centered on my mother's inability to bring any money into the household. He reminded us both of this fact on a continual basis.

"It's all up to me to bring home the money," he said, lowering his intensity to plead for mock sympathy. "Without me, where would you two be? On the street is where you would be! When do I get some help?"

We had heard this rant from my father with unfailing regularity, but it had never stopped my mother—she refused to quit. But today's rant was more hostile, and we both knew why. My father had evidently discovered a secret she had kept from him—a secret that originated with the parish priest.

• • •

"*Who are you trying to please?*" the priest asked my mother.

Without knowing my father's relentless opposition to my mother's sewing, Father Romano had decided to take action. He wanted my mother to display one of her baby quilts in a Philly craft show.

"You have a talent that is God-given," he told my mother. "You aren't glorifying your talents—but glorifying the gift God gave to you. Who are you trying to please?"

"But you don't understand," she said. "I do it for a child—not for any other reason."

"There's a time for humility, and there's time for sharing," he said. "You need to share your gift with the world." Embarrassed to tell Father Romano about my father's disdain for her sewing, she allowed him to show the quilt.

The baby quilt won first prize in the craft show. After seeing it on display, a member of the planning committee for the 1976 Bicentennial celebration invited my mother to work as part of a quilting team. Their objective was to create the Philadelphia Quilt, a massive thirty-foot square containing images of historic landmarks in the city. It would be on display during the Bicentennial and thereafter at the Philadelphia Museum of Art. Again, Father Romano insisted she participate.

"This is something that will live on for years," he said to her. "It's obvious God wants you to use your talents. This is more than a gift—this is part of history and will be seen by thousands of people. You must do it! Not for you—but for God!"

She finally agreed to take part, but never told my father about her participation. It was the only time my mother had ever kept a secret from him—and the secret was now exposed.

• • •

"Why did you lie? It's one thing to give a blanket to a family, but you've lied to me!" my father shouted with a level of rage neither my mother nor I had witnessed in the past. "You've been spending your time away from home working on a big blanket with a bunch of women. And for no money!"

We knew how he unearthed her clandestine project before he told us. Unexpectedly, a photo of my mother and several of her partners working on the Philadelphia Quilt appeared on the front page of the Lifestyle Section of the *Philadelphia Inquirer*. Afraid and embarrassed, she had tried to hide it from my father, but one of his drinking buddies at O'Malley's Saloon had evidently called his attention to it. Seeing the photograph had led to this epic explosion of cursing and swearing.

"You're wasting your time and my money!" he yelled, pounding his hand on the nearest wall as he paced the living room. "You weren't doing anything worthwhile sitting on your ass for hours, working on fancy blankets and then giving them away. Now you found a new way to waste your time. Now you're a big shot—in the newspaper. All that means is that everyone knows what a waste you are. Aren't you special?" Pausing for a breath and refocusing his threats, he pointed his finger at my mother, who sat motionless and expressionless. He shouted at the top of his lungs, "I want you to promise me you'll stop this waste of time! Your life is a waste!"

Backed into a corner, my mother responded. Leaping from her chair she was suddenly standing face-to-face with him, staring into his eyes without any appearance of fear. With a voice nearly as stern and cold as my father's, she said, "I'll not stop quilting—it's one of the few things I do that makes me happy. Joseph, your mother would be ashamed of you. Shut your mouth and leave this house—now!"

Fearing what would happen next, I wished I could disappear. But her response worked. He shut up and went to the garage to sulk and drink.

After she heard him walk out the back door, she looked at me and said, "Jack, never give up on your dreams no matter what happens. If you don't have dreams, life isn't worth living." She put her hand on my shoulder and then seemed to freeze. As if embarrassed by her show of emotions, she sat down in the chair and cried. I stood frozen not knowing what to do.

• • •

My father never said another word about her time spent quilting. He remembered what she said.

And I remembered her advice. I had dreams. I had already decided what I wanted to do in life. I wanted power and wealth. I wanted to be in control. I wanted to be something that would make my father and mother proud.

I wanted to be a banker.

It was hard to believe that dream had come true. But now the dream seemed more like a nightmare. I remembered what happened when I told my father about my career objective. A scar remained from one of the few honest moments I shared with him.

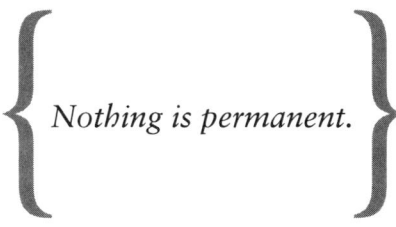

Nothing is permanent.

—BENJAMIN FRANKLIN PRICE

4. What Do You Want to Be?

"WHAT DO YOU WANT TO BE?" my father asked with his sarcastic laugh. He had heard me clearly but was acting surprised. I realized I had made a mistake being honest.

"A banker," I said. I had returned home from school and was excited to share my vision of a career as a financial intermediary. I thought my father would be impressed with his teenage son's ambition—he wasn't.

At first laughing and now almost scowling, my father said, "Bankers are crooks. They feed off other people's misery. They're like buzzards, pecking away until there's nothing left but bones. Or they're like a leech, sucking people dry to make money for people who are so rich they don't even count their money. They pay someone else to count it! Is that what you want to do in life? Count their money? Be a buzzard or a leech?"

Before I could defend my dream, he continued with his rant.

"I hate bankers!" he said using his loudest and harshest tone. "So does everyone else in the world. The only people who like bankers are other bankers."

I would never forget his words. His tirade stayed in my memory because despite his urgings, I became a banker. But was he right? I hated where I was at and what I was doing. My well-thought-out plans for my life had seemed to fail.

. . .

"What holds me back?"

The question was haunting me. I had encountered my fair share of obstacles, but I had always found a way to get what I wanted. But my situation at Merchants was different. Surrendering to an unworthy foe was out of the question. "Jack Oliver never quits," I said, using my oft-repeated phrase that helped motivate me. But it didn't help—I still felt stymied. Maybe it wasn't Merchants that was making me feel trapped, I reasoned. Was it my failure to achieve? Arriving back in my dingy apartment, I pulled the book Benny had written from the cluttered pile of hardbacks and paperbacks by my recliner. I opened it to a place I had previously marked, forgetting why I had marked it:

> Many times we get our emotions confused with reality. I've heard many people say they want to climb higher, feel free, and see the horizon, but they find themselves anchored, unable to lift off and reach their dreams. They ask themselves, "What holds me back?" Think about a kite. A kite appears to soar, climbing with the wind. What a sensation! The thrill of defying gravity, flying high and seeing a view of the world you would miss if you were on the ground. You want to go higher, but realize you can't. Why?
>
> There's a string attached.

Now I remembered why I had marked the passage. The "strings" and "attachments" Benny addressed were issues I fought with. The metaphor of the kite fit me perfectly. It also made me think of my father. I felt pride in my achievements—but I felt trapped in the success I had created for myself. I definitely had a lot of strings attached.

The strings went far beyond my career. I had been separated from my wife, Tina, for three months. My two teenage children,

Jessica and Joshua, were like strangers. I had a girlfriend, Cassie, I spent most of my off-work hours with. But even my relationship with her had slowly deteriorated over the past few months. While Tina had blamed her for our separation, it wasn't Cassie—it was me. I had given up hope. In my surrender I had given each of them a string, one they could pull at will. I felt like a kite. The wind was dying down, and I was in a downward, out-of-control dive.

While we had never seemed to get along, I missed Tina. "Why am I missing her?" I asked myself. Sitting back in the recliner with the first of my evening drinks in hand to take the edge off the pain of my life, I thought about how we met.

Like so many things it seemed like a lifetime ago.

• • •

"What are your plans?"

Until recently, this had been one of my favorite questions. I had always been a planner—everything had to have a plan. I had a plan to attend the University of Pennsylvania. I had a plan to obtain my MBA from Wharton. I had a plan for my career. I even had plans for the type of cars, clothes, and homes I wanted to possess. Yes, Jack Oliver was a planner.

While so many things in my life were planned, relationships definitely weren't one of them. Relationships appeared to be one of those things in life that did not want to be scheduled and planned. They just happened. I was in the last year of graduate school, and I was lonely. My plans changed when I met Tina.

Tina was practically the exact opposite of me. She was athletic. I wasn't. She could walk into a room and heads would turn. No one ever noticed when I walked into a room—I looked like a banker. Tina was taller, fitter, and outgoing. I was shorter, out of shape, and more comfortable in my introverted personality. She was politically a left-wing liberal. I was a far right-wing conservative. I loved Nixon, she loved McGovern and Mondale. She came from a wealthy family—I didn't. Music, food, hobbies, you name it; our choices always differed. But the extremes that existed between us created a source of energy that fueled our interest in each other. Whether it was curiosity or some other force of nature it was magnetic. And I was the negative.

I fought to control my feelings. To deal with the challenge of someone invading my world, I developed a new plan for my future. Until I got everything I wanted, love was on hold. Once I achieved what I wanted, I would have women falling over one another to get my attention. There would be time for love and sharing. That was my plan.

But then there was Tina.

• • •

"What would you suggest?"

It was the first question I asked Tina. The question, like so many things in our relationship, was not sincere—it was just a way to get what I wanted.

I met Tina in a record store, Books, String & Things, near the University of Pennsylvania campus where I was a graduate student. Tina was working at the record store part-time while she finished her graduate degree in political science at Temple University.

It was a Saturday afternoon, and Bill Clemmons, my roommate at the university, persuaded me to walk down to the record store with him. Bill was anxious to buy the new Led Zeppelin album. I was not as anxious. I didn't enjoy the early seventies music of the Rolling Stones, Led Zeppelin, or the Who. I liked country music. That left me doomed to listening to music I enjoyed only when no one else was around. Country music wasn't cool in 1974, at least not in Philadelphia. So there I was walking into what I viewed as a "hippie head shop," a real fish out of water.

As I walked in the store I saw a young woman standing in front of the jazz album section. She was tall—taller than me—with long, strawberry blonde hair that meshed perfectly with her blue sundress. I saw a name tag identifying her as an employee but could not read the name. Her eyes, focused on a customer in front of her, were amazing. They were the bluest eyes I could imagine, sparkling and piercing at the same time. I was immediately smitten. Trying to be as cool as possible, I worked my way around the store's bargain stacks of albums to get close enough to hear her voice. I can't remember ever wanting to hear what a woman sounded like, but at that moment it was all I could think about. As I got closer I could hear a voice that was smooth and calming, with a rich, deep quality, full of confidence. Her voice was just like the rest of her—beautiful. She was telling the lucky guy about a new jazz fusion album she highly recommended.

Right or wrong, I thought a person who loved jazz had to be very intelligent. So, when I heard her velvet voice describing the music on the album it signaled a person of incredible intelligence. *Beauty and brains,* I thought as I stood looking down at the albums. *I've got to talk to her!* Looking at the album bin in front of me, I realized I was challenged finding common ground to initiate a conversation with a beautiful woman who obviously loved music that was a far cry from Buck Owens. How could a guy who enjoyed listening to Merle Haggard and Glen Campbell impress her? I suddenly felt shorter and fatter.

I could only think of one jazz musician, Miles Davis. Like a moth flying into the burning flame, I was ready to go where I had not ventured in my life. As soon as she finished talking with the jazz-loving customer I made my move.

"Hi. I'm interested in buying a Miles Davis record but really don't know much about his music," I said clumsily, connecting with her blue eyes. "I heard you talking, and you obviously know jazz. What would you suggest?" I immediately wished I could have spoken more eloquently. I took a quick glance at her name tag: TINA.

"Well, *Bitches Brew* is my favorite Miles Davis album. What other types of music do you like?" she asked.

I was not ready for her response. *Bitches Brew?* Is that a song? Still in semi-shock, I let out an honest "I really like Johnny Cash."

Tina laughed and said, "I doubt if you would like Miles if you like Johnny Cash, but I may be wrong." After pausing to flip her hair back, she asked, "Are you flirting with me?"

For whatever reason, I could not lie to her about my intentions—I was flirting. "I'm going to be honest. I think you're the most beautiful woman I've ever seen," I said. "Would you like to get a cup of coffee after work?"

"You don't do this very often do you?" she said and smiled.

"No, honestly, I don't. Otherwise I would have scars and bruises from getting slapped," I said, laughing and gaining more confidence.

"I don't see any scars or bruises," she said, looking me over with a sly grin.

"So, is that a yes?" I asked.

"Yes," Tina said. We both laughed.

We met for coffee and immediately became a couple. The stark differences in our personalities, beliefs, and even physical appearances formed the magnetic current that pulled together two totally different people. We married one year after that first meeting. Neither of us knew how we were going to make ends meet.

The two of us were never very good at agreeing on a joint plan. And that never changed.

· · ·

Being different can be exciting, but having differences is a problem, I thought. I loved Tina with all my heart. But I soon realized love was not enough. I didn't know how to share my life. Worse, I became a less-than-honest person.

Now, Tina wasn't with me. I had lied to her.

I had also lied to myself.

5. Who Do I Believe?

WHO DO I BELIEVE? I thought, as I poured another drink. It was a question I asked myself a lot. I didn't trust anyone. I had heard too many lies to assume anything a person said was honest. There was always a hook—something the other person wanted and would lie to get. As I took a drink and felt the warm sensation of the alcohol melting away my inhibitions, I remembered that it wasn't just others I distrusted. I didn't trust myself.

With a Houdini-like mastery of the art of escape, I recalled my history of self-deceptions. But the past had finally caught up with me. I took another sip to gain more clarity. Dishonesty had ruined my relationship with Tina. Now I was facing a choice in which I could not afford to be anything other than honest—especially with myself. Was working with Benny a realistic option or just a distraction? *Now's the time to be honest,* I thought.

Benny was over seventy years old—close to my father's age if he had still been alive. I rarely thought about my father, but now seemed like a good time to open up the mostly painful wounds of my relationship with him. I couldn't ignore the fact that thinking of Benny made me think of my father. Shutting my eyes I visualized my old man. One of the most consistent images of him was his time in front of the television watching the evening news.

I was sitting with my father as he watched Walter Cronkite on the *CBS Evening News*. It was part of my old man's evening ritual. The year was 1968. It was election year. In politics, my father was ahead of his time. He was Archie Bunker before there was an Archie Bunker. My father's ultraconservative political perspective would have made Archie proud. Likewise, my father enjoyed Archie's character, thinking it represented the norm. He never understood why Archie got so many laughs when he talked about religion, racism, and politics. My old man believed Archie was right.

"If Richard Nixon loses to Hubert Humphrey, we may as well turn the country over to the communists," my father said. "Humphrey is like every Democrat—he has no backbone."

I was barely eleven years old, but I had a voracious appetite for reading about the lives of American presidents. History fascinated me. Before I thought about the risks, I ventured into the uncharted waters and asked my father a political question. "Did John Kennedy, Harry Truman, and Franklin Roosevelt have backbones?"

He gulped his Schlitz beer to wet his throat and paused before telling his barely teenage son about backbones. "Jackson, those men were different. Humphrey and the Democrats you see now aren't the same Democrats you're asking about," he said, using my complete first name, a tactic he unfailing adhered to his entire life. He had named me after the Confederate general Stonewall Jackson, a very unusual choice for the son of an Irish plumber in Philadelphia, but it was something he enjoyed saying to make a point and remind me of his control.

"Nixon is a person you can trust," he said, continuing with unbridled confidence. "You can bet your life that Nixon will never lie, cheat, or steal. Nixon will go down in history as the greatest American president. You can read about him someday in those books you read about presidents and realize your father was right. Nixon's for the working man. Take my word on it, Jackson, life is a job—you have to work hard and never quit! Take what you can before someone else takes it. Trust me Jackson—I know what I'm talking about."

"Life is a job" was one of my father's favorite expressions. He believed it. But I didn't want a job—I wanted a career. I had never wanted to be like him. If Benny was similar to my old man and the rest of his generation, how could I work with him? We'd be complete opposites. Just like with Tina, opposites may initially attract; but they didn't do very well long-term. Not in my world.

• • •

"*What have you learned?*" my father often asked me, mocking my desire to achieve more than a high school education. "You spend all your time in school reading books about life. The only way to learn about life is to live it outside of books."

Attempting to learn the way my father had learned would have been impossible. My father's father had died long before I entered the world. A first-generation Irish immigrant to the United States, my grandfather passed through Ellis Island with nothing. After failing to achieve the American dream, he left his wife and son with the same thing he had brought entering the country—nothing.

My grandfather departed from his family following an Oliver family tradition. He put a .38 revolver in his mouth and pulled the trigger, the same departure his father before him chose to escape the challenges of the world. The only positive thing I can say about this bit of family heritage is that they were evidently good shots. My father found his father dead on the kitchen floor when he returned home from school. My father kept the gun.

He never returned to school. With an eighth-grade education, the role of breadwinner fell on his thirteen-year-old shoulders. He became a plumber's assistant, learning his craft from a person I viewed as my substitute grandfather, George Schmidt. Without any children of his own, "Old George," as most people knew him, looked at my father as his de facto son. George operated Schmidt's Plumbing Service from a storefront shop where he had started the business in the early 1920s. Old George had weathered the Great Depression and a World War by being both frugal and excellent in his work. He passed along these traits to my old man, along with the enjoyment of alcoholic beverages and gambling.

Joseph Oliver basically inherited, in name alone, George's business after George passed away suddenly of a heart attack in 1963. Not too surprisingly, he had died at a poker table in a back room of O'Malley's Saloon. When Old George died, it was the only time I remembered seeing my father cry.

After George died, my father followed the same practice of keeping the business a two-person proposition: him and an apprentice. The apprentices changed so often I can't recall any of them lasting more than a couple of years. Working for my old man was not easy. He demanded hard work, but paid little. He never told them they were doing anything right, but took every opportunity to criticize. At least he was not any different at work than he was at home.

"You can't find good help anymore," he said routinely after witnessing the departure of another apprentice. "People won't listen. I'm the boss—I know more than they do. Just do what I say is all I ask!"

As each apprentice left, they started their own businesses and took a slice out of the revenues. The continuing erosion of his business over the years spurred my father to drink more and then joke about what he would do if things got too rough on him.

He had two fantasy getaways. In his first get-away-from-it-all fantasy, he would buy a train ticket, one-way, and go to Alaska. Alaska was a place holding some kind of magic for my old man. He had never been to Alaska and was not a fan of ice-cold weather. He certainly wasn't a nature lover. Why he fantasized about Alaska, I could not imagine.

He had a second, much more disturbing fantasy, given his father's exit from this world.

"If things get really bad, I'll just take a nice long walk to the Ben Franklin Bridge," he would begin. "I'll take my time—enjoying every step along the way. Then I'll walk out on the bridge to the middle to enjoy the view, then climb up over the rails and stand on top with nothing between me and the river. I'll be in control. I won't be afraid. Then I'll jump head-first just like I'm in the Olympics, straight down into the river. I'll do a dive better than Tarzan could ever dream of doing. If I die, at least I'll die the way I want to."

He understood no one could survive a dive from the bridge. Unlike his Alaskan getaway, when he discussed his Tarzan dive, he was always sober.

• • •

"*What's wrong with my life?* You think you're smarter than your old man, don't you, Jackson? Try walking a few steps in my shoes and see how smart you are."

I never liked my father's shoes or the idea of retracing his steps. I was totally the opposite of the son my father wanted. He wanted a son who was athletic. I enjoyed playing sports, but I was fat and slow. I didn't like to lose, and I especially didn't want to be used as the reason my team lost. But as a student, I got straight As. I loved math and the sciences. I took pride in my grades. My father didn't understand. "You can read till your eyeballs pop out of your skull, Jackson, but you'll never make a living from reading. I never dreamed I would have a son like you."

• • •

At least he was honest, I thought to myself. He wanted a son who aspired to be his apprentice, learn the plumbing trade, and take over for him when he decided to quit. That was not for me. The thought of crawling under floors with sewage ready to spew in my face suffocated me. Even worse was the idea of hearing him remind me a hundred times a day that he knew more than me.

Instead of trying to please him, I had decided to best him. I wanted to show him *my* way was better. While I had never said it aloud, I wanted my father to respect me for being *different*. If he would not say he was proud of me, at least I would earn his respect with my accomplishments. That was my plan.

I had never let up or let go of that strategy as I progressed through school and tried to make my plans a reality. I held onto the belief that I would reach such an unquestionably high level of success that my father would be forced to finally say, "That's my son. He's a success—I'm proud of him." But I had fooled myself. *It didn't work out that way*, I thought as I drained the glass of the last drop of fluid with a single gulp. I remembered the last time I saw my father alive.

6. Who Are You Fooling?

"WHO ARE YOU FOOLING?" my father asked. "The rich get richer, and people like us just hang on to what we've got."

We were standing on the front porch of my parent's home. I had visited my mother and father infrequently after entering the University of Pennsylvania. Maintaining a 4.0 GPA took time. That was part of my excuse. The other was my part-time job at PT&G, which helped support me, along with student loans. Even though my parents lived less than thirty minutes from Penn, I left home and lived on campus. I had minimal tolerance for my father's criticisms of my life, especially when he was drinking. Seeing my father drunk was now the rule instead of the exception.

"You're fooling yourself if you believe you'll be one of them," he said garbling his words. "The rich will never accept you—you're still Jackson Oliver from Southwest Philly, son of a plumber, and they'll never forget it. You're no better than a slave to them. The only thing you'll be like them is heartless—willing to do anything to get what you want."

This was a radical change for my father. "Life is a job" was not working for him now. A failing business had given him reason to drink and gamble more. Neither one was helping. He believed he had failed in his "Life is a job" mantra.

"I'm not heartless," I said defensively. "I've worked hard for everything I have."

You could not fault my father's work ethic or his honesty. He had never cheated anyone. He was a hard worker and had achieved a lot for someone with only an eighth-grade education. While he had not fully admitted it, he was implying he was a failure in not only his job, but also in life.

"Cheaters aren't lazy, Jackson—they work hard," he said. "It's their job."

He always had an excuse—he had been cheated. Bankers had cheated him by not lending him money when he needed it, and now I was a banker. His former apprentices had tricked him and taken his business.

"I don't cheat," I said. "I'm different." The years had made me impatient with his taunts. My old man treated the people he hired like animals. He was cold and uncaring with everyone he met.

"They're heartless, and you're going to be like them," he said, shaking his head side to side. "You're not the type of son I thought you would be. You would do anything to get ahead—anything."

My goal had been to earn his respect, but now, standing on the front porch looking at my father, I had a different perspective; I felt sorry for him. Maybe I *was* like him. Was I heartless? *No, I have a heart*, I thought. *I have feelings.* "I'm not like *them*, and I'm definitely not like *you*," I said. "Why can't you admit you're jealous of what I can become?"

"You can become anything you want, Jackson," he said, turning to enter the house as the outward anger subsided. "But if you aren't happy what's the point?" He looked unhappy, as if he had given up. But I wasn't going to let him have the final word.

"I'm happy. The point is you're jealous," I said defiantly. "Admit it—I'm going to be more successful than you, and you hate the thought of it. And you hate me for it."

"No, you're wrong, *son*," he said, stopping to turn and face me before stepping inside the house. We made brief eye contact. "I don't hate you. What I hate is the thought you'll be like me. That's what I hate."

I walked away, vowing I would not speak to him until he apologized and admitted I was successful.

I kept my promise.

• • •

"How could I be like him?" The question had survived many years. While I did not know it was the last time I would see him alive, the conversation was a deciding factor in making me the successful, but unhappy person I was now. I did not heed his warning. I never tried to be like my father, but in so many ways, I was seeing his image in the mirror.

"I'm not like him!" I said as I left my parent's home and drove back to campus in my Volkswagen Rabbit. I was still angry. Fueling my rage was the fact that I could not find the right response to a drunken old man's words. *I am educated, socially connected, and have the rest of my life in front of me, not behind me like him,* I thought, as I navigated my way through the heavy traffic. The old guy sounded as though he had given up on his life. *I never want to be like him. I still have hope.*

"He's jealous," I said as I moved onto the freeway, pulling every bit of horsepower available from the Volkswagen's engine. "It's what I can become that bothers him." I looked off to the side to see the skyline of modern Philly. "Jack Oliver—you have potential. Philly is yours for the taking!"

If there was one comment that echoed through most of my life, it was "Jack Oliver has great potential." While I was not the most popular person in high school, I made an impression on my fellow classmates. In the senior poll for Person Most Likely to Succeed I was the hands-down winner. Everyone knew I had the potential to do great things in my life. I reminded them if they forgot. I was a fan of potential. I would rather be named Person Most Likely to Succeed than Best Looking or Most Athletic.

Planning's the difference, I said, continuing the conversation with myself as I weaved between cars to be positioned for a quick start at the next traffic light. Being first in line at the light was always important to me. *I'm driving like I'm living,* I thought. *I'm getting ahead by staying in front. I'm thinking ahead.* Looking at the cars behind me in my rearview mirror gave me an advantage.

One big advantage was that from a relatively early age I knew what I wanted to do. Unlike thousands of other young people in my generation, I did not want to be an athlete, politician, movie star, or astronaut. Those were just silly dreams that only one in a million may realize. The few who said they wanted to be a doctor or lawyer did it to sound important, I thought. I wanted something I could obtain—a position of power and respect—a banker. There weren't as many people queuing up for jobs as bankers, which allowed me a clearer path. "It fits," I said as I forced my way between cars to access my exit ramp, ignoring the sound of the horns blowing at my driving tactics.

I was not being selfish or heartless as my father had implied. I increased my speed to pass a Cadillac. There was nothing wrong with wanting more. My plan was rational and realistic, I reminded myself. No one was going to help me. Life was a game, and it was me against everyone else. Unlike my father, if I lost, I knew I had no one to blame but me.

That is the American way, I thought, looking up at a billboard for the Platinum Lounge touting "Philly's Sexiest Girls." I was playing the game the way the game was meant to be played. "I'm not greedy," I said out loud staring at the silhouette of the PT&G office tower, a place I wanted to rule in the near future. To reinforce my belief, I leaned over to see myself in the rearview mirror and smiled. I had potential. I had a plan. I was prepared. *All I had to do was win the game,* I thought as I drove through the campus entrance heading for one of the more remote parking lots.

I didn't want anyone to see me in the VW Rabbit . . . I was embarrassed.

I was not the person I hoped to be. I had missed my mark—barely. *But* almost *doesn't win in the game of life,* I thought, looking around at the four walls of my small apartment. "Life is a game." I remembered the first time I had heard the term. The person who said it inspired me to become a banker; and the person I am now.

• • •

"Who inspires you?"

I remembered the classroom assignment as if it were yesterday. Ms. Faulkner, my twelfth-grade English teacher, had asked us to write a brief essay about the person who inspired us the most. While others moaned and groaned, I felt very comfortable with the task. One person stood out. The person had encouraged me to choose my profession, changing my life forever. He was the president of a large Philadelphia bank. He had visited our eighth-grade class and spoke about basic economics and how a bank functions. Everyone thought he was boring—except me.

He inspired me.

His name was Chad Jefferies, the president of Philadelphia Trust & Guaranty. Actually his full name was Chadwick Arnold Jefferies IV. "I don't like being called Mr. Jefferies because that's my father's name, and he's dead," he said with a smile in his introductory remarks. "I'm afraid of being mistaken for a ghost so please call me Chad."

No one else laughed, but I remembered what he said. I understood the thought of not wanting to be like your father. I thought that Chad was very young to be a bank president. I guessed he was probably in his thirties, younger than my parents and most of my teachers. He answered my thoughts by explaining in his introduction that he "inherited the job" from his father, the former president of the bank. *At least it was not a plumbing business he inherited,* I thought to myself. Some people have all the luck.

What I learned later was that Chad's father had inherited his job from his father. This hand-me-down bank presidency went much deeper into their family history. The Jefferies name was one of the most prominent names in Philadelphia business history, spanning back over one hundred years. Chad was tall, and immaculately dressed in a dark gray suit that included a vest and pocket watch, the gold chain dangling. To my classmates, Chad was a rich guy who was forced into coming to our class to bore us with a talk about banking. But I was not bored. I was impressed.

I was focused. I used my role as editor of the school's junior high newspaper to interview Chad. The way some people would climb the gate at Graceland to get a glimpse of Elvis, I wanted the opportunity to tell him my career objective. After asking a few basic questions, I told Chad that I wanted to become a banker.

"That's interesting. I rarely hear young adults talking about being bankers," Chad said.

"Young adult" made me feel even better about Chad. I asked him what I could do to prepare for a banking career.

"You need to be an excellent student," he told me. "Banking requires a person to know a lot about everything."

Asserting my qualifications I told him I was an excellent student. To further my cause I talked about my job delivering papers and how I invested the money in coins. Trying to impress him, I rattled off several of the more valuable coins in my collection. To my surprise, he did not seem to know anything about coins. But he was impressed with my knowledge of money.

"Your name is Jack?" he asked, as if he had forgotten my name after the introductions only a few minutes earlier.

"Yes, sir—Jack Oliver."

"Jack, I think you're starting off on the right foot to be a banker," he said.

I told Chad of how he had influenced me when he spoke to my eighth-grade class a year before.

"Jack, when you're old enough come to PT&G, and we'll give you a job. Tell them you know me. Just keep making As and working hard." Then he said it. "Life is a game. You have to know more and work harder than anyone else to win," Chad said. "I have a gut feeling you're that type of person."

I told him I would be back as soon as I was old enough. I was going to hold him to his promise to give me a job.

The game was on.

• • •

"Who's ahead?"

The question had a much deeper meaning for the teenage Jack Oliver than whether the Eagles, 76ers, or Phillies were winning. As the son of a plumber and a resident of one of the less affluent neighborhoods, I felt that I was on the bottom, always looking up. I wanted to be one of the people on top, looking down at everyone else. They were the winners, and I wanted to join them. The view from the top had to be much better.

I obviously wasn't the only person with this goal in mind. Who didn't want to be rich and powerful? I arrived at the same conclusion Chad reached about the meaning of life—"Life is a game."

I reasoned that my father had failed because he had believed "life is a job." If you treated life as a job, you were admitting that someone else was in control. If all you had was a job, you would be working your entire life for others. I knew even then that I would never be satisfied with just a job—I wanted to be in control of my life. Chad was right—life is a game, and the winners were in control. He was living proof.

But how can a poor kid win? I wondered many times, trying to find a way to take command of my destiny. From my brief life experiences, I could plainly see that rich people had power, and powerful people were rich. I concluded winning was dictated by how much power and money a person could gather. You could never get too much of either. It was me versus them in a competition to see who could gather the most. I was living to win, not lose.

But I was having trouble finding a way to get into the game. I needed to find a way in—a course of action, a plan. After thinking as deeply as a teenager could think about attaining power and riches, the answer came to me on a snowy midwinter weekend. Stuck inside the house with two feet of snow and bitter temperatures forcing everyone indoors, I found myself playing a game with several of my snowbound friends.

The game was Monopoly. I decided to develop a strategy—a plan that would help me win the game of life. I wrote it down and added to it as I moved through the game over the years. With some minor changes, I adhered to the strategy for most of my life. While I had lost the notebook paper I had written it on, I remembered my tactics.

The first step was understanding that getting into the game wasn't impossible. Everyone who chose to play could be on the board. But space was limited, so you had to decide quickly.

You didn't need a lot of money to start. But there was a price to pay. Players had to be willing to lose whatever they had to win. That wasn't a problem for me. I never felt that I had a lot to lose.

Winning was also relatively simple. To win at Monopoly you had to take advantage of every opportunity. Gather all of the property and cash you can carry, and be sure to buy Boardwalk and Park Place. Only the best property is worth the effort. Be prepared and keep a Get Out of Jail card handy for those moments the roll of the dice doesn't go your way.

Never be afraid to take risks. Draw your Chance card and hope it's something beneficial. Don't rely on luck—be ruthless in your pursuit of winning. Beat the other players before they beat you. Take their money before they take yours. When it comes to rules, know the rules so you can bend them.

Speed was important. Get around the board as quickly as possible, and do your best to avoid paying rent or owing anything to anyone. Never stop to enjoy what you own—it can all be taken away. Pass *Go* and earn your money. Always stay on course no matter how long the game takes. Distractions will result in defeat.

In Monopoly there was only one role other than being a player— the banker. Everything revolved around money, so being in control of the money was important. Be the banker!

Finally, it's time to cash in and count your money at the end of the game. Who has the most? If you do, you win, and *now* you can be happy!

It was hard to believe someone not even old enough to drive could concoct a plan for life based on Monopoly—but I did. There would be only one winner, and I was determined to win.

According to Chad's game plan, "know more" and "work harder" were the two keys to success. Obtaining the best education would be my first step according to Chad's advice. I had always been a good student, but I started focusing more on math and business classes.

As soon as I was old enough, I decided to see if Chad's promise of employment was valid. During my junior year of high school, I applied for a job with PT&G. After filling out the job application I told the PT&G human resource representative that I knew Chad personally.

"Chad promised me a job two years ago," I said. "He told me

to make excellent grades. I have. I'm at the top of my class. I want to work for PT&G."

"You know Mr. Jefferies?" she asked, doubting my story.

"He told me to call him Chad because everyone called his father Mr. Jefferies," I said. "Just check with him and tell him Jack Oliver is ready to go to work. He'll remember me—I'm positive."

"I'll get back with you, Mr. Oliver," she said, smirking.

As I slid the pen I used to fill out the application back across the counter, I said, "I look forward to working with you."

I got the word the next day. Chad remembered me. I was hired part-time in the operations area. After a few months sorting mail I was trained as a teller and began my banking career in earnest. I loved my job. I handled money all day.

Instead of being proud, my father remained steadfast in his open distaste for my early career choice. "You dress up in a nice suit and work in a big office building. You count out thousands of dollars to people while you work, but you are paid nickels and dimes. When are you ever going to be paid some real money? You're wasting your time, Jackson. Only rich people's children will get ahead."

I decided I would show my father what could happen when his son pursued a goal. I would not only be a banker, but the president of the bank. Chad was my role model, the person I wanted to emulate. If I could be like Chad, then I could have it all . . . and ultimately my father's respect.

• • •

If my old man could see me now, I thought, alone in my small apartment, *what would he think of his boy now?* Knowing the answer to my question, I poured another drink. I had a choice to make. Do I stay on the same path that put me here, or do I change directions?

What happened to my potential? I asked myself, rubbing my hands through my thinning hair. *Is there no hope for me?*

I thought about the confrontation with my father. I needed help—something that could give me hope and guidance to make a better choice now.

I remembered asking a priest about hope.

> *Hope isn't all we have—*
> *but if we lose hope,*
> *nothing else works.*

— BENJAMIN FRANKLIN PRICE

7. Where's Your Hope?

"WHERE'S YOUR HOPE?" the priest had asked me long ago. The question asked then was pertinent now.

"I don't know, Father," I had replied. "I've lost hope. I don't see any hope—any way that life will get better. I'm ready to give up." I was attending my first confessional in years. Father Romano was very concerned.

"Giving up is never a solution," he said. "That's what happened with your father—he gave up hope. You must never give up hope, Jack."

"What's left to hope for? Finding a more humane way to kill myself?"

"Hope is the foundation for all we do," he said. "Your life can be different than your father's if you choose to make it so. You don't have to share his fate."

Since that conversation with Father Romano, I had done my best to maintain hope that I would be a success. I had accomplished a lot in my career, but now I was feeling the same way again. I was losing hope.

I was scheduled to call Benny in less than one hour. Before I called him, I wanted to prepare. I had a number of questions I wanted to ask. I had reviewed his bank's Web site and profitability statements. While successful, it appeared that the success had come in spite of a radical approach to doing business. I had already drawn the conclusion that the way Benny conducted business was years behind Philly. But how he ran his bank was not my biggest concern.

My biggest concern was Benny the man. He was old and did things in a different way. I imagined he had the same stubbornness and adherence to sticking to the "old ways" that I had always scorned. I had thought about the past and tried to understand how I could work with someone in a new venture that might remind me of my father. What had given me hope earlier in the day, the idea of working in a new environment, now seemed like only a dream or a wish—not something that could be realized. I put down the note pad full of questions about his business practices and thought again about the reason I had visited Father Romano.

• • •

Death was a part of life I had never found a successful way to cope with. My only surviving grandmother had passed away six years earlier. I struggled with her death more than I allowed others to see. While she had lived to be over eighty, her death still frightened me. Now I was dealing with an unexpected death. Unlike my grandmother's, my father's death wasn't at the end of a long life.

It was sudden.

My mother called me at Tina's apartment late one night and told me my father had not come home. He was known to drink at a local bar, O'Malley's Saloon, but the bartender always made sure he had a cab ride home. It was a routine—something we all accepted. That night, he had slipped out of the bar, and according to the bartender, was sober. The bartender said he left before nine o'clock, but now he was nowhere to be found. My mother was worried—so was I, but I wasn't going to show it.

"Okay, I'll be right there," I said. "He probably got into an argument at O'Malley's and went to another bar. I'll find him."

We got dressed and drove to my parent's home. "What do you think has happened?" Tina asked as we drove through the narrow streets.

"I don't know," I said, not wanting to show any extraordinary concern. "That's my father—always making sure he gets everyone's attention."

"I hope nothing has happened," Tina said.

"Maybe he went to one of his girlfriends' and passed out," I said, actually hoping that was the case.

"How is your father doing?" she asked. "I haven't heard you say anything about him for weeks."

"The last time I went home he jumped me—he said I was heartless," I said. "He doesn't understand why I wanted to go to college and be a banker. He doesn't understand because he doesn't know any better. Poor guy, he can't admit he's jealous."

"Your father never seemed like the jealous type," Tina said. "I wish you two could get along."

"That's not going to happen," I said, as we pulled into the narrow driveway. "That's his choice, not mine."

As we stepped inside, my mother said she had not heard anything from him. It was almost 1:00 A.M.

"Have you checked the garage?" I asked.

"No—but I haven't seen a light on all evening," she said. My parent's home had a detached garage. It had a workshop that he seldom used, except to sneak a drink of whiskey. My mother would not allow alcohol in the house, so my father used the garage as his getaway.

Looking out the kitchen window, I saw no lights in the garage. The door was closed, but I went to check it anyway.

"I'll just go take a look," I said. I wanted my mother to believe that my father would return home, but I knew better. Something terrible had happened—I could feel it. But I had to convey some hope for my mother.

"Okay Jack, I'll make some coffee," she said. She knew what I was doing.

"Mrs. Oliver, I'll do it—why don't you sit down and rest," Tina said.

"Thank you Tina, but I can't sit down right now—it helps to keep busy." Looking at me, she asked, "Do you think we should call the police?"

"You know what they'd say," I said. "I'll go out looking through the neighborhood in a few minutes."

As I stepped off the back porch, I remembered the many times I had jumped off of it when I was a kid, my vault carrying me over the bottom two steps, into the yard to shoot basketball. The old man had fashioned a backboard and rusty rim on the side of the garage. It was still there. My mother did not like the way the grass died on our backyard court, making the yard a dust bowl in the summer, but she tolerated it. Shooting basketball with me, while rare, was one of the few times my father interacted with me while I was a kid.

I opened the garage door and stepped inside, reaching for the light switch. I flipped the fluorescent lights on. After blinking quickly, they beamed light into the cramped and cluttered garage. I did not see any signs of my father. I walked around and everything looked normal. As I turned to walk out, I looked at the workbench, where my father kept his liquor in the overhead cabinets. I was getting ready to open the cabinet to check out his supply, when I noticed something different. On the top of the bench was an envelope. As I stepped closer, I saw the envelope had my mother's name written on it. It was my father's handwriting. I picked the envelope up and saw that it was sealed.

While it was addressed to my mother, I did not hesitate a second before opening it, my heart pounding faster, not knowing what to expect. He was capable of just about anything. For all I knew this could be a good-bye note telling my mother he had run off with another woman. He had a history of indiscretions. Or maybe he was finally following through on his fantasy getaway to Alaska. That was unlikely.

But as I unfolded the lined 8 ½ by 11 sheet of paper, I thought of another option for a getaway he had discussed. There was a family tradition to be upheld. Unlike his father and his father before him, my father said if he wanted to end it all, it would not be with a gun. He would be different.

I turned the light on over the workbench and read his message to my mother:

Dearest Carolyn,
    I'm sorry I have never been the husband you deserved.
My life has been a waste. I was selfish. You and Jackson
have suffered too long. I can't seem to let go of the past. I

can't change. I'm lost. No hope. Forgive me.

I only have one option. I love you forever.

Your Loving Husband

I rushed out of the garage, across the yard and into the kitchen thinking about what was I going to say. I knew which getaway option my father had chosen. My mother stepped into the kitchen as I was getting ready to pick up the phone.

"Would you do me a favor and turn on the television to see if the Phillies won?" I asked my mother, hoping she would go into the living room so I could call the police without her hearing the conversation.

"Are you all right, Jack?" she asked.

"I need to make a private phone call," I said. My mother looked shaken. "Tina, would you and mother step out for just a minute?"

"What are you holding in your hand, Jack?" my mother asked, looking at my father's note I clutched in my left hand.

"Let me use the phone," I demanded. "Both of you please go into the living room, and I'll be right with you."

They left the kitchen, and I heard Tina turn on the television—both of them knew something had happened. I picked up the phone from the wall mount and dialed the police number on the adhesive strip on the phone's handle. The strip had been on the phone as long as I could remember, along with all of the other emergency numbers. This was the first time anyone had used any of the numbers. A lady at the police department answered the phone. I told her what I had found and my suspicions. She said they would assign a car immediately to check out the area around the Ben Franklin Bridge. Even at this time of the night, driving across town from southwest Philly would take twenty minutes, so a police car dispatched in the area would be on the scene immediately. At least I hoped so.

I walked quickly into the living room. My mother was sitting motionless with her hands folded in her lap with Tina beside her. "I'm going out to look for him," I said. "I won't be gone long."

"Do you know where he is?" my mother asked as I opened the front door.

"I think so," I said. "I'll be right back—I promise. Tina will stay here with you." Tina nodded and put her arm around my mother.

I jumped into the Volkswagen and drove as fast as I could to the Ben Franklin Bridge. It was early fall—a mist from the river was rising, making the bridge less conspicuous as I closed in. I parked on the side of the road and climbed over the barrier to the walkway. I saw no one in the light fog. I started running down the walkway hoping I would see him.

At the third light on the bridge I stopped abruptly. I leaned over the railing and aimed my flashlight toward the river. The fog made it difficult to see anything other than the swirling mist in front of the light. I aimed the beam of light to the left toward one of the bridge's massive concrete supports. I thought I saw something so I ran closer and leaned over, beaming the light downward. I could not believe what I was seeing. Lying against the concrete base jutting out from the bridge was my father—his body twisted from the impact. I shouted out "Dad!"—something I never called him before—but there was no response.

Just then I saw a police car making its way across the bridge. I waved my light at the police car. They saw me. I showed the policeman where he was and passed him the note. The moment did not seem real.

I stayed at the bridge with one of the officers while they sent a patrol boat to the base of the bridge to retrieve his body.

As I drove to Jefferson Hospital behind the police cruiser, the reality of this nightmare began to emerge. I had yet to call my mother and Tina—I did not want to tell them over the phone. Before I called them I had to identify my father.

The police officer stepped into the waiting area and asked me to follow him. We walked through a maze of corridors until we entered the morgue. We walked into a room with four corpses covered in white sheets, lying on metal tables. The officer directed me to the fourth body. I did not know how I would react. He pulled back the thin white sheet from the face. It was my father. I could not look for more than a second. I looked up at the officer and said, "It's him."

"I'm sorry, Mr. Oliver," the officer said, pulling the sheet over my father's face.

"Can I go?" I asked. "I have to tell my mother."

"Do you need a ride?" he asked.

"No, I'll be all right. I need to use a phone to tell them I'm coming."

"There is a phone right outside," he said as we walked out of the room into the hall.

I called home. Tina answered. "I'll be back in a little while," I said. "Is she okay?"

"Jack, what's wrong?" Tina asked.

"I can't say—just stay with my mother," I said.

"Where are you?" Tina asked.

"I'm at Jefferson, but I'm leaving now. Don't say anything to my mother, okay?"

"Okay, Jack," Tina said. "We'll be fine . . . please be careful—I love you."

"Okay," I said, my mind still locked on the vision of my father's face.

• • •

How do you tell your mother her husband had fulfilled a nightmare and jumped off a bridge? I had yet to show any emotion, and I knew that was not the issue. I had to be strong when I told her.

Arriving back home, I saw Tina looking out the window. As I stepped onto the porch Tina opened the door and met me. We hugged. "Jack, what happened? Is your father all right?" she asked.

"Let's go inside," I said.

We stepped inside. I felt like I needed to hug my mother, but an invisible wall seemed to rise up and stop me. Our family never hugged each other. Affection wasn't something you exhibited at the Oliver home. The closest we ever got to one another was in one of the rare family photos. Seeing my mother sitting on the couch as I entered the room, I remembered the last family photo. It was when I was twelve years old. We were sitting on the same couch. The photographer kept trying to get us to sit closer. That was a struggle. It was like we had the home under a mandatory emotional quarantine. No show of emotions allowed—house rule.

Forgetting the rules, I decided to embrace her and stepped toward the couch. I didn't know what else to do. Before I could make the second step across the room, she said, "He's gone—isn't he?"

"Yes," I said as I stopped.

"The bridge?" she asked.

"Yes," I said. I reached in my pocket and handed her the note.

I sat down beside her on the couch. Tina rushed and sat down beside her on the opposite side putting her arm around her. My mother read the note. She had tears in her tired eyes, but remained composed. She kept her emotions in check, like me.

"Poor Joseph," she said, continuing to look at the note. "He never could find peace."

"I'm sorry," I said. "I don't know what to say."

"There is nothing to say," she said. She sat on the couch with Tina holding her. Tina was sobbing.

I sat back, keeping my distance, the way it had always been in the Oliver home.

● ● ●

"Jack, it's all right to talk about it—talking might help," Tina said. Since the funeral two weeks before, I had not said a word to her about my father or his death. Instead of taking time off from work or school, I only missed the afternoon of the funeral. No tears, no show of emotions. "You know I'm here for you," she said, putting her hand on my shoulder.

"What good would come from talking about him?" I asked, withholding the many things I wanted to say but had promised I would never utter. "I'm fine. It wasn't a surprise. I knew he would do something like that—it was only a matter of time."

"Jack, I'm worried if you're holding all that inside," she said. "Please let me help you."

"I don't need any help with my feelings, Tina," I said angrily. "Just let me deal with this in my own way."

Talking about him would unleash the flood of emotions I had contained inside. His suicide exaggerated all of the paradoxical emotions I had about him. I loved him, but never told him. He never told me he loved me either. I was hurt and angry, but had no way to communicate it to him. I wanted to hate him, but couldn't. He was my father.

I would never see him again. The few times I visited, he was abusive and dismissive of my lifestyle and career choice. We were from different worlds, and neither could accept the other's viewpoint. A wall had been constructed, both of us working hard to build higher and wider. How could I miss him now when he was dead when I did everything to avoid him when he was alive?

He had never given me what I sought the most. I evidently had not given him what he wanted. I desperately wanted him to be proud of me, but for twenty-two years I was never able to get his attention unless he wanted to criticize me. I hated the way he had lived, drinking, gambling, and womanizing, but I was not too dissimilar. He was selfish, and so was I. He spent all of his time and money in the pursuit of his own pleasures and left my mother and me behind to wonder if he would come home. I wondered if that was the kind of man I would ultimately become. I felt sorry for him but could not understand why. He had never been a person who expressed himself—other than with anger—but I always hoped that he would change. Of course, I never expressed myself either, so it may not have mattered.

While I suffered from a confused array of emotions there was one issue on which I had perfect clarity. I vowed that this was a family tradition that stopped with him. *I'll never let myself get into that condition*, I promised myself. When my father's casket was lowered into the ground, I decided that all of my emotions were being laid to rest and buried with him. But it didn't take long for me to realize I was wrong. The unsettling wave of emotions I had held back finally surfaced.

• • •

It was almost a month after my father's death. I was walking across campus and saw a maintenance van, like the one my father drove. From a distance, the man who was carrying a tool box up the steps into the university building looked like my father going on a call. Instantly I missed him. I regretted not doing more to mend our problems. In that moment I understood him and felt pity for him. Tears began to stream down my face; I could not stop them. I ran toward my car hoping no one would see me. I sat down in the car and wept, realizing there was no hope. I could not fix what had been broken. I couldn't hold back the guilt any longer.

Why didn't I do something to help him? How could I have missed the warning signs of his depression? Why didn't I spend more time with him? What was the last thing he said to me? He saw that I was just like him.

"I don't hate you. What I hate is the thought you'll end up like me. That's what I hate." My father's last words to me were a warning.

"Now look at me," I said to the four walls of my apartment as I rubbed tears from my eyes. In true Oliver family fashion, my mother and I never discussed it—never. What could we do? He was gone. Life moved on. I never shed another tear over him. It wasn't because I was strong. I was empty.

I got up to get another drink before I called Benny. *This will be a waste of time—there's no hope*, I thought. I picked up the phone and started pushing the buttons.

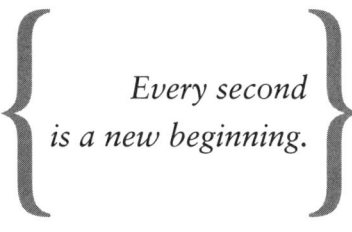

*Every second
is a new beginning.*

—BENJAMIN FRANKLIN PRICE

8. What Are You Looking For?

"WHAT ARE YOU LOOKING FOR?"

Benny's question took me off guard. The memories of my father had fueled a frustration and anger that I could not contain. I had been in attack mode for much of the conversation. I was out to prove he was a relic from a bygone era, lucky at best to find success. At first, I had challenged his simplistic business approach.

"How can you put your Purpose Statement on the front page of your Web site and expect people not to complain? Haven't you set yourself up for failure?"

The simple Purpose Statement for Citizens Bank read:

At Citizens Bank we promise to exceed the service you expect and the trust you demand. Our goal is to be the best bank in your world. If we fail to live up to our goal, let us know. We are here for you.

"Well, Jack, if a business doesn't make a commitment to a client, then how will clients ever trust the business. That's what we do—right up front we make a promise. Then we do our best to practice what we say. If you keep your word, you keep your clients. Does your bank have a Purpose Statement?"

"Yes, but we call them *declarations*: value declarations, service declarations, ethics declarations, client acknowledgement declarations, code of conduct declarations."

"Jack!" Benny said laughing. "I'm not being critical, but you sound like Bubba from the movie *Forrest Gump* describing all of the ways shrimp can be served."

I laughed. *That was funny,* I thought—*I need to remember that one.* Merchants had a declaration for everything. I was glad he didn't ask me to recite any. "Yeah, I guess our way appears a little complex, but all big banks are the same. It's the same in all big businesses, not just banks."

"Simplicity is our organization's goal and my own personal objective," he said. "If we don't understand what we're doing, how can a client?"

"What I don't understand," I said, "is putting *your* direct line phone number as the number to call if someone is upset. You must stay on the phone all day hearing people gripe." I thought listing his direct line number on the Web site as the client's helpline was stupid, but refrained from saying so, waiting to hear his answer.

"Actually, I don't hear complaints all day—and that's a good thing," Benny said, "but if I did, what better use of time could I find, Jack?"

"Hearing complaints doesn't seem like a good use of time to me," I said.

"If you don't listen when someone complains, you're admitting failure," Benny said. "I encourage complaints! I want every client that is having a problem to complain—we then have the opportunity to fix whatever is broken. If they don't complain, they typically leave quietly to a competitor. I call that 'silent death' for a business."

Silent death? That was almost funny, but it occurred to me that was what was happening to my group in Philly after the Merchants takeover. We weren't hearing complaints—people were simply leaving, quietly. Unable to persuade Benny, I changed subjects.

"Everything is so simple in your products," I said, looking at a copy of the types of accounts Benny's bank supported. "How can you continue to grow your business being so simple? People need a wider variety."

"Do they, Jack?" Benny responded. "We have three types of checking accounts. How many does your bank have?"

Thinking rapidly so he would not see my own trouble keeping count, I said, "We have six different personal checking accounts, five interest-bearing accounts, and six business checking accounts—seventeen total."

"Can your people explain the difference in the accounts to your clients?" he asked.

"They're supposed to," I said. "If they can't, we find someone who can."

"Is that working for you?" Benny asked.

"What do you mean?"

"Are you growing? Are your clients happy?"

"Well—no—but this is a different world from Virginia," I said.

"I looked at the number of competitors you have in Philly," he said. "Interestingly, we have more competitors here. Your market has been the target of considerable consolidation. For a small city, we have a remarkable number of competitors, and the list expands every day. But we're continuing to grow—not because we offer everything—but because we keep it simple and allow the clients the confidence of feeling good about their choices."

We, however, were shrinking rapidly. Customers were leaving us in droves. It was not an area I wanted to debate. I tried to find another subject to discuss, but before I could, he continued.

"If clients don't have confidence, they'll leave. Client confidence isn't found in more—but in less. Freedom is the same. More choices don't equate to freedom. More is less, and less is more."

"With that type of thinking you'd get run out of Philly, Benny," I said, frustrated with his perspective.

"What works, works, Jack," Benny said.

"Well, Benny, we'll have to agree to disagree on simplicity," I said, trying to move away from the subject. It was time for my secret weapon. I was sure I would expose Benny as something much less than the tremendous leader John and many in the industry believed him to be.

"Why are you looking outside your organization to fill your position?" I asked. "I would've thought you had a succession plan in place when you retire."

"Over the years we developed people to be specific in their functions," he said. "The goal was to have clarity and simplicity as the foundation for everything we do. You don't get that having, pardon the pun, jacks-of-all-trades in key positions. We also paid our people very appropriately to do a good job. We are now faced with the interesting challenge of having very satisfied, successful people doing what they love. We looked very closely and discussed the opportunity with a good number of people. No one was interested. They love what they do and are doing it very well. The other reason I am looking outside the organization is to find someone with a fresh approach—an objective perspective—on how to do business. We can all get stuck in a rut, even when we're successful, so bringing in someone with the leadership, experience, and knowledge to do better is our goal. I'm looking for an energetic, brave leader, a person that can take Citizens Bank to the next level."

"John said you're being pressured to sell to a large bank. I know you can't tell me who, but why is that happening?" I asked.

"Pure and simple greed," Benny said. "Several of our directors have forgotten their commitment to why we formed this business. They see an opportunity to make some fast cash. I understand their greed but do not agree with it. We have a number of banks that would love to acquire us. But, Jack, you said it yourself; the big banks do business differently. I don't see that working here, and I can prove it. I'm dedicated to keeping the bank independent, not for greed, but because of a promise I made and the fact we are doing pretty well."

I didn't know what to say in response. I could only ask a more personal question. "Why would you consider me?"

"I respect John Helm's opinion, and he says you're the best available person. You've been very successful, obviously, in your career. But Jack, I have a question. What are you looking for?"

That was the question I had been afraid to ask myself. Now, after arguing with Benny for over thirty minutes, the simple question of what I wanted emerged, and I paused. "Actually, I'm not sure. I have roots here in Philly. I have been successful, but I'm not sure I can continue forward with Merchants."

"You may fit here or somewhere else—that is something you must choose. But from our brief time chatting, I believe you could use a change," Benny said in a calm, reassuring voice. "It sounds like you don't fit into your new environment."

After a pause, he continued, "I'd like to extend an invitation to come visit us. I'll pay for the plane flight and all expenses for you and your family. I would like you to come down to Roanoke for a weekend so we can talk outside of the office. My wife Ann and I will show you the beauty of our little corner of the world in south-west Virginia. No obligation. We can fish and hike. Look at it as a weekend in the country away from Philadelphia. I promise you'll enjoy it. You can bank on it! Are you interested?"

The offer surprised me. Before the conversation began, my goal had been to identify Benny as a living dinosaur in banking. I had not been able to do so. Not yet. Now I had an invitation to visit. But he said my family, something that wasn't possible. Fishing? Hiking? It sounded more like a Boy Scout expedition than a job interview. "I appreciate the offer, but I don't think so right now," I said. "I do appreciate the offer."

"Jack, will you do me a favor?" Benny asked. "Sleep on it and then let me know. I promise you'll have a great time. I feel like I know you from talking with John over the years. You need a getaway weekend I'm sure. Will you consider it?"

Before I knew what I was saying I responded, "Okay, I'll think about it and get back with you tomorrow."

"Great! Do you like to fish?" he asked.

"The only time I ever went fishing was with my father at Penn's Landing. We sat there for an hour before he got frustrated and decided to pack up and leave. I doubt if fish could even live in the river because it's so polluted."

"Pollution is not a problem here," he said. "Sometimes it gets a little crowded at the lake, but I'm learning to live with the company."

"I'll give you a call tomorrow," I said, trying to reclaim control of the conversation.

"I strongly believe in fate, and it's at work here," he said. "You need to know what you want in life. Searching for the answer is never a waste of time. You need to do what is right for you and your family. I'm sure you will."

"Thanks, Benny, I appreciate the offer," I said. "I really do."

After hanging up the phone, I looked across the room and saw my reflected image in the blank television screen. I could see the outline of a person. I could not see the face in the reflection. My weight had ballooned to over two hundred fifty pounds. The bloated form was not the Jack Oliver I expected to see. What I saw was a lonely, alcoholic, obsessive man on the verge of failure. I had achieved almost everything I wanted in my career but was not allowed to take the final step—the one that would signify my ultimate success: I wanted to be a bank president—and answer to no one. But I had failed. The person I married and loved was not by my side. Instead, she was living in the home I had worked many years to give to my family—but I wasn't there. I had no real connection to my two children. I was not where I thought I would be.

What am I looking for? It wasn't this. I needed to talk to someone. I was feeling hopeless.

I called Cassie.

9. What Happens If I Quit?

"WHAT HAPPENS IF I QUIT?" I asked.

Cassie was mad. I had to talk to someone about the conversation I had just had with Benny. I had too much alcohol in my system to drive to her apartment, so I called hoping to get her opinion on the idea of leaving Merchants Bank. She made her opinion clear.

"How could you even think about giving up your position with Merchants and your bonus?" Cassie asked. "Jack, those are some huge dollars. I would have to work ten years to clear that much money. Ten years! You only have another year. I'm not so sure you appreciate what a good job you have."

"What good is the money if I'm not alive to spend it?" I asked.

"Your job isn't killing you—it's your ex and the kids that are putting the pressure on you. You're goin' through a rough spot," she said. "You're tough—you can find a way to cope."

"Coping is what I've done all of my life," I said. "I want more from life than money." The sound of what I had just said shocked me—*it must be the alcohol,* I thought as soon as I said it. It shocked Cassie much more.

"What did you say? That doesn't sound like the Jack Oliver I fell in love with and adore. You got where you're at because you're ruthless—you never give up. So now you're ready to quit because some old man in Virginia offers you a job?" Cassie asked with frustration dripping from every word. "You're ready to stop what you're doing and start over in some little hick town in Virginia?"

"What happens if I quit? What would you think of me?"

"I have always admired you for the way you play the game of life," she said, a terminology we shared. "You're the best player I know. But talking about tossing away a quarter of a million dollars when you're only a year away from getting it doesn't make sense. I'm worried about you, Jack. That's a lot of money."

"Is that all there is to life?" I asked. "Money?"

"To me—yes—because that is how I can live the life I want," Cassie said with a firm conviction in her voice. "You've forgotten how tough it can be. Do you know what it's like to not be able to buy something like food? You know, life's necessities, Jack. You may have forgotten, but I remember what not having money is like."

"I would make plenty of money in Virginia," I said.

"Maybe you would, but you would be in Virginia," she said, "and I'll be here."

"Is that the problem?" I asked. "Would you want to move to Virginia?"

"I would never consider moving to Virginia or anywhere else," she said. "This is my home. Philly is where I'll die. I thought you felt the same way."

"Well, that's still what I think, but I am in a rut at work—I hate my job," I said, allowing my emotions to find words. "At PT&G I was a heartbeat away from the top. At Merchants I'm a role player, someone they want to keep for a while, then I'll be expendable. I don't like that feeling. I'm better than anybody at Merchants. Nobody in their organization can handle the Philly operation like I can."

"I know, Jack," Cassie said, "but with a quarter of a million you could leave and find something else to do in Philly. There are other banks here. You could get even with Merchants by working for another bank. You don't have to go to Virginia."

"This is a unique opportunity. I could be in charge of the bank after one year. The bank has great potential. I could make a lot more money than the bonus. I would have a future," I said.

"A future?" she asked. "Maybe you could in banking—you

know more about that than me. But when I think of the future, I'm not thinking about banking. Is there any future for us?"

"I didn't know we were committed to a future," I said, growing weary of the conversation.

"You're right, Jack, we aren't. There's no future for us; how stupid could I be?" she said. "You do what you think is right for you, as always. Take care of number one. But don't come crying around to me about making a mistake. If you go to Virginia, you're makin' the biggest mistake of your life. I promise you that, Jack Oliver!" She hung up the phone.

Maybe Cassie was right.

• • •

Am I a quitter? I asked myself. I had never been a quitter. I was the opposite.

The job advertisements demand it: *Must be a self-starter!* Guilty, as charged. I was always ready. I felt comfortable starting something, going as fast as possible, and I only considered stopping after passing under the checkered flag, winning the race. I deplored the idea of stopping. Stopping allowed others to pass you. Quitting was for wimps. Quitting was failing. No one would ever beat me.

That is why I loved NASCAR races. Braking was something you would do only when the yellow caution flag dropped or you had to go into the pit to fill the tank up and change the tires. I lived my life like I was in a NASCAR race. I would pit only when I had to do so. I never allowed anyone to pass me. My foot was always on the accelerator.

Benny had started my mind racing. I kept hearing his question, "What are you looking for?" Was it Cassie? How had Cassie become such a prominent person in my life? Was Cassie part of what I was looking for?

I got up from the recliner and put a frozen dinner in the oven. Feeling thirsty and needing some relief after the argument with Cassie, I decided to pour another drink. Cassie was one of the things I would leave behind if I left Philly. As the oven began to heat the turkey dinner, I sat back down in the recliner, drink in hand. Would I miss her?

Cassie had been a part of my life for many years. While we had never talked about the future, she had become one of the most significant people in my life—till now. How did Cassie and I connect?

Turning the television around so I didn't have to see my reflection, I sat down in the recliner. The beginning of our relationship was something that started innocently. It started with a choice I had made years ago and had consequences I never expected.

• • •

"*What do I expect*?" Tina repeated my question. "I expect you to want to spend time with me and enjoy our time together."

The world can change with a few words. Tina and I both expected more than what the other person could deliver. Our brief conversation opened a subject we had avoided—our expectations. What did we expect from each other? Unfulfilled expectations finally doomed our marriage. What Tina expected of me I could not give to her. I had other things I wanted more. Cassie was one of them.

When I couldn't get what I wanted from Tina, I looked outside our marriage and found Cassie. But meeting her was not the beginning of the end for Tina and me. It all began in the days leading up to the birth of our daughter, Jessica, long before I met Cassie. The choices I made in those few days proved fatal for my marriage and opened my mind to desires I had held at bay for years.

• • •

Less than a week from the due date of the birth of our first child I was working late every evening. I felt backed into a corner. I had to choose between doing my job at a critical time in my career or sitting around with Tina while she complained about being fat and her feet hurting. At that moment, there was not much of a choice.

"What should I do?" I asked, pulling out my best defense. "You tell me, Tina, what should I do?" I had already made up my mind—I had to go back to the office that evening to finish a report.

"Be happy, Jack," she said suddenly, appearing to exhibit some concern about my welfare in the moment of a harsh interchange. "I want you to be happy. If you really think work is more important and that makes you happy, go for it. At least one of us will be happy."

There are moments in life when you know that what you are doing is wrong but convince yourself you are right. That was one of those moments. After eating a sandwich and chips and gulping down a beer, I went back to the office at 7:30 P.M. to do paperwork, leaving Tina alone. I enjoyed working when no one else was in the office. I could get more accomplished. I stayed until midnight and came home to find Tina asleep on the couch.

What do I expect? I wondered as I stepped into the kitchen. I wanted some understanding and compassion. I had the pressure of the world on my back. Why couldn't Tina see that? Granted, I had set out with some lofty expectations. But I could see the light at the end of the tunnel.

Obviously, Tina didn't share my vision. The light she saw at the end of the tunnel was a train barreling down the tracks on a collision course. All I heard at home was how I was working too many hours and not spending enough time with her. Tina's negativity was something I had never noticed until after we were married. Now, Tina's demands were forcing me to choose. I wanted to be excited about the birth of our first child, but I could not enjoy the moment. All I could do was worry about the future and my career. I could never get ahead in my career if I spent all my time with Tina. My career demanded that I put everything into my job to ensure a bright future. That was my priority. Why didn't Tina see that?

After throwing together a bologna sandwich and opening a fresh beer, I walked back into the living room and sat down in a chair facing the couch. As I gazed at the sleeping figure, I remembered the passion that created the life she carried inside. That night was special. We had celebrated my first promotion at PT&G—I was named a management trainee. The years of sacrifice were finally paying off. Things seemed so perfect then. But as the memories of that night faded, my frustration returned. Why couldn't she see that everything would work out? I wanted to be happy with Tina and the baby. Why didn't she trust me? I wanted to give our child everything that my parents couldn't afford, a better life.

Still, I sat looking at Tina and remembered how she made me

feel. I was in love with her. Maybe she was right—I couldn't keep working at the same frantic pace after the baby was born.

Feeling guilty for leaving Tina alone night after night, I promised myself I was going to spend more quality time with her and the baby. I was going to relax and take a different approach at work. Life wasn't a hundred-yard dash, it was a marathon. I needed to pace myself and enjoy the scenery on the long-distance run. I was not going to risk my marriage over my career. I was going to change. Now was the time.

I stepped over to the couch and knelt on the floor, putting my head gently against her stomach. Tina awoke and was surprised to see me so close. "What's wrong?" she asked.

"Nothing is wrong," I said. "I think I've got things figured out. You'll see."

"Jack, I worry about you," Tina said. "I love you."

"I love you too," I said. "Now, let me help you to bed."

By the time I had shaved in the morning, I had already forgotten those promises. My focus was back on my career. How could I forget so easily? It just happened. I went to work early that morning to win the game of life. I had to keep up the pace.

As soon as I entered the office that morning I saw a yellow sticky note on the top of my computer. CHAD NEEDS TO SEE YOU ASAP! It was hand written by Chad's assistant.

• • •

"*Why now?*" I asked myself. It was the first time I would meet with him since being named the bank's management trainee. While I was not expecting the meeting, having an audience with Chad could never hurt.

"Jack, have a seat," he said as I entered the room. Chad remained seated behind his desk. "You're doing a great job. In fact, I'm giving you a special assignment. It is somewhat of a test."

"I'm ready to do whatever you need me to do," I said.

"I know. That's what I like about you, Jack. But this is a little different." Chad proceeded to tell me that a car dealership, Frank Smith Ford, one of the bank's largest clients, was having cash flow problems.

The owner, Frank Smith, was a friend of Chad's, and he wanted to help his friend. "While Frank is a friend, I have a fear that he is selling cars out-of-trust. Do you know what that is?" Chad asked.

I knew what out-of-trust was for a bank and a car dealer relationship. The bank loans money to a car dealer to purchase vehicles from the manufacturer. The dealership assigns the car as collateral for the amount they pay the manufacturer. When the vehicle is sold, the dealership agrees to immediately repay the bank the amount owed on the vehicle. If they don't repay immediately they are out-of-trust. I summarized this for Chad.

"Right," Chad said. "I think Frank is selling the vehicles and withholding payment to us for several weeks—maybe longer. While we are making money on the debt, he is violating the agreement, and in the process we lose our collateral. So Frank is getting our best interest rate on an unsecured, much riskier loan. If he is doing this, he's being dishonest. I need to find out."

"What do you want me to do?" I asked.

"To add some complication, I think someone in our loan department is overlooking this situation—on purpose. Why, I do not know. I want you to go to the dealership on Saturday and perform a surprise check of the inventory. I want you to get proof of what happened to any vehicle that is not on the car lot. Ask questions, and get an answer on every missing vehicle. Did they sell it? Where is it? Frank won't be there. He's out of town. So you can be tough on his son, Frank Jr., who will probably be called off the golf course to meet with you while you're doing your surprise check of the vehicles."

This sounded important; here was something that would not generally be handed off to a rookie. I wondered why I was being chosen.

"I want you to do this because you can get the information without raising any suspicion of your intent in our loan department, who may be in on this. You're new to this area, so if Frank complains about your surprise visit, I can blame it on your inexperience. But what I really want to know, other than what Frank is doing, is how you handle a situation like this. How do you respond to pressure? Can you handle a delicate situation? Can I trust you? This is the real world, Jack. This is a test. Are you ready?" Chad asked.

Without hesitation I said, "Yes." After gathering the information from the bank's database without anyone questioning what I was doing, I planned my Saturday excursion. Tina could give birth at any moment, but that was not in my thoughts at work.

I had a job to do.

• • •

On Friday afternoon I received a call from Tina. It was time for Jessica Elizabeth Oliver to enter the world. I raced to our apartment and took Tina to Jefferson Hospital. After thirteen hours of labor, Jessica was born at 5:35 Saturday morning.

In the middle of the labor cycle, I remembered what I had to do later that day. How could I not do it? It was crucial to complete the inspection while Frank Smith Sr. was out of town. Chad was counting on me. Or would he understand about the birth of my child? I am sure he will.

Sometime before 9:00 A.M. I found a few minutes to call him. I called Chad's home number, a number he gave me to call after I completed the inspection later that day. His daughter answered the phone and after identifying myself I waited several minutes for Chad to come to the phone.

"Jack, is there a problem?" Chad asked immediately.

"Mr. Jefferies, I mean, Chad, I'm here at the hospital," I began, stumbling over my thoughts after a night without sleep. "My wife just gave birth to our daughter, our first child—a few hours ago. I was wondering . . ."

Before I could get out another word, Chad interrupted. "Jack, that's great. Congratulations to you and your wife. So this timed perfectly. You'll still be able to do the inspection later today, right?"

"Well, sir, that is why I was calling you," I continued, but was interrupted again by Chad's forceful voice.

"Well, you could do it another day—but that would be too late! I need it done *now*," he said. "If you knew that this could be a conflict, why didn't you tell me?"

"I'm sorry. I've been up all night. I'll do it—I'll call you after I finish the inspection," I said, caving into the pressure.

"Good," he said. "This is something you'll face often in your career. You were there for the most important part. Your wife will understand. Don't fail me. I am counting on you."

"I'll never fail you—I promise. You can trust me," I said.

"That is something you'll have to earn, Jack," he said. "Now, go back to your wife and baby. Enjoy your family."

After hanging up the pay phone, standing in the empty hospital corridor, I thought, *how am I going to explain this?* I was again stuck between my family and my career.

I went to the recovery area still unsure of what I would say. "I have to leave the hospital for most of the afternoon. I just talked to Chad and he wants me to do a very important inspection on a client who may be cheating the bank. It's a secret assignment. Chad says it's a test to see if he can trust me. I've got to do it, Tina. He's counting on me." Tina looked like she had seen a ghost. She was in shock. Then she was angry.

"How can you leave your new baby and wife to go to work on a Saturday afternoon? And for what—a secret assignment? You say this is a test? What is wrong with that man? Is he crazy? I cannot believe you're doing this," Tina said with tears streaming down her face.

"I have to do this for our future, for the good of you and Jessica," I said meekly.

"Jack, be honest," Tina said. "You're doing this for you."

• • •

I conducted the inspection. As Chad anticipated, the dealership had sold twenty-three new cars without paying the bank, leaving the bank exposed for almost a half a million dollars. Frank Jr. showed up in a panic. He looked like a spoiled rich kid, just what I expected.

"We are having some accounting problems," he said. "That's why we haven't paid on time."

"From what I'm looking at, you haven't paid on cars sold three weeks ago," I said. "That sounds like more of a business decision than an accounting problem."

"Are you implying we're crooks?" he asked, raising his already high-pitched voice.

"No, I'm not implying anything. I'm just looking at the facts. Your father's business signed a contract that says when we must receive payment. I need a check now for all of the cars you've sold. Otherwise, you're in default," I said, never changing my gaze into his eyes.

Frank Jr. begged for time.

"You're out of time," I said. "You owe us the money. Pay it and I'll leave." I didn't flinch. I felt power, real power for the first time in my career. I had to hold back a smile.

"My father will be back in town late tomorrow," Frank Jr. said. "I'm sure he'll want to come to the bank and talk to Chad about the situation."

"Tell him what he needs to bring—a check covering all of the out-of-trust cars," I said. "That's what we expect." After leaving the dealership I found a pay phone, called Chad, and reported on what I found and what I had told Frank Jr.

"Excellent job, Jack," he said. "Come to my office at seven o'clock on Monday morning and we'll plan our next step. You did a great job. You also proved what was important to you. I won't forget it."

• • •

Tina and Jessica were scheduled to leave the hospital on Sunday, but a complication in Jessica's breathing warranted the doctor keeping her till Monday for observation. My schedule was now very complicated. I had another choice to make. I told Tina I had to be at work on Monday morning early, but would then come to the hospital and take her and the baby home.

"No, my sister is in town. Alice said she would help, so you go ahead and take care of more important things," Tina said, almost as if she expected me to not be available. "I'll take care of things here— the less-important things in your life."

I swallowed her sarcasm. I knew in my gut that Chad would make things more difficult the next morning if I was a minute late. I thanked her for being understanding.

"Oh, I understand Jack," she said. "I understand."

• • •

When I met with Chad Monday morning he was in a great mood.

That wasn't what I expected from a person who just found out that someone was cheating his business and putting a half a million dollars at risk. I went over the details with Chad. He took notes and asked questions to understand every detail of what I found and did not find. He then called Frank Smith Sr., and put the call on speaker phone.

"Frank, this is Chad. You're out-of-trust. I want your line of credit paid off by noon today or I will repossess every car on your lot and put you out of business," Chad said in a cold, matter-of-fact voice. I was in as much of a state of shock as Mr. Smith.

"That's impossible!" Mr. Smith replied. "You know I can't do that. Why are you doing this to me?"

"Read your loan contracts. You have two options. You can either bring me the money, or you can execute the agreement to sell your dealership to Andy French. One or the other by noon, or I will own your dealership for a lot less than what Andy is offering to pay you."

Andy French was on PT&G's board of directors. He owned several car dealerships in the Philadelphia area. I had never heard his name associated with Frank Smith. What was Chad doing?

"You're a bastard, Chad," Smith said. "Just like your father, you don't care about anyone but yourself. I'll sign the papers—French can own this place. You got your way. I hope you burn in hell."

"Thanks, Frank, for seeing it my way," Chad said. "That's the best thing for everyone, and you know it. Thanks."

Smith had already hung up before he heard the final "thanks" from Chad.

Chad had just forced a client to sell his business to a member of the bank's board. Chad had used the defaulted loan as leverage. He used me to get the job done because he didn't want anyone else to know, and he knew I'd be quiet. I was numb.

"Jack, you now have a taste for real banking. You liked doing this, didn't you? I could see it in your eyes. You liked having the power to tell Frank Smith's rich, stupid son that he had to pay up or get out, didn't you?"

I didn't know what to say. "I was just following your instructions. It was my job," I said.

"And that is why you'll get ahead," Chad said. He smiled. "Follow my orders, and you and I will have a great relationship."

I felt at that moment I had sold my soul. It was something I had never expected.

• • •

The timer went off on the stove. My turkey dinner was ready. I walked into the kitchen and using a dish towel pulled the meal from the oven. I looked out the window and saw the steady traffic passing on the street below. It was raining, blurring the lights on the cars, as if they were connected.

Where were they going at this time of the night? Home? What is home? I sat down at the small table. Taking the first bite of potatoes I realized the dinner was not done. I threw the tray in the trash can and decided to opt for another drink. I told myself that I'd stop after this one.

Making my way back into the small living room, I turned the television around facing the recliner. Sitting back in the recliner I hit the remote, but nothing happened. I saw again the reflection on the darkened television screen—a wave of hopelessness poured over me. I wanted to talk to Tina, but it was too late and I was too drunk. I threw the remote control across the room, barely missing the television. The remote was in pieces.

As meticulously as I had planned my life I had somehow gone off course. "Is this all there is?" I said aloud. I leaned the recliner back with a thrust that almost tipped the chair over. *Maybe this was why my father killed himself,* I thought to myself, mentally stepping toward the abyss.

I opened my eyes and looked at the ceiling, which was marked with stains from a leak. I needed a plumber. A plumber—that's what I could have done with my life.

It was after midnight. While exhausted, my mind continued to run full throttle. I thought back to the first time I met Cassie. My life's journey was littered with events that signaled I had reached a fork in the road. Was it coincidence or fate?

"Timing is everything," I said aloud, shutting my eyes and remembering that day and that fork in the road. Like many other times, my timing was off.

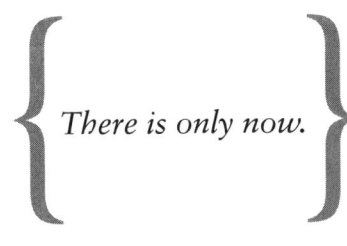

There is only now.

— BENJAMIN FRANKLIN PRICE

10. What Time Is It?

"WHAT TIME IS IT?" Tina asked still in a half-sleep.

"You don't want to know," I said. "It's early." It was four-thirty in the morning. Even for a late-to-bed-and-early-to-rise Jack Oliver, this was early.

"Why are you going in to the office so early today?" she asked.

"I have something to do, something unpleasant."

"So, what's new?" Tina said, rolling over and covering her head with a pillow. In a muffled tone I heard her say, "You would think you were a mortician instead of a banker."

The day before, Chad had called me into his office and given me the news. I had earned a promotion and management assignment after my one year in the PT&G management trainee program. Even though I had received a pay raise along with the promotion, I didn't feel like celebrating the event—strings were attached.

"Jack, you've done a great job in everything I've asked. You're dedicated, and I trust you. I want you to have a challenge— something you can really sink your teeth into," Chad said. He gave me a rare smile. "I am putting you in charge of our Fifth Street office. The office has been underperforming for years. You've worked there before, haven't you?"

"Yes," I said. "I worked there as a teller before you promoted me."

"I thought you had—that's good. I think you know that the people in that office are the same people who started there when we opened it. It's time for a change. They need a fresh approach. You're the man, Jack."

The Fifth Street office was located on the edge of one of the trendier sections of Philly. The area had been almost in ruins until Thomas Skeens, a respected developer in Philadelphia, bought everything he could find and began a refurbishing campaign. Skeens was one of PT&G's largest borrowers, with several million in loans outstanding. At first, his efforts had seemed doomed to failure. But his idea finally caught hold, and one of the worst neighborhoods became one of the gems of Philly residential markets.

"You have one year to get the office up to my expectations. Don't let me down," Chad reminded me. "The future is now, Jack—make good things happen."

I was listening and thinking about the office. Chad hadn't mentioned what he was going to do with Henry Starnes, the manager of the office since it opened.

"Chad, I appreciate the opportunity and will not let you down. The office does have a lot of potential," I said, "but I'm curious. What are you going to do with Henry?"

"One of the first things you need to do is clean house," Chad replied. "The cleaning starts at the top. I want you to fire Henry tomorrow. That will get everyone's attention."

I didn't know what to say. Henry was one of the nicest people in the organization. Everyone at PT&G liked him. Henry was one of the first people I worked with and had given me recognition for doing my job as a teller. I liked him.

"Why is he being fired?" I asked.

"You do want the job don't you?" Chad responded gruffly.

"Yes sir—but why are we firing Henry?" I asked.

"We aren't firing Henry—you are," Chad said.

"Why am I firing him?" I asked.

"Are you questioning my decision?" Chad asked.

Knowing I had crossed a very clear line with Chad, I said, "No.

I wouldn't question you. I have never fired anyone. I just want to know how to handle it."

"Here is your short lesson in firing people. Call it Firing 101," he said. The smile made its second appearance. "Walk into Henry's office. Tell him I just made you the new manager and he no longer has a job. Tell him to clean out his desk, turn in his keys, and be out of the office by closing time. That is all you say. Never say that you're sorry or blame it on me or anyone else. Just do it exactly like that, and everything will be okay. Can you do that?" Chad asked, leaning back in his chair.

"Yes—I will do what you told me," I said. "I won't let you down."

"Good—I know you will," he said. "Get that dinosaur out of there and do some business."

I didn't tell Tina about the new assignment. I felt guilty for the way I was getting the promotion. I couldn't sleep that night and went to work early and reviewed reports comparing the PT&G offices to see how the office matched up. My stomach was in knots.

• • •

I still didn't understand why I was firing Henry as I drove to the Fifth Street office. *Don't you need a reason to fire someone?* I wondered, making my way through the maze of stoplights. My hands were visibly shaking and my heart pounding rapidly. I had never fired anyone. Why did it have to be Henry? What was even worse was I was taking his place. Henry had been at PT&G for thirty-six years. While his performance may not have been great, it was never terrible. But I had a job to do.

I entered the office and spoke casually to the tellers and Sherry Hall, the receptionist. Sherry had moved from Georgia years ago but had kept her accent. People always made fun of her, labeling her as "slow" because of her speech, but the customers seemed to like her. She reminded me of Scarlet from *Gone with the Wind*. "You must be lost, Jack Oliver, comin' to this side of the city," Sherry joked. "How ya doin'?"

"I'm doing fine," I said. "I need to talk to Henry."

"Henry is in the back makin' coffee—doin' his morning chores," she said, laughing. "Do you want me to get him for ya?"

"That'll be fine," I said. "I'll just wait in his office."

Walking through the lobby on my first real step up the company ladder should have been something I wanted to always remember as a special moment. I knew I would always remember the moment, but now for unhappy reasons.

I had tried my best to find common ground with Chad regarding Henry's fate. I looked at every piece of comparative information on Henry's office. The office was slightly below average among the bank's fifty-four offices. But you could make a strong case that almost one-half of our managers could be facing the same fate as Henry, based on their performance.

So why was Henry being singled out? Maybe it was his lack of leadership? He was making coffee. He had other people who could make coffee. Sherry was teasing Henry about "doin' his chores." At his salary he was wasting the bank's money. *That is it,* I realized. *Henry is old and does not have the strength to lead. He is a dinosaur who needs to go.* That is what I kept telling myself as I stepped into his office to wait for him to finish his chores.

The first things I noticed were the family photos on his credenza. Henry obviously had a lot of children and grandchildren. I counted at least four children from the older family portrait on the corner of the bookcase. What I was getting ready to do would not make me popular with any of these strangers. They would probably curse my name every time they heard it. But I had a job to do.

I started thinking about my own family. Jessica was a toddler. In one year I had spent a grand total of one evening alone with my daughter—forced to do so when Tina attended a baby shower for one of her college friends. My work had kept me busy. I was trying to get experience in every department. It had taken its toll on my home life, but Jessica was a baby and wouldn't notice I wasn't there. *I'll do better,* I thought.

Henry stepped into the office without his jacket on, wearing a rumpled white shirt with the sleeves rolled up to his elbows. It looked like he had slept in it.

"Hey Jack!" Henry said, extending his hand. "We miss you coming in and subbing on our teller line—you were the best."

"Yeah, I miss it in some ways," I said, shaking his hand, still unsure of how I could get to the reason I was visiting.

"You're moving up the ladder," he said. "Congratulations on the promotion to management trainee. I'm sure your family is very proud of you." He released my hand from his firm handshake. He seemed very sincere.

"Well, that's been almost a year ago—I've been busy," I said, feeling awkward.

"Has it been that long?" Henry said. "You've got a new addition to your family, don't you?"

"Yeah, a little girl, Jessica," I said.

"Ah, that's great! I love 'em when they're little and they can't talk back," he said, laughing. "You'll see what I'm talking about when she gets to be a teenager."

Still trying to find a way to change the conversation, I muttered, "I haven't got to spend a lot of time with her. You know how work is."

"I'll give you a little advice from someone who made a mistake," he said, turning his head to look at the pictures on the credenza. "I spent too much time at work and not enough with the kids—I know that now."

I did not know what to say. "Would you mind shutting the door, Henry?" I asked as I sat down in one of the chairs facing his desk.

"Sure thing, Jack. You act like someone just run over your cat or something," he said as he shut the door and sat down behind his desk. He remained leaning forward with both hands folded on his desk. "So, what brings you to Fifth Street?"

"Henry, you're fired," I said as slowly and carefully as I could, trying to hide every emotion from my voice and expressions. I made sure to keep looking into his eyes, hoping he would not see my own fear. "You need to get everything out of the office by four o'clock today," I continued without any hesitation or stammering.

"What did you say?" Henry asked.

"You're fired," I said.

"Is this some kind of joke?" he asked, nervously laughing and hitting the top of the desk with his hands. "Jack, you gotta be kidding?"

"I would not kid you about something like this," I said. "Henry, you're fired." I wanted to say I was sorry, but Chad was right. I could see how saying I was sorry would only open up a huge Pandora's box of comments. I stuck to my preprogrammed routine without compromise. *I must be strong,* I kept telling myself.

"Wait a minute. You really aren't kidding are you?" Henry said as his mouth grew taut and most of the color faded from his face. "Why are you doing this?"

"I have been promoted as manager at Fifth Street," I responded, with the most emotionless tone I could muster. "The office has underperformed. I'm going to fix it."

Henry's face was now a crimson red. "You little weasel. You did this, didn't you? You wanted this office and got me fired," Henry said.

"I had nothing to do with the past problems," I replied, holding back my anger and frustration with the situation. "I'm here to make this office a high performer."

"I think I know what this is about," Henry said in a much calmer voice. A grin grew on his still crimson face. "You're just doing Chad's dirty work. I'm being fired because I wouldn't sign off on one of Chad's loan deals. It's making sense now. You're just his henchman."

I didn't have a clue what Henry was talking about. I really was afraid to ask. I didn't. "Whatever you say won't change the fact I have a job to do," I said. "You need to pack up and leave."

"I'm disappointed in you," he said as he sighed and shook his head from side to side. "I would have never thought that the same young kid who was so happy to have a job at a bank and come in dressed like he got the clothes at a thrift shop would ever have the balls to walk in my office and fire me like this. You know, at first, everyone was pulling for you—but we started to see through your act. I bet you didn't know that everyone was on to your game—but we are, Jack. We see you for what you are. You'll do anything to get ahead and you met a willing partner in Chad. You two are quite a team."

"Well," I responded, "that's life." Wanting to end the nightmarish situation, I repeated, "You're fired. You have until four o'clock to clear out of this office or I'll have security help you." As I got up, Henry stood and reached out and grabbed my arm, gripping it tightly.

"Congratulations, Jack, on your promotion. You earned it doing Chad's dirty work. I know you're going to go far in this business. You have exactly what an executive needs—no feelings. I think you enjoyed firing me. You don't act like you care about anyone except your job."

"Let go of my arm," I said. "I do care about my job—maybe you should have cared more? What's your excuse?"

"I don't need an excuse," he said, releasing my arm. "I know why this is happening. Good luck when everything catches up with you—it will. Now, if you don't mind going back to whatever hole you climbed out of and leave me alone I'll pack up and get out. But first, I have to tell my family." I walked toward the door.

"You know this will happen to you someday, don't you, Jack? What goes around comes around."

"I don't think so," I said, avoiding looking back at Henry. I was just doing my job.

• • •

What will they think? I wondered as I walked out of his office. I heard Henry's door slam as I exited the lobby. Stepping into the sunshine, my thoughts returned to what was most important—survival. I had one year to improve the office's performance, or I would be just like Henry—fired. Firing Henry would definitely get everyone's attention in the office. Maybe it would help me. I walked aimlessly down Fifth Street toward the parking garage. If they are afraid of me, they'll at least pay attention to what I say. Or would they be resistant, resentful? Regardless of what I had hoped for in my first assignment, this was something I couldn't change unless I changed the entire staff. I stopped at the corner and looked up and down the street. Maybe that's the solution? I needed loyalty to be a success.

I needed to get something to drink. Walking down the busy street, I saw a coffee shop on the corner, Rude Awakening. I liked the name, and it looked like a place where I could have a few moments to collect my thoughts. As I entered the small shop, a warm, friendly voice greeted me.

"Good morning!" the young lady said from behind the counter. The morning rush had left the shop with only a few customers.

"Good morning," I said, making my way to the counter. "What would you suggest?" I looked up at the menu above the counter. Looking back to the attractive brunette, I noticed her name tag. It read, CASSIE.

"It depends on what you like," Cassie said. "Are you someone who likes something different?"

I was Mr. Stuck-in-the-Mud, as Tina referred to me. I rarely tried anything new, sticking with whatever I was used to—especially coffee. I hated the various flavored coffees. While I knew what the true answer to her simple question was, I felt the need to let Cassie know that I was willing to try something different.

"Sure," I said. "I like to try different things. Surprise me."

Cassie's face glowed with a bright, engaging smile and eased away some of the horror I had just endured. "Comin' right up!" she said, making sure to have eye contact with me for a split second. As she mixed the drink I realized I would be a regular in the neighborhood. I was now the Fifth Street office manager.

"Cassie is an unusual name," I said, as she began to work on my surprise drink.

"It's short for Cassandra," she said. "When I was little, Cassandra was too long for my mother to get out when I was getting into trouble—so she shortened it to Cassie."

"I like that," I said. "Cassie—that's a really catchy name."

"Thanks," she said. "I still get in trouble so that's why I go by it," she said. Her playful attitude was just what I needed. Before I could utter a response, the door opened and out of the corner of my eye I saw a familiar face. It was William Crabtree. We looked at each other at the same time. He was with a well-dressed gentleman I didn't recognize. Crabtree was in charge of PT&G's loan area. While he had never said anything critical to me directly, I knew he was not a fan of Jack Oliver.

"Jack, what are you doing in this part of town?" Crabtree said as though he had caught me in the bank vault with a bag full of cash. "I didn't know we let you out of your cell during the day." His weak attempt at humor only highlighted what I believed was, at best, a contemptuous regard for me.

"I'm visiting the Fifth Street office," I said.

"Tom, this is Jack Oliver, our management trainee at the bank," he said as I shook the stranger's hand. "Jack, this is Tom Skeens, one of the bank's best clients," Crabtree said as he finished the introductions.

After exchanging the minimal pleasantries, Cassie inserted herself into the conversation, saying, "Your surprise drink is ready." The comment embarrassed me in front of Crabtree and the client.

"Thanks, Cassie," I said without thinking, turning toward her and opening my wallet.

"And your name is?" Cassie asked still smiling, knowing she had made an impression on me.

"I'm Jack—Jack Oliver," I said. Without thinking I said, "I'm the new manager of PT&G's Fifth Street office."

Crabtree, still standing within earshot, heard my comment. I turned to leave the coffee shop, but he stopped me. "Jack, can I speak to you for a second," he said. We stepped back into an unoccupied corner of the shop as Crabtree excused himself from Mr. Skeens.

"Did you say you're the new manager at Fifth Street? What happened to Henry?" Crabtree asked.

"I fired him this morning. He's clearing out his office," I responded.

"That's a surprise," he said. "Chad never said a word about it to me. I think a lot of Henry. He's worked at the bank as long as I have. What happened?"

"He was not doing his job," I said, not knowing what else to say.

"So you're going to take his place," he said. "That's interesting. Well, good luck—you'll need it."

As I turned to leave, Cassie said in a noticeably friendly voice, "Do you like your surprise drink?"

I took a careful sip of the drink. I liked it. "It's great!" I said. "Thanks."

"See, trying something different is fun. Nice to meet you, Jack. Come back again," she said, smiling.

"I will," I said. "Nice to meet you, Cassie."

• • •

That evening I told Tina about my promotion—a day after the fact.

I didn't tell her about anything else. She said "great" with as much sincerity as she could muster.

"I have some news," Tina said without emotion. "I'm pregnant."

I was shocked. "You're pregnant? How?" I asked.

"You still don't know how women get pregnant?" Tina asked. She looked at me with a sarcastic grin. "We need to get you back in junior high health class, Jack Oliver!"

It wasn't funny. We had agreed to a plan to not have another child until we could get our finances in better shape. I knew Tina wanted another child. So I felt like I had been set up. My feelings showed. "I thought we agreed—"

"Now sex is an agreement?" Tina asked. "You can't have a family as a hobby, Jack."

I withheld the many hurtful comments in the back of my mind. Talking had never worked; arguing surely would not. I put my head down and remained silent.

"Congratulations on the promotion," she said after a few seconds. "I know that's what you think was the big news today. I'm glad you're happy about something."

I was not happy about anything. My only happy moment on what should have been a great day was meeting Cassie.

Turning out the light I thought about Cassie. Something about meeting her had a sense of déjà vu hanging over it. What was it? After lying in the dark for what seemed like forever, I remembered. The first question I had asked Tina was the same first question I asked Cassie—"What would you suggest?"

• • •

Now, the memory of meeting Cassie had faded into the same pit where the rest of my best plans had fallen. The years had seemed to evaporate, leaving bits and pieces of memories where I had chosen the wrong fork in the road. My mind was racing, pulling back the years. There was one other day where my life spiraled down to a choice.

It was a day I would never forget.

11. How Can I Make My Life Better?

"HOW CAN I MAKE MY LIFE BETTER?" I asked Father Romano. My previous confession had followed my father's suicide when I lacked hope for the future. I felt the same way again, but I was twenty years older.

"You must confess your sins. Pray for forgiveness and change your ways," he said through the confessional screen. Even though I was now almost where I wanted to be in my career, I wasn't happy. I felt the guilt settling around me, smothering every move, like the dirt around a casket.

"I thought I was doing the right thing, Father, for my family and for me," I said, "but somehow I can't get it right."

"What are you doing to make it right?" Father Romano asked.

"I'm trying Father—I swear I'm trying," I said.

"Until you want to change you won't," he said. "You know you *need* to change, but you act as if *want* is more important than what you need."

"I do, Father, I do need to change," I said, avoiding listening to what he had just said.

"You must make the right choices," he said. "You need to care more about your family. Focus more on them than on your job. You must stop your relationship with the woman—nothing good can come from it. And, most of all, be honest with yourself. Otherwise, Jack, you'll never change."

· · ·

Fifteen years had passed since I had been promoted into my first management position. I felt that I was nearing my professional peak. Everything in my career seemed to be going great. Every challenge looked like a great opportunity. I framed challenges in the context of my next step. The path seemed so clear and well-defined. At least it felt that way.

I had been promoted to executive vice president, the second-highest position at PT&G. Chad was closing in on retirement. I was his acknowledged successor. My time was coming, soon. Everything should have been right in my life, but it wasn't.

My children, Jessica and Joshua, had grown into unhappy young people. They appeared to suffer from the Jack Oliver disorder; they wanted more than life was offering. They were never satisfied with what they had. I had tried to give them everything I missed out on growing up in South Philly. But giving them everything hadn't stopped them from wanting more. It was my fault. I had confessed that to Father Romano, but saying it aloud only made the hurt more of a reality. I was in pain.

Home was not a sanctuary. It was where the pain resided. There were only two places I could escape the hurt. Work was my primary sanctuary.

The other was with Cassie.

· · ·

The relationship with Cassie took many years to evolve. We shared some type of connection from the very first time we met. At first we just talked about work, current events, or Philly sports. She would make me try a new coffee drink, at least once a week. The game we played continued, then moved into flirting. I made sure to visit her shop every morning. Then when my schedule allowed me I began to go at lunch. Still not getting enough time with her, I would visit the shop on Saturday. Saturdays were my days of catching up on paper-work in the office. Seeing her on a day when everyone else enjoyed their families made working on a Saturday easier. She became like so many things in my life—an obsession. I wanted more from her. And like everything else, I had wanted in my life, I finally got what I wanted.

Cassie inherited the ownership of Rude Awakening. Her mother, who had started the business, had succumbed to breast cancer, leaving her in charge. This transformed her into a very tough, conservative businessperson. I admired those qualities.

In many more ways than Tina, Cassie was similar to me. She had to fight for everything she had in life. She viewed life as a game, just like me. She knew what it was like to be poor and have nothing. She wanted more out of life. She understood me.

"Jack, you're just like me—the only person I've ever met that thinks like me and wants the same things in life," she said the first time we were alone. "I don't know what I would do if you didn't come in every day. Every time I hear the door open, I look over and hope it's you."

No one had ever told me how much I meant to them. Tina was never one to say much about how she felt about me, afraid I would find a way to use it to get my way. And we didn't have much to talk about anyway since I was at work more than I was at home. In fact, after knowing Cassie more than a few months, I'm sure I talked more to her than to Tina.

Our friendship began to move toward an affair. She gave me a birthday card that said, "I want more." I did too, but I didn't want to risk losing the wealth and reputation I had worked so doggedly for over the years. I thought I may have stronger feelings than simple lust, but I tried to break off whatever relationship we shared. I abruptly stopped going to the shop and would not take her phone calls at work. The break up didn't last.

• • •

One evening several months into distancing myself from Cassie I was having dinner with a client. I heard a familiar voice—I knew instantly who it was. I turned and saw Cassie across the room. She was with a man. I did not know if she saw me, but I couldn't take my eyes off of her. She was smiling and looked so beautiful. I heard her laugh and her voice at different points. I completely lost track of the discussion with my client over his loan request. I couldn't stop looking at Cassie.

When Cassie and her escort got up to leave, a wave of jealous frustration poured over me as I continued to sit and learn what my client wanted from me. *Her escort was going to have what I always wanted,* I thought to myself. *I should be the one with her.* At that point I made up my mind that I would talk to Cassie and explore my feelings for her. I believed I owed it to myself.

I went in the shop the next morning. She looked up and smiled, keeping her composure, and kept waiting on the long line of customers. As I neared, she looked over and said, "Hi Jack—long time, no see."

"Yeah, it's been a while," I said. "But that won't happen again." I started talking even though a small crowd of people was standing and listening. "I miss you, Cassie—I miss you so bad. I'm sorry. I'm sorry I was afraid. But I'm not afraid anymore. Can we have dinner tonight?"

Everyone near us stopped what they were doing. It was as if someone had hit a pause button, freezing everyone in place. "Yeah," she said. "That would be nice." The crowd started moving again.

That night, we met at a small restaurant where I was sure no one I knew would see us.

"Why are you here?" she asked as we sat in the candlelight, drinking wine, paying little attention to the food on the table.

"I miss you," I said. "I saw you with a guy—it just about killed me. I knew you two were going to be together. I realized it should have been me."

"You're jealous? Jack Oliver, the man always in control of every emotion, jealous? I don't believe it," she said, laughing sarcastically. "What did you think? When you quit I quit living? Did you think I was going to wait for you?"

"No—I didn't expect you to wait for me—I didn't ask you to," I said. "Are you in love with him?"

"Jack—I love you. You know it. I've told you in so many ways.

You broke my heart hundreds of times. Every time you walked away from me, I knew where you were going—home, to be with your family. I can't wait for you forever. If you love your wife and want to be with her, you shouldn't be with me. But at least tell me, so I can go on with my life."

"I do love—I don't know what I feel about her. I need to know if you and I are supposed to be together," I stuttered. "I know I miss you and think about you always. When I wake up in the morning and when I go to bed at night, you're on my mind. I think you're beautiful and the perfect woman for me. Is that love?"

"You tell me, Jack," she said. "Do you love your wife?"

"I did," I said. "But now, well, we don't talk. I don't know."

"Are you going to leave her?" she asked. "I need to know."

"Yes," I said. "But I need some time. My career is moving in the right direction. I have a lot of assets tied up with her. But I will—I'll leave her soon. I promise."

"I want you, Jack Oliver," Cassie said, reaching across the table and gripping the top of my hand. "I love you."

I had never kissed her until then. I leaned over and met her halfway across the table. We kissed. I then heard a noise. It was the waiter.

"I'm sorry to interrupt, but would you care for anything else?" the waiter asked.

"No, thank you, we have everything we need," I said, smiling at Cassie, feeling one of the most joyful moments in my life.

"Yes—I can see. You and your wife are a beautiful couple," he said.

Cassie looked up and said, "Yes—we are, aren't we?"

As the waiter walked off, we both laughed. I still had a question on my mind.

"Why, or I mean how, could you love me? I'm married and have two kids. I'm an overweight, balding workaholic who doesn't know when to stop," I said. "What attracts a beautiful, young woman like you to me?"

"I'll tell you Jack, honestly. It's your power. I see you as a person who gets what he wants in life. That makes you the most attractive man I could ever find. You're like me. We could get anything we wanted in life! We would be incredible together—I know it."

"What do you want from life?" I asked, peering into her sparkling eyes.

"More," Cassie said. I knew what she was talking about. That's what I wanted.

"I know what you mean," I said.

"Jack, that's why I know we're perfect for each other," she said with a content smile. "We want the same things."

We left the restaurant and went to her apartment. I had told Tina I had a late meeting with a client. As we walked up the steps toward her second-floor apartment, I felt freer than I could ever remember. We stopped on the landing and kissed. As she opened the door I heard a beeping noise. "It's my phone messages," she said.

"Do you want me to step out while you check them?" I asked, assuming she would want her privacy.

"No," she said. "It's Scott." Her boyfriend had left a string of messages. After playing all of them, with me standing by her, she picked up the phone and dialed his number. "Scott, here's what I need to say—I'm with who I want to be with now. Never call me or come in the shop again. We're over, so over. Good-bye, Scott."

After years of teasing and lust, we finally consummated our relationship. I did not get home until 2:00 A.M. Tina didn't ask why I was late.

I don't think she cared.

• • •

While I promised to make every effort to be with Cassie, my marital exit strategy took much longer than expected. Cassie did not like keeping our relationship a secret. I still loved Tina but without passion, something I never divulged to Cassie. At the time, I wanted to be with Cassie but was not willing to give up my reputation and the financial rewards I had struggled so hard to obtain. But, I still had to see Cassie—I was addicted.

I began to lie to Tina in order to spend more time with Cassie. It was one of the few times in my life that I reduced the number of hours I was at work. Finally, Cassie was demanding I leave Tina.

Instead of going to the office on Saturdays, I would go straight to Cassie's apartment and stay there all day. On a Saturday, October 28th to be exact, Cassie confronted me with a choice.

"I've given you my heart," she said. "I've been waiting for you for years and you're still with a woman you say you don't love, but you go to bed with her every night. I'm at my breaking point. It's time to choose—me or your wife."

We talked for hours. Finally, I told her what she wanted to hear. "I'm going to leave Tina," I said. "I'm going to tell her tonight."

"If you don't, Jack, we're over," Cassie said. "I can't wait any longer."

"I understand," I said. I drove back home. It was getting dark. Halloween decorations were up throughout the neighborhood.

"Is this the last time I'm going to drive home?" I asked myself, pulling into the driveway. Surprisingly, no one was home.

I stepped inside and found a note.

12. Where Have You Been?

"WHERE HAVE YOU BEEN?" Tina sobbed through the phone.

"That doesn't matter right now—what happened?" I nearly shouted. Tina had left a note telling me my mother was ill and was taken to Jefferson Hospital. Tina had gone to the hospital to be with her. Jessica and Joshua were at one of our neighbors. I was alone with my guilt in the kitchen.

"Your mother got really sick and called me," Tina said. "I called for an ambulance. She's in intensive care. They think it's a stroke."

"I'm coming," I said.

I had spent very little time with my mother over the years. The demands of work, Tina and the kids, and Cassie had kept me busy. I turned on my cell phone and saw that Tina had left ten messages. I listened to each one. I felt sick knowing where I had been, what I was talking about, and now, seeing what was happening.

I put the emergency lights on and drove to Jefferson running through red lights, trying to make up for lost time. I called Cassie on my cell phone.

"My mother is in the hospital," I said. "She's had a stroke."

"Do you want me to come be with you?" Cassie asked.

"No—that's not possible now. I'll call later."

My guilt was churning. I drove faster.

I crashed.

The velocity of the air bag had smashed my glasses into my face. I felt blood trickling down like tears. I looked around and realized I had run into the side of a black Chevy Tahoe. Running the red lights had caught up with me.

As I got out of my car I heard the angry voice of the driver of the Tahoe. He was screaming at me. I then saw the blue lights of a Philly police cruiser.

"What happened?" the officer asked me.

"My mother is at Jefferson. She had a stroke. I was trying to get there as quick as I could and I must have run a red light. It's my fault. But please, I need to get to the hospital."

After a few minutes, I was sitting in the police cruiser. The officer took me to Jefferson. "You need to get those cuts on your face checked, Mr. Oliver—your glasses cut you pretty badly when the air bag hit you."

"I will," I said. "But I've got to see my mother."

•　•　•

Getting off the elevator I saw Tina. "What happened to you, Jack?" she said as she walked toward me.

"I was in a wreck driving here," I said. "Where's my mother?"

We walked back into the intensive care area. A nurse gave me a towel to wipe the blood off my face and led me back to my mother's room.

She was unconscious, with tubes and wires connected to monitors. Tina stepped into the room beside me as I stood and looked at my mother from several feet away. Tina then walked over to the opposite side of the bed and held her hand.

My mother looked small and tiny, like a child in a king-size bed. In my few infrequent visits I could tell she was looking thinner, but she was getting older, I had reasoned. I always told her to call me if she needed anything. But she never called—neither did I.

The tubes and monitors created a soundscape of drips and beeps in the room. I finally stepped to her bedside. I reached out and held her hand—the first time I could remember holding her hand in mine. The nurse reentered the room. I stood until the nurse asked me to move while she checked the gauges and tubes. I didn't want to let go.

After the nurse left the room, Tina asked, "Are you all right? You look like you need to get those cuts bandaged. You may need a couple of stitches."

"I'm all right," I said. "This doesn't seem real."

"I'm sorry I was so nasty on the phone. I was so worried. Your cell phone was off. You weren't answering in your office. I didn't know where you were."

I didn't say a thing. I hoped Tina would change the subject. She did.

"I'm sorry. I know you have a difficult job. I worry about you, Jack. I don't want to see anything happen to you. I love you."

Standing at the bed holding my mother's hand, I couldn't look at Tina. If I had not been here, I would have been in the process of telling her I wanted a divorce. Instead, I was here. Not knowing what else to say, I said, "Thanks, I appreciate you being with my mother."

"Do you want me," she hesitated, and then said, "to stay while you get someone to look at your cuts?"

"No—why don't you go back home and be with the kids. I'll stay here with Mother."

"Are you sure?" Tina asked.

"I want to be alone with her—please," I said.

"Okay, Jack," she said as she walked around the bed and put her arms around me. I didn't move. "Call me later. Promise?"

"I will," I said. As Tina was walking out of the room, I said, "Tina, I—I want to thank you—I mean it."

"I know," she said. "I love you."

I turned my head back toward my mother. "Ditto," I said, feeling lost for words.

• • •

I stayed at my mother's side, moving a chair beside her, still holding her hand. I did not know what to do. Father Romano had been at the hospital when she arrived. Her condition was so poor; he administered last rites. She had not been awake since then, and was clinging to life. I was clinging to her hand.

As I sat beside her, the regrets that had been lingering below the surface began to rise. I felt tears beginning to fill my eyes. I gulped and leaned my head back, taking a deep breath. *No tears*, I said to myself. My father had jumped off a bridge, taking his own life. He said he was worried I would be like him. At that moment I knew what he meant and was afraid he was right.

Now I was sitting by my mother, blaming myself again for what was happening. No one else was in the room. I stood to brush back her hair from her forehead. I leaned over the bed and kissed the top of her head.

Still leaning close to her ear I whispered lightly, "Mom, I'm so sorry for being a terrible son."

I choked back the tears and guilt of forty-plus years and said, "I love you. Please don't leave me now, Mom, please. I'm going to change. I promise. Please don't die. I want to make you proud of me. Don't leave me here alone."

I cried.

I sat back down in the chair, tears streaming down my face, holding her hand. I sat for several hours not moving, listening to the whir of the monitors. The exhaustion and pain caught up with me.

I fell asleep.

• • •

The nurse tapped me on the shoulder and stirred me.

"I'm sorry—I must have fallen asleep—I'm exhausted," I said groggily. "I must have just dozed off."

I immediately noticed two other nurses entering the room. "Mr. Oliver, I'm sorry, your mother is gone."

"What?" I said. "Gone?"

"She passed while you were asleep," the nurse said.

I stood and looked at her—I was still holding her hand. I had never let go. My heart, whatever was left, broke apart.

I'd never felt so alone.

The nurse escorted me into the hall. "Is there anything I can do?" she asked. I felt numb. I knew I had to call Tina. Then I remembered Cassie. Even in my sorrow I had conflict.

"Is there a phone—in a private place—I need to make a couple of calls," I said.

The nurse led me to a small office at the end of the corridor. "Take your time, and if you need anything, I'll be at the nurse station," she said, closing the door.

I called Cassie.

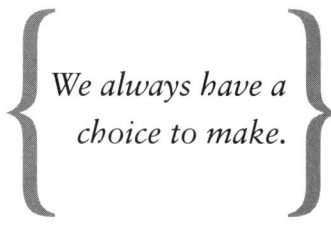

We always have a
choice to make.

—BENJAMIN FRANKLIN PRICE

13. Where Are You Going?

"WHERE ARE YOU GOING?" Tina asked.

"I need some time alone," I said.

"Now? You've been in a car wreck—your mother died—you need to be here at home!" Tina said through her tears.

"I'll be back," I said. "Trust me. I need some time alone."

I drove to Cassie's apartment.

• • •

The pounding on Cassie's door awakened us. My heart began to race.

I knew who it was.

"I know you're in there Jack!" Tina screamed. "I know about you and your friend. If you don't let me in, I'll wake up everyone in the building."

We struggled to get dressed. I felt like I was in a nightmare but could not wake up. Cassie stayed in the bedroom, and I opened the door. Tina's hand landed firmly on my already bruised cheek, knocking my glasses across the room.

"You bastard! How could you do this? Your mother died, and you go to your whore for a shoulder to cry on."

I stood still—frozen like a statue, afraid to respond. The door remained open, allowing anyone nearby to hear the end of my marriage.

"I want to talk to your friend. I know all about her. Did you think I was stupid, Jack?"

"That's not going to do any good," I said. I heard the bedroom door behind me open.

"If you'll shut the door and not attack me, we'll talk," Cassie said in a very unemotional voice. I was still looking at Tina. She reached back and slammed the door, leaving the three of us standing in the living room. I decided to not move, keeping a barrier between the two.

"I knew you couldn't help coming out of hiding," Tina said. She shifted her gaze back to me. "So this is what you're giving up me and your children for? You're giving up everything you worked for to be with her? I want to hear it from you—now!"

Before I could say anything, Cassie said, "I'm sorry you found out like this. I really am. But we love each other. You two have been over for a long time. Your marriage didn't work. It's time we're honest. Right, Jack?"

"I don't want to hear anything out of you," Tina said, pointing her finger at Cassie. "It's funny you said *our* marriage didn't work. Jack is married to his work—his career comes first. If you think you're going to get anything better you're a bigger fool than even what I think am! Tell us, Jack. Is she what you want? Are you going to change the way you've been to spend time with her?" Tina growled a sarcastic laugh that made the hairs on the back of my neck stand up. "Answer me, Jack Oliver. Be honest for once in your life!"

I couldn't respond. I did not know what was going to happen next. I expected the worst and got it.

"Do you love her?" Tina asked. "Honestly, that's all I want to know."

The word "love" was something I rarely used. I used the word much more in reference to my work—not in relationships. Now—with the question hanging in the air—I could not connect to the meaning.

"I don't know what I feel about anything or anyone right now," I said. "I just lost my mother—both of you forgive me for thinking about something else right now." I turned to Cassie. "I'm going home to talk to Tina—I'll talk to you later."

Before I could turn back toward Tina, she was walking out the door saying, "You can have him. You two belong together." I still had my back to Cassie who was standing looking at the open door.

"You're not going over there now, are you?" Cassie asked as I put my jacket on.

"I have to," I said, still not exchanging even a glance. "I'll call you."

"I'm sorry all of this happened," she said. "But you must make a choice. You can't have two lives."

"I know," I said.

• • •

Returning home I did not know what to expect. Tina was sitting in the kitchen, her hands holding up her head while she leaned over the table, staring downward. I wanted to say I was sorry, but she spoke first.

"We're over, Jack."

"Is that what you want?" I asked. "Honestly?"

"Honestly? That's a word you don't seem to understand the meaning of. Why are you asking me what I want? You have what you want. Go for it."

"I didn't want this," I said. "You quit caring about me. You acted like I didn't matter anymore."

"You're blaming me? I don't want to hear your excuses," she said, lifting her head up and looking at me. "I don't want to hear anything. I can't believe I was such a fool. I thought you would change. I thought your power trips were confined to work. But that ego of yours just has to keep being fed, doesn't it? I'm sure she's not the only one you cheated with." She paused a moment. "I just have one question—did you tell her you love her?"

"No," I answered, not knowing what love really had to do with what was happening. "I still love you, Tina."

"Love me? That's funny, Jack. So that's why you spend all of your time away, never talking to me about anything other than your power—how together you are, how people respect and admire you. Love is something you share, Jack, not something you do to yourself. I don't want to argue anymore. I'll get an attorney tomorrow. Then we can discuss how much you are going to lose. I am sure that will keep your attention."

The thought of losing everything I had worked for had my attention. Not Cassie. Not my mother. Not my kids. I felt like everything I had built was being destroyed. If I lost it all, my life was a waste. How could I lose what I had earned—what I gave to my family to make their life better? How was this fair?

"Go ahead and get an attorney," I said. "That's what it comes down to. All you care about is money—the house—everything I've bought for you! You don't care about me."

Tina began to laugh hysterically. "Oh, it's me that wanted this house? It's me that wanted the cars? It's me? Who are you trying to fool? I'm sorry your mother is gone, I really am. I loved her. She had a hard life. But here is some honesty for you. Do you know why she never told you she was sick but she told me? Do you know why she never told you anything about how she was feeling? It wasn't because she was mad at you. It wasn't because she was hurt. She didn't tell you because she didn't want to bother you! Can you believe it? She wanted for you what you wanted so badly all of your life—to be a success! She didn't want you to worry or be distracted, just get what you wanted. Well, I'm not going to make the same mistake. I don't need all this stuff you've worked so hard for, but I'm going to take it so you remember how you've hurt everyone. Get out, Jack, now. This is *my* house. You gave it up. It's the price you're going to pay for your success."

I left my home without saying another word.

• • •

That's how I got here.

The small apartment felt more like a prison than a safe haven. I had refused to move in with Cassie, despite her urgings. "I need space," I kept telling her. Space? Why would I want space? I had lied. I was lonely, but not for her.

I had taken, not given, all my life. I was truly reaping what I sowed.

The relationship was no longer convenient. Cassie was not what I was looking for, I realized in the haze of too much alcohol and minimal sleep. I used her, just like almost everything and everyone I had met in my life—to get what I wanted.

I felt nothing.

I still have a choice to make, I thought to myself as I allowed the exhaustion to have its way.

Benny needs an answer.

14. Why Won't This Work?

"WHY WON'T THIS WORK?" I asked my father.

I rarely dreamed—or at least remembered dreaming. Especially dreams about my father. After he died I had a few recurring dreams about him. He never spoke. He would walk into my office and look at me. No expression or words. He would just stare, watching me. I would wake up almost immediately with a feeling he was still alive. I wanted to ask what he was doing, but my dream always ended without words.

This was a much different dream. It was more like a memory that somehow was being replayed in my sleep. The memory was of one of those few and far between times when I was trying to help my father. He had asked me to come along on a plumbing job. It was a Saturday, and I could not find an excuse to avoid it. It wasn't that I was lazy; I simply didn't want to have anything to do with plumbing. He knew I did not relish the thought of being a plumber, especially as his apprentice, but he still tried to get me to go with him on a couple of jobs when I was a teenager. I gave in and went with him. We were putting in a new hot water heater in a home over one hundred years old.

"Are you sure that's how it fits?" I asked, thinking I knew more than my father who had spent most of his life working on pipes and fittings. "If you can press those pipes together it'll save a lot of time."

"Jackson, you sound like you know what needs to be done on this job," he said sarcastically. "Do it."

My father backed out of the cramped, dark corner, handed me the large wrench, and bowed and pointed toward the corner as if the Queen of England was approaching.

"Show me what you are talking about," my father said.

I was not going to be embarrassed. I thought I saw what was missing. The connector fitting between the two pipes lacked only an inch from connecting. If I could get the two pipes pressed together to connect, it would save removing and replacing a long pipe and all of the fittings. I was already into efficiency. At least I thought so.

With all of my teenage muscle I tried to force the pipes closer. My father didn't say a word. He just stood and watched with a smile etched on his face. The smile should have been a giveaway. But I kept on. "Jack Oliver never quits," I said to myself under my breath.

"Why won't this work?" I finally asked after struggling for more than ten minutes, the sweat dripping from my brow.

"You tell me," my father responded.

This only made me more determined to prove I was right. In doing so, I broke one of the basic guidelines of being a plumber: don't force it.

I did.

As I tried one last time to push the pipes close enough together to secure a fitting, the remaining water that had not drained from the overhanging pipe showered me with a burst of pressurized H_2O.

"You asked me, why won't this work?" my father said. "The answer is it wasn't meant to. Some things are not meant to work, Jackson. They won't fit."

● ● ●

Recalling the dream as I woke up in the recliner, I applied it to what I was facing. Some things were not meant to work—they won't fit. How true. I was realizing what ill-fitting meant every day. But recalling that conversation with my father only made me feel worse than I already felt.

I looked at my watch. It was 5:30 in the morning. I had a staff meeting this morning. The thoughts of standing in front of fifty people and trying to find a way to motivate them didn't help my already sour stomach. Looking in the bathroom mirror as I turned on the faucet to let the water warm, I thought: *Just another great day at Merchants Bank.*

Over a year had passed since the acquisition of PT&G by Merchants Bank. I was miserable. I was trying to make something work. The problem was trying to fit in the Merchants mold. I was trying my best, working longer and harder than at any time in my career. But nothing worked. I didn't fit.

After shaving and taking a shower, I walked into the living room and looked at the stack of papers lying on the floor. I pulled *Bank on It!* out of the pile and I opened the book to one of the places I had marked with a small, yellow sticky note. The passage was about "choosing."

I have found one of the toughest things to do in life is to admit something isn't working. Why do we try our best to make the square peg fit in the round hole? Typically it's because the square peg may have worked before—it might have been round—so we try to hang on to what has worked in the past, even though it may have changed.

Why do we hold on to our experiences of what worked and fail to learn from our failures? When we look to the past for answers, memories of our mistakes make us feel guilty. We try to avoid the weight of our past, allowing history to repeat itself. We make the same errors again and again, burdened with guilt. Instead of a compass, our past serves only as baggage weighing us down. There is only one way to escape the circle of suffering we created—drop our guilt baggage.

Dropping the "guilt baggage" was the problem. I had a lot of baggage. I could have filled up every luggage carrier at the airport and more. I had been able to carry everything till now, but I was getting tired. The past year had worn me down. I was going in a circle. A slight pain flashed across my chest. I had been getting a few of the brief pains lately, but no wonder, given my diet and lifestyle. *It must be stress,* I reasoned as I put the book in my briefcase and left for work.

I wanted to be the first one there—as usual.

• • •

What changed? I wondered, as I walked down the steps to my car. I recalled the many changes that had occurred in my career. The biggest change occurred without me having a voice in the matter. The sale of PT&G took place, barely passing the shareholder vote. The deal was not nearly as financially rewarding as anticipated after the immediate surge in the stock value. If anyone had looked back on Merchants' other acquisitions this would have been predictable. *Another case of failing to learn from history,* I thought. But the deal was done and the name changed to Merchants Bank. The change in name paled in comparison to what happened within the bank.

Chad was gone. At first I couldn't understand why someone who was so connected to the history of a company would decide to sell, but then I remembered something Chad had told me years before. "If you're unsure of why something is happening, just follow the money. Everyone does everything for money," he had said.

I followed the money. Chad was at the money trail's end. Chad received a payout of one million dollars per year for the next ten years, in addition to other bonuses and stock options. In total, Chad would receive over thirty million dollars from the deal. Thirty million dollars. The number almost sounded absurd. Chad wasn't worth that kind of money. "Who is?" I said as I pulled my Jaguar onto the freeway.

In Chad's last public announcement, he bid farewell to "his family at Philadelphia's oldest bank" and declared he would be part of the Philadelphia community "forever." Within two months of the shareholder vote, Chad moved to Phoenix, Arizona, selling his home in Philly. Chad took the money and left the rest of us behind. If he had any guilt baggage, it was nowhere to be found.

Several of the PT&G executive committee directors received positions on Merchants' board of directors and lucrative stock options and perks afforded to them for their part in selling PT&G. Norman

Scruggs, our CFO and the person who had clandestinely worked with Chad and a few of the directors constructing the sale, received the second-largest payout: five million dollars paid over the next ten years, plus stock options. He left Philly for Fort Myers, Florida.

The rest of our executive team had essentially been forced to sign new employment contracts that kept us as indentured servants for the next two years. A bonus of $250,000 was waiting for us if we "played for the Merchants team." But we did receive small raises and ample amounts of stock options. The Merchants stock continued to slide, making the value of the stock options we received worthless. Given the history of the bank's less-than-sterling stock prices, we would be waiting an eternity for any return from the options. I told John Helms about it and he told me it was Merchants' re-creation of "Confederate dollars."

"It looks like a lot, but isn't worth the paper it's printed on," he said. "But you got to give 'em credit—it's nice paper!"

Their public relations in Philly didn't make us feel any better. PT&G's operations centers were closed within six months following the purchase, something the Merchants CEO, Andrew Ledger, promised would not happen. Twenty percent of PT&G's employees were laid off within twelve months of Merchants taking over, and that was just the beginning. I wondered if Andrew Ledger was selling the same line to the next bank on the target list.

My career had been built around one scenario. After Chad retired I would replace him. That was my plan and the structure of our management. But selling to Merchants changed what happened when Chad left. Somehow my career had been put in reverse.

I now essentially had two bosses.

Merchants had sent "one of their own," as they referred to the new "City President" they sent to Philly, to coordinate the transition. His name was Rex Nessman. Rex appeared harmless. But like a snake, he preferred to stay low to the ground to avoid detection and would strike if you threatened him.

My other boss was Bill Hopkins. He had never appeared harmless. He relished every opportunity to bring people "down to size" as he said (which reflected on his own shortcomings). Bill was dangerous 24/7.

As I pulled into the parking building and entered the Merchant Bank Tower I felt another brief pain in my chest.

"I need to get on a diet," I said, as I hit the elevator button.

• • •

Arriving well before anyone else, a habit that continued even though my enthusiasm had gone, I turned on my computer to clear out my e-mail before I left for my staff meeting. I began my routine of reading the "overnighters." Overnighters were e-mails sent by corporate that typically had little value but were policed to ensure everyone read them. The content focused on two areas: *regulations* and *culture.*

Regulatory e-mails were reminders of how to cover up mistakes that would result in fines for violating banking regulations. Merchants had learned the hard way over the years. The bank had paid millions in fines for overcharging customers with improperly disclosed fees and finance charges that benefited Merchants and hurt consumers. Instead of trying to focus on meeting regulations, the bank focused on keeping any mistakes covered up.

"More CYA e-mails for the team," I said to myself, forwarding each of the e-mails to over forty people on my e-mail list.

The e-mail reminders about adhering to the Merchants Culture were more numerous and nearly as ridiculous as the CYA e-mails. I often referred to the people composing the e-mails as the "culture police." They appeared to work night and day to remind everyone what to do so "all Merchants' team members would respond to customers in the same manner." To me it was clear what they wanted—robots.

I started to count the number of overnighters but stopped at twenty-seven seeing an e-mail from Rex. He never sent e-mails. I wasn't sure if he was computer challenged or simply never wanted to go on record about anything.

I opened the e-mail and my blood pressure began a rapid increase. The e-mail said, "We need to talk today about how to enhance growth. It appears we are the worst team in Merchants." A copy of the monthly Production Report was attached.

It wasn't new that we were on the bottom of the heap in Merchants. We were dead last. As badly as I wanted to tell Rex to replace the

Merchants signs with PT&G and for him to go back to North Carolina and play golf, I knew that was not an option. It would only get me an early exit ticket, well before my bonus.

While I hadn't always agreed with Chad, I respected him. We had shared the same insatiable lust for power and money. He was my role model. But I had no respect for Rex. He bothered me. He only had one vice—golf.

Rex was ten years younger than me. While I had always been considered young in banking circles to be an executive at PT&G, Rex by comparison was fresh out of diapers. He grew up in Pinehurst, North Carolina. His entire life revolved around golf. When I told Cassie that Rex was born with two silver spoons in his mouth and a golf club in his hands, she said, "It must have been a difficult birth."

He appeared to have it made. He had climbed the Merchants corporate ladder quickly, carrying his golf clubs every step of the way. Unlike Chad, who was discreet about his privileged upbringing, Rex reeked of money and privilege, something that did not help his credibility as Chad's successor. Neither did his slow, Southern drawl. Most of our staff called him "Richie" as in the cartoon *Richie Rich*. If he was forced to choose what others would think about him—great banker or golfer—I was certain he would want to be known as a great golfer.

Rex's golfing skills were so advanced he probably could have played professionally if he had not been so easily distracted. I really didn't believe people suffered from Attention Deficit Disorder—I just thought they were lazy or enjoyed using the idea of ADD as an excuse for never finishing what they started. But I changed my mind after working with my new leader. It was impossible to carry on a conversation with him. Everything was a distraction. He would change from one subject to another and back again in the time it took to sneeze. He was consistent in one area—he always finished every conversation with a golf story.

"Well, I guess I have something to look forward to after the staff meeting," I said.

I felt another sharp pain.

"I've got to start exercising," I said to myself, rubbing my bloated stomach.

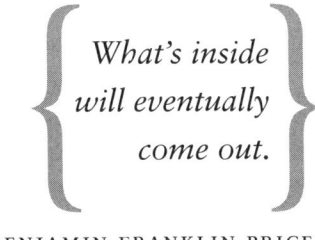

*What's inside
will eventually
come out.*

—BENJAMIN FRANKLIN PRICE

15. What Are You Hiding?

"WHAT ARE YOU HIDING?"

Of all the questions I feared to respond to in my life, this was the one that made me the most anxious. Being honest was never as simple as I wanted it to be.

I dreaded being in front of my team. I felt that they could see through me. While I may have never been a beloved leader, I was respected and feared. Now I had the feeling everyone looked at me as a hypocrite—that I was biding my time for the bonus money. It was my job to tell everyone that Merchants is the best bank in the United States. Of all the lies I had told in my life, this was one of the biggest and most revolting. The truth was that I hated Merchants and almost everything about them.

But I had a job to do.

The structure of the staff meetings was part of the Merchants culture. Each month Merchants required every person in my position to conduct a staff meeting. The entire meeting was scripted by my other boss . . . Bill Hopkins.

After finishing the e-mails, I put all of the handout material in a banker's box to take to the meeting. "I'm going to need a forklift," I said as I made my way toward the elevator and my team waiting in the crowded second-floor conference room.

The weight of the reports reminded me of why I disliked Bill as much or more than Rex. "Everything equal—everything the same" was one of many pieces of propaganda that sprang from Merchants Memory Minders (MMMs in the bank's lexicon) forced on all team members in order to have everyone behave in the same way. I entered the room trying to smile.

After opening the meeting, as I was instructed, I turned the next portion over to Bridgett, another fresh-faced Merchants up and comer from Charlotte who served as our culture coach. I moved to the back of the room. Hearing Bridgett begin a Merchants pep rally nearly made the sausage biscuit I had devoured earlier almost make a second appearance. I was sure Bridgett's photo was in the dictionary beside the word *perky*; I was also sure her picture was in the dictionary beside the word *naïve*.

Bridgett believed every bit of propaganda given to her that had the Merchants logo on it. A photo of her with the Merchants CEO, Andrew Ledger, at her graduation from the corporate management training school sat on her desk. While Bridgett wasn't mean spirited, if you said anything negative toward Merchants, she would make sure people at HQ in Charlotte heard about it. I found that out the hard way when I said in a private conversation that Merchants could save money by not printing so many reports—especially in color. "They're already on the computer system and printing all those reports costs a ton of money," I had absent-mindedly said to her after lugging the weight of paper into a meeting. "If they want to find a way to save thousands of dollars why don't they quit printing the reports." I didn't realize my faux pas until I saw the agonized look on her face.

"What do you mean?" she gasped. "Do you know how many people it takes to prepare all of these reports? Do you know how much time it takes?"

"Well, then it's even more of an opportunity to save money because no one pays attention to them and they really have no use," I said. "Just stop the presses!"

"I'll have you know, Mr. Oliver, that was my first job after I finished management training," she said. She probably thought she would embarrass me. Instead, I wanted to laugh some more. But she continued her passionate defense of the bureaucracy. "I put my heart into creating those reports when I worked there. The reports are the foundation for everything we do. What would we do without our culture? That's what makes us special."

"I thought it was about making money from serving customers," I said, enjoying seeing Bridgett squirm.

"If Bill Hopkins heard you say that you would be in a lot of hot water," she said with an evil smile that should have warned me I would be hearing from him sooner instead of later. I had forgotten about the conversation until I felt the hot water from Bill later that same day when he called to discuss my "attitude."

"I understand you don't like my reports," Bill said as soon as I answered. Annoyed that Bridgett had ratted me out for something so small and, in my mind, insignificant, I struggled with a response.

"Whatever gave you that idea?" I asked. I already knew the source.

"Bridgett told me," he said. "Jack, just a reminder, I know what happens up in Philly, 24/7, every minute of every day. People think they can hide what's going on, but I know. Loyalty is the key component to our culture. So never think I don't know everything that's happening just because you're several hundred miles away."

"Well, that's great, Bill—how do you like my tie?" I responded without thinking.

"That's clearly insubordinate," Bill said.

"No, I was just wondering if you really knew everything that happens here," I said. "I bought a new tie—it has a golfer on it. Rex liked it, but I didn't know if that was professional enough for Merchants. Since you know everything I was just asking for your advice."

"Let me give you some professional advice—don't rock my boat," he said. "I see a bad attitude in you, and I'm not going to let your poor attitude affect my team's performance."

"Thanks for the professional advice, Bill," I said. "I'll keep it in mind. 'Don't rock Bill's boat.' Where does that fit in the MMMs? Should I put that one at the top of my to-do list?"

"I'm not a gambler, but if I bet on anything, I would bet you won't be here much longer," Bill said. "If you keep that attitude, I promise I'll make sure you don't."

Things only got worse afterwards. While I had to put on a good front, I had never been a good actor. It was frustrating to hand over one hour of my meeting to Bridgett, who was called the "Kool-Aid Kid" by the majority of my team. While almost all of her presentation lacked value, if you failed to at least act like you understood the corporate culture, your career was in jeopardy.

• • •

How important am I? I wondered.

Sitting in the meeting room in the back corner gave me an almost out-of-body experience. If I got up and left, who would notice? How easily could I be replaced? Does anyone care anymore? With all of those questions ringing in my head, I looked down at my guidebook and saw Bill's name. *He is worse than Rex,* I thought to myself. *Bill is Merchants.*

Bill was a few years younger than me, six to be exact. I had met him face to face only one time. He was probably no more than five feet tall. So while I was just average height, I towered over him, but so did everyone else. Most of the people I had met since joining Merchants called him Napoleon; but not to his face. His features may have made him appear Napoleonic but unlike Napoleon, he was no leader. Of all the people I had met in Merchants, Bill concerned me the most. There was something about him that made you think, "What is he after?" I didn't trust Bill, especially after challenging him. He was dangerous.

The only job he had from the time he left college was Merchants Bank, just like almost every executive in Merchants Bank. Bridgett called it being "homegrown." I thought it meant that Merchants execs were spawned from an incestuous professional breeding pool.

While Bill had little field experience, other than several years as an office manager and a business lender, he had made sure he was at the right place at the right time. In a company that was far outgrowing its own internal "homegrown" talent as it bought bank after bank in rapid-fire deals, Bill was recognized for being both homegrown and decisive. And being decisive stood out in the Merchants system. Decisive meant he not only did everything exactly as he was told, but he somehow got results from following orders.

If you cut Bill, he would spill the corporate blue instead of anything that looked like blood. I was certain he could recite each of the corporate Mission and Service declarations from memory.

Unlike Rex, there was no ADD detectable in Bill—he was focused on looking good to the corporate executives. His real skill and talent was for taking credit for the right decisions and being able to blame the faulty decisions on others.

To maintain control of the Merchants culture, Bill's job was much more like a policeman than a coordinator.

While I reported directly to Rex, Bill's name had a strong dotted line on the organizational chart to me. His job was to ensure his assigned cities and regions would hit their performance targets. While Merchants had grown in size, the real value of the stock remained pegged to growth in profits. As he loved to remind me every month, "Everything comes down to numbers."

To my detriment, the numbers had worsened over the past year. Behind the numbers was a near mass defection of the PT&G managers I had relied on for years. The best had left for greener pastures, with competitors willing to offer more money and less pressure. Without anything to hold them, like my bonus, they left and took as much business with them as they could to impress their new employers.

I'm stuck with my employment contract, pretending to be part of Merchants, I thought as I continued to survey the room. Chad had left for Arizona, taking millions of dollars with him. I was the only executive from PT&G left to hold things together. I was getting tired of trying to work miracles.

But Bill expected one.

• • •

"And now Jack will review the reports for this month," Bridgett said. It was my turn to take the stage and do my best to recite Bill's talking points.

After a PowerPoint presentation furnished by Bill's team, showing our team as the worst in Merchants, I felt another twinge of pain across my chest, and I opened the floor for questions. I sat down on a folding table to field questions. The Q&A was very important in Merchants culture. Bridgett kept notes of who asked what. The questions were not as important as the questioner's attitude. If the question was perceived as "questioning corporate culture," Bridgett would notify Bill. "Bad attitudes equal bad numbers," was something Bridgett often quoted. It was not quite Big Brother, but it was getting close.

As I looked out into the room, I saw only a small number of faces of dedicated PT&G managers. I was dealing with a group of newbies—outsiders who had been brought in to fill the void left after the PT&G exodus. I felt alone. Still looking into the crowd, I saw a hand go up.

It was Bruce.

Bruce Kellogg was one of the newbies who had tried to paint himself as a Merchants clone. He nicknamed himself "Special K." At first, everyone thought it was cute, but he used it to the point of annoyance. No one wanted to hear him speak in his weird third-person manner.

"I'm Special K, and I'm here to save the day!" This was just one of his overused, self-promoting raps pulled from his repertoire. While no one liked it (other than Bridgett) in Philly, Bill *loved* it. Bruce's attempts to be a Merchants kind of guy were working with the right people. He was now the highest performer in Philly on paper.

I couldn't stand him.

"Jack, Special K has a quick question! I was wondering why we are having such a problem opening new accounts in Philly," he said, seeing his name at the top of several reports in new accounts and wanting to make sure everyone realized he was the best on our team. "My team isn't having any problems—if they have a doubt, Special K throws it out." Much of the room did their best to avoid rolling their eyes.

Before I could respond by pointing out that even though he was the best in our team, he was well below the company average, Bridgett jumped in and asked, "Special K, could you please share your success story with us?"

"Special K is happy to share his success with everyone!" he said. You could hear the entire room groan. "It's a super success story!"

Success stories were something Merchants loved us to share, supposedly to motivate the team. But just like most stories, they were fictional. I could see this was something Bridgett and Bruce, the Merchants clones, had worked out ahead of time. Fifteen minutes into Special K's storytelling, I felt another twinge of pain radiate from my chest into my neck. I winced. *When is he going to shut up?* I thought.

After Bridgett and Bruce finally finished their preplanned impromptu performance, I ended the meeting, reminding everyone to "Never stop being the best!" This was another Merchants' piece of scripting. I had hoped it was the last time I had to utter those words.

It was.

16. Who Cares?

"WHO CARES?"

I could almost hear my words echoing in the room. After finishing the staff meeting, I had returned to the top floor to meet with Rex. As usual, Rex was late for a meeting he called. As I sat and looked around at the space Chad had occupied as PT&G CEO (and the office I had intended to move into) now cluttered with golf decor, I remembered one of the many strategy meetings we'd had in the office.

"Who cares?" I had responded to Chad. "We're going to make a ton of money in fees." The conversation was one of many that played into the hands of Chad's greed. I had told Chad about my idea for charging higher overdraft fees to the bank's less fortunate clients. "Higher fees won't drive good clients away—they never overdraw their accounts. But the people who overdraw their accounts don't have an option; they will pay the fee and go on with their lives. It's a penalty fee, not a service," I argued. "They're stuck, and we have every right to make money from the situation."

"I'm not so sure I agree," Chad said, trying to mask his lack of care as a client advocate. "Can you imagine someone on a limited income getting charged three hundred dollars in fees because they overdrew their account by a penny? It doesn't sound fair, Jack."

"Who cares about fair?" I said. "That's business."

• • •

"That's business," I said aloud as I looked around Rex's golf museum. Merchants had probably spent twenty thousand dollars decorating his office. It bore little resemblance to the space Chad had inhabited for years.

I had trusted Chad. I had literally done everything he asked me, much of it bordering on unethical behavior. The debate over fees and fairness was basically staged. I was given information by Chad prior to the meeting and told to come up with a plan to increase income. This was a familiar role-play that grew out of the give and take in our work relationship. I did his dirty work and expected payment, but accepted promises. The promises disappeared when he sold the company to Merchants. He got what he wanted and left everyone else behind. I felt betrayed, as if I had been sold.

Most of my team had left for greener pastures. Now I had an opportunity to do the same. But I didn't want to quit. Aside from the money, I had something to prove to Merchants. Hearing Rex talking outside his office I decided that I would stick with Merchants, no matter what.

Working with Benny was not an option. Jack Oliver wasn't a quitter.

• • •

Still waiting for Rex to enter, I saw a thick document package on the edge of Rex's desk. It was from the corporate offices and even sitting back from the desk looking at it upside-down, I could see the RE: JACK OLIVER on the packet. Rex opened the door.

"Jack, how ya doin'?" Rex said, entering the room as I stood up to shake his hand. He looked away and stepped behind his desk without shaking my hand. *Classic ADD*, I thought to myself.

"I'm doing okay," I said, still standing and anxious to get back to work with a renewed vigor for the first time in months. I felt a new focus and wanted to tell Rex.

"I appreciate you dropping in. We should spend more time together, but I've been so damn busy," he said, shaking his head and adjusting the golf balls sitting in a stand beside his desk. Without blinking he changed the subject. "Did you see Phil blow it yesterday? Mickelson is one of the best but gambles way too much."

Not knowing exactly what he was talking about, I said, "I didn't watch any TV yesterday."

"You missed a heck of a golf tournament," he said, shifting his gaze to the stack of golf magazines on the floor behind his desk. He picked up *Golf Digest* with Phil Mickelson on the cover.

"Mickelson could have won twice as many golf tournaments if he had been able to control his urges to do too much with a shot," he said. "Mickelson is in some ways a lot like you."

The comparison took me by surprise. Was he actually making a comparison of me to a golfer? Had he planned it as part of our meeting? I hated the game. "Like me?" I asked, still searching for an understanding of where he was taking the conversation.

"Yes—it's a lot like your difficulty assimilating into the Merchants culture," he said, looking over my shoulder at something that caught his attention, distracting him for a moment. "I think Phil Mickelson is a good comparison. He's got all of the skills but he lacks one thing—discipline. Phil wants to play the game Phil's way instead of just playing along like everyone else. He tries to change the game, attempting shots that no one can hit. That's when he makes mistakes. I think that's your problem, Jack. You're a gambler, and you think you can exert your will to change something you don't like. All you have to do is play the game, but that's the problem. You don't like the game, do you?"

While I would have never admitted it, he was right. *But how do I respond to a golf analogy?* I waited to see what he would say.

"The game changed. I understand your frustration—I really do. You would have been CEO of PT&G. Chad told us he had groomed you for that position. But he also told us you were stubborn and would likely have problems fitting in at Merchants. He was right. You were great under the old rules and the old game, but this is something new."

My anger got the best of me. "I'm still a damn good banker but you won't listen to me. We have lost our best people. Your company laid off people who were told they wouldn't be laid off. The employees here in Philly don't trust Merchants. Now you talk about my problems? I want to work and do my job. So why don't you trust me and let me do it?"

"I don't trust you, Jack," he said, looking around the room as if he was gazing at a buzzard circling over me. "For one thing you just said this was my company. Guess again—you're part of Merchants now, but you don't think so, and that's one reason I don't trust you. But there's a much more compelling reason. The reason I don't trust you is because the last thing Chad told me before he left Philadelphia was to not trust you. He told us about your affair with a bimbo that works at a coffee shop. He said it cut into your hours. He also said you would do anything to get ahead. I haven't seen anything to think any differently than what Chad told me."

I was stunned. "Chad said that?" I asked. "Let's call him and see if he'll admit to that."

"It will do no good," Rex said, smiling. "He's probably out on the golf course right now, where I would love to be. But you really can't deny any of that, can you?"

He was right. I couldn't deny anything he had just said without opening even more problems. "I wish you were playing golf, Rex," I said, picking up a miniature golf club from his pen holder. "Then I could be doing some good for Merchants and you would be to."

He glared at me. "What are you implying?"

"Nothing," I said. "I meant it exactly how I said it. By the way, no one trusts you—especially me. I hope that clears the air."

"No, it doesn't, but this will I'm sure," he said, pulling a document from the envelope I had noticed before Rex entered the office. "I thought while you were in here alone you might take a look at it." He slid the stapled bulk of papers across the desk with his right hand while simultaneously reaching into his desk drawer and pulling a document from it.

"What's this?" I asked, picking up the document. Then I saw the title. It was a Performance Enhancement Plan or PEP as they referred to it at Merchants. It was basically a written warning, a document that would be placed in your personnel file for anyone of consequence to see. The warning positioned Merchants to be able to begin a process of delivering warnings that would ultimately end with the termination of the employee.

"Jack, take your time and read it—then we can discuss it," he said as he began to look at his copy.

I leaned back and began to read the PEP. In my entire career I had never been "warned" or told I was "less than satisfactory" in anything. I had always been a star performer until Merchants. I could not believe what I was reading. The document asked me to complete a near thesis-type plan on how I was going to reach goals that were realistically impossible. It was like being shoved out of an airplane and told to fly. I did not have a parachute.

I felt like I was ready to implode. My face was red hot, and my head began to hurt. "You know the challenges I've faced. Why are you doing this?" As I said the words I remembered the same phrase being said to me years earlier—by Henry—a man I fired for no apparent reason.

"Honestly, you asked for it with your bad attitude. You said too many negative things about Merchants to the wrong people. You're formally on notice. If you don't improve, you will be released."

I wanted to say a million things, but none of them would be correct. I stared at the document. A quick pain shot across my chest. I kept looking down at the document even though I had quit reading it. My vision was blurred.

"I'm sorry it's coming to this, but you're being given one last chance," Rex said. "I know a lot of people still look to you for leadership here in Philly. I need you, Jack, on the team—but working for me, not against me. Understood?"

I knew the process required for a PEP to take effect. I turned to the last page, pulled a pen from my jacket pocket, and signed and dated the document. "Do you have a copy for me?" I asked.

Rex slid the copy he was holding across the desk as I slid the original back to him. "Now, I'll wait for your plan. If you need any help, you know where to find me."

I got up with the copy and didn't look at Rex. Instead I saw a picture of Ben Hogan in a framed picture by the door and stopped and looked at it. As if he had forgotten everything that happened, Rex turned his attention to the photo. "You like that photo? It's my favorite. Ben autographed it, and I bought it on eBay. I got a good deal on it."

I read what was barely legible on the old photo above the golfer's signature. "I don't really care about the photo, but I like what he wrote. 'Never give up!' I think that's something to think about," I said.

"Yeah, Ben made one of the greatest comebacks ever," Rex said. "That's something you should think about."

● ● ●

As I left the room I heard Rex's secretary tell him Bill Hopkins was holding on the phone for him. I felt like I was a time bomb and the last second had just ticked. Somehow I made it to my office in the far corner of the building.

Sitting alone in my office I tried to control my anger. I shut my eyes and leaned my head back, thinking about what had just happened. I leaned forward and saw the PEP document on the desk in front of me. Beside the document were the only photos in my office—Jessica and Joshua. The photos were a couple of years old—from a happier time in my life. The kids were younger and my hopes were alive and appeared within reach. As I looked at their photos I realized how much of their lives I had missed—choosing to be at work instead of spending time with them. They were distant, just like the hopes I had for being the top banker in Philadelphia.

The past offered no comfort.

I pulled the cell phone from my briefcase and hit the speed dial for Cassie's number, but I stopped short of hitting the Send button. What would or could I say to her?

I thought of Tina, but Tina was out of the question. As I put the cell phone back in my briefcase I saw the top of Benny's book. The title, *Bank on It!*, stared at me from the tightly packed quarters it was sharing with Merchants reports. Just like earlier in the day, I needed to find some sanity in the madness of my world. I opened the book to the list of chapters and found the chapter titled "Effective Attitudes."

What makes us different? It's our choice of our attitude. Never underestimate the power of choosing your attitude. Our power to choose is our greatest strength as humans. It's more important than our IQs, education, experience, jobs, or net worth. You cannot control the conditions, but you can choose your response. Being effective is choosing an effective attitude—the right response at the right time.

The first time I had read the passage I disagreed with his judgment. I tended to define attitude as either positive or negative. A good attitude was more of a sedative or appeasement instead of a smart solution. I liked absolutes—good was good and bad was bad—even though I somehow found my life always in the gray as Chad had counseled. I still did not know what I was going to say to Benny. I felt another pain in my chest. "Maybe I need a healthy attitude," I said to myself.

Then the pain worsened.

As I leaned forward to try to find a position to control the pain, sweat rolled off my forehead and dripped on the PEP lying on the desk. I felt a wave of nausea. I looked at the photos of Jessica and Joshua.

Then—nothing.

> {
> *Reality can be painful—*
> *the truth can hurt.*
> }

—BENJAMIN FRANKLIN PRICE

17. What Happened?

"WHAT HAPPENED?" I asked, trying to understand where I was. I could see people around me and had the sense I was moving.

"Mr. Oliver, you're at Jefferson Hospital—you're at the best place you can be," a male voice responded. "Just relax and enjoy the ride," I heard him say with an air of humor.

But this wasn't funny. I was flat on my back on a gurney racing down the corridors of Jefferson Hospital. Being at the hospital was a shock, but my memory of the hospital and my mother's death made the trip down the hallway unravel me even more.

"What happened?" I asked again. I had a variety of monitors hooked up to me and saw an IV stuck into my left arm. The ammonia-like smell that seemed to permeate any type of clinical environment had always been difficult for me to stomach. I held back the compulsion to become ill on the paramedic pushing me down the hall.

"Calm down, Mr. Oliver, and relax," he said. "You're going to be okay."

Relax? Is that what he told me?

"Am I having a heart attack?" I asked. "How did I get here?"

"We don't know exactly what's wrong, but we're going to find out," he said calmly. "Relax—we'll take care of you."

After being parked in a room, a male nurse came in and introduced himself. His name was José. José looked like a bodybuilder, with thick arms, wide chest, and a football player's neck. He smiled and continued to take all of my vital signs, writing them down on my chart.

"How are you feeling, Mr. Oliver?" he asked.

"Feeling? I just want to know what happened," I said. "Can you tell me why I'm here? Am I having a heart attack? What's going on?"

José said with a reassuring grin, "I don't know exactly why you're here—yet. But you're at the right place. This is where you need to be. You passed out at work, and your secretary did the right thing. She called and got you in to see us. Now, take some deep breaths for me and just focus on getting yourself relaxed and calmed down. Take a deep breath . . . okay, another . . ."

Now I was being told how to breathe. As the memories of what was happening at the office began to filter into my thoughts, the monitors responded with a quickening number of beeps.

"Mr. Oliver, please relax," José said, patting my shoulder. "I need you to take slow, deep breaths. It's important. Don't think about anything else except breathing—slow, disciplined breaths."

The deep breathing and José's calming influence finally helped to slow down the monitors' beeps. I asked again, "Why am I here?"

"Don't worry about why you're here—you are where you need to be," he said. "We'll take excellent care of you. I promise. It's my job."

It would be sad if talking to Rex Nessman could put me in a hospital or even kill me, I thought. Why should a conversation—even worse, a piece of paper—put me into this kind of condition?

The thought embarrassed me. Then I was mad. *How dare that idiot!* I thought. That SOB! My anger started to resurface. "Mr. Oliver," José said, "I don't know what to tell you other than you need to relax. You're letting your fear take control—think only about right now—breathe. Take deep breaths. Your doctor will be here shortly to talk with you. Until then, I have one word: relax."

José continued to look at every possible gauge, tube, hose, and machine hooked to me, maybe sensing the potential for the Jack Oliver volcano to blow at any time. *I'm sure he has experience dealing with overachieving, overweight, overstressed workaholics before,* I thought. I was easy to figure out.

"Rex isn't worth losing your life over," I said to myself when José stepped out of the room. *Something this insignificant should not put me in a hospital,* I thought, leaning forward to find a remote control for the television.

I briefly fell back to sleep.

• • •

When I awoke, I saw Tina standing over the bed. "Hi, I didn't expect to see you," I said, rubbing my eyes. She had obviously been crying, but now had a lost, vacant appearance as she stared at me.

"How are you feeling?" she asked. "We were pretty worried about you for a while, but the doctor says you're going to be fine."

"What is it?" I asked, not knowing what to expect.

"The doctor will be back in later," she said, still standing several feet away as if I had a communicable disease. "He said all of the signs at first pointed toward a heart attack—but, it wasn't your heart. He thinks you had an anxiety attack."

"An anxiety attack?" I asked. "That doesn't sound right."

The doctor had to be wrong. *I'm a mentally tough guy who has survived everything life's thrown at me,* I thought. For a moment I almost wished it had been a heart attack. An anxiety attack sounded like something people who cannot deal with stress blamed for their inadequacies. *Jack Oliver doesn't have anxiety attacks.* The more I thought about it, I was certain I was misdiagnosed.

"They must be wrong," I said. I loved stress and pressure. Stress made me stronger. It separated the wimps from the pros. Like the saying goes, "What does not kill you will make you stronger." I believed it my entire adult life. *Anxiety cannot attack me—I feed off of stress. Pressure is my friend.* Just like a drug, stress had juiced me to go to the next level in my career time and time again. But I hadn't expected Merchants. I realized I was afraid.

"They're going to check you out," Tina said. "You haven't had a checkup for years, so maybe this is a good thing."

"What causes an anxiety attack?" I asked.

"The doctor didn't explain it to me, but he said he felt like you needed to stay overnight to make sure your system was settling into a normal rhythm. He'll be back in a few minutes to talk to you," Tina said, looking at me as though she had a mix of pity and anger.

"Thank you for coming to the hospital," I said. "Do the kids know I'm here?"

"Yeah, they were there when I got the call from your office."

"I'm sorry to put them through this," I said, thinking of how I would have felt in the same position.

"Jack, they're not surprised. They expected something like this at any time. You're not living a healthy lifestyle, and it shows," she said, pausing for a moment. "I didn't come down here to upset you or to say I told you so, but your lifestyle is killing you. All you do is work long hours, drink liquor, and eat the worst kind of food. You're eating and drinking yourself to death!"

I didn't respond. I wanted to tell Tina she was wrong, but I was in no position to lie to her. Everything she said appeared to be true.

"It's a miracle you have survived this long," Tina said, shaking her head side to side. "Everyone sees it. Why can't you?" Tina started to cry tears of rage and what may have been some amount of sympathy. She regained her composure.

"I'm sorry Jack. I don't want to upset you," she said in a calmer tone. "I'm saying this for your own good. You need to change the way you're living, or you won't be here much longer."

Hearing this at any other time might not have left much of an impression. Or I would have blown up and accused Tina of wanting to see me in this condition. What had she done over the years to help me? But my prone position in a hospital bed with tubes and monitors hooked to me slowed down my normal response. Tina still had anger with me over the past, but hearing her say that I needed to change struck the same chord I felt talking to Benny the night before and John Helms before that. I needed to change. Tina was right. If I didn't change I would die.

"I know," I said. "I'm trying to do better."

"I'm sorry, Jack, but I honestly don't think you can," Tina said.

"You've created a monster, and now you're paying the price for living the life you chose."

"A monster," I said. "That's a new term of endearment." My anger started to surface, but I remained determined to show I was in control of my emotions.

"Endearment isn't something that can be applied to us," she said. "I'm sorry. I didn't mean to lose my temper. You're still the father of our children, and I do care about your health." Tina stayed for a few more minutes, standing in silence a few feet from the bed. She got up to leave saying she needed to go meet Jessica at the high school counselor's office.

"Is there a problem with Jessica?" I asked.

She responded with a laugh, "When isn't there a problem with Jessica?"

I did not ask any more questions.

"Let me know how you're doing," Tina said.

"Thanks again for coming here," I said. "It means a lot to me that you would check in on a monster," I said, smiling, hoping she would do the same.

"No problem," she said, turning away. "Good luck, Jack."

She left without making any eye contact with me. No hug or even a pat on my hand or shoulder. As she turned and walked out of the room, I thought to myself, *No one cares.*

I lay in silence with the sound of the beeps and drips to keep me company. I fell back to sleep.

18. What's in This for Me?

"WHAT'S IN THIS FOR ME?"

It was a question I regretted asking Chad so quickly, but I was accustomed to being part of his "deals," as he referred to them over the years. After hearing him call it the "Merchants deal" several times in the executive committee meeting, the first question that formed naturally in my mind was "What's in this for me?"

Over my career Chad had asked me to do some questionable things. A couple of his large stock purchases—or "deals"—left some doubt about what actually happened in the transactions. Whether it was complicity or being forced to do so, I signed documents as a witness without seeing the people involved. I trusted Chad. He had simply asked me to sign as a witness to expedite stock transactions. But the bottom line was that had Chad realized significant gains by knowing what was going to happen in the near future and buying stock at reduced prices ahead of events. My part was to alter the timing of the transactions, back-dating documents, relying on his word about when the person had signed over the stock.

Lying in the hospital bed, I replayed the situations surrounding my part in Chad's dubious transactions. Was I wrong? Yes, but what do you do? Tell your boss, a person who has put you in charge and trusted you with the reins of a huge organization, that he is a liar and a cheat? Do you say "No!" and know you will have ruined your career by uttering a two-letter word? I never gained any financial reward from these blind acts as a witness, I reminded myself.

While the rationalizations allowed me to overlook my participation, the truth was that I was afraid to say no. I *did* receive something from it—Chad's promise to make me his successor. Finally, I confronted him but it was too late. I was paying the price now. Where had I gone wrong?

• • •

"What's in this for me?" I asked Chad as I sat down in his office.

"I guessed you would ask me that. I know you, Jack. I could see it in your eyes in the meeting. You're worried. Why? You know you'll be fine after this merger. You're one of the prizes for Merchants Bank. Plus, I know your value. Have I ever let you down?"

"No, you haven't let me down," I said, "but what's going to happen to me?"

"What will happen to you? Why don't you ask first what will happen to me? My family has served as leaders of this bank for the past seventy-six years. Do you think it was easy for me to sell PT&G? Don't you think I've been the person all along with the biggest stake to lose? This has been very difficult for me—more difficult than anyone knows."

"So what will happen to you?" I asked.

"I don't know yet, but I think it's safe to say I'll be stepping down and letting you run the show for Merchants," he said.

"I'm sorry," I said, trying to appear sympathetic as I tried to find the positives he was tossing to me in his comments. "But I assumed you would be taken care of in a deal this size."

"Assuming again, Jack!" Chad nearly exploded. "Money doesn't mean everything. I have pride. I have a history. You have a job. Do it!"

I did not expect his response. I was still mulling over what I would be doing taking over for him, under new management. Hearing Chad say, "Money doesn't mean everything," surprised me. But when he said that I "have a job" it hurt me to my core. Chad was basically putting me in the same group as every other person at PT&G. I thought I should mean more after I had given him my trust and more. I had given him my heart and soul. I was his successor—or at least thought I was his successor.

"Since it's just a job, what will happen to my job?" I asked, barely containing my anger.

"You'll be fine," Chad said, calming his voice to his normal, mellow tone. "Merchants Bank will want to guard their investment by keeping people like you. You'll be a key person in this operation, their largest outside of North Carolina. They don't know a thing about Philly—so you're very valuable to them. You're far enough away from Charlotte so I'm sure they'll leave you alone and let you run things for them."

"Do you really believe that?" I asked, hoping he was telling the truth.

After pausing for a minute, Chad changed his tone to the same tone I had heard when he asked me to help him in his "deals" over the years. "You do need to do one thing for me—without fail," he said, leaning forward and pointing toward me. "Don't let me down. Keep up the positive attitude, or your staff will lose faith in this deal, and everyone will suffer. I'm counting on you, Jack. So are they."

He leaned back into his chair and paused to hear my reaction. This was classic Chad. I had seen him use this tactic before. I knew if I waited without responding a compliment was coming next. I was right . . . and wrong.

"You're the best young banker I know," he said and then paused. "But you do have a weakness. You're always worried about *Jack Oliver*. You care more about you than anyone else—you have no loyalty, other than taking care of you. I have heard this from your managers—they don't trust you. They believe you would not go down with the ship like a captain should, that you'd take the last life preserver and swim as fast as you could from the sinking boat leaving everyone else to drown. That's almost the exact words from one of your managers. How does that make you feel?"

"I don't believe that," I said immediately.

"Believe it," Chad said. "As a CEO, I can't afford to do that. I had to look out for the shareholders and seven thousand employees. If you were CEO, I'm afraid you would have one focus: yourself. I'm looking at what's the best for everyone—not just me."

His words were like pouring salt into an already open wound. I was selfish, but not to the extreme Chad was telling me. "I have always done everything you asked without question and succeeded in every task," I reminded him. To move away from strictly "me" as the issue, I brought up my concerns about others: shareholders, customers, and the community—and the bank's employees. "What will happen to the institution that PT&G is for Philadelphia?" I asked. "What about our customers—our employees? People are counting on us. Are we going to preserve that image?"

"Who was it said that 'image is everything'? You're not the first person to ask those same questions. Merchants will make this work. They have done it over sixty other times. They know how to maintain an image," Chad said, raising his tone. Then, almost chuckling, he added, "They're the buying experts in banking. You don't need to worry, Jack. They know what to do. They have a job and you have a job to do."

"Why did we sell to Merchants—now?" I asked, not wanting the discussion to end on that note. "We don't have that big of a problem in our loan portfolio that would force us to sell—I know that. So why sell now?"

"They made us an offer we couldn't refuse," Chad said with an alarming similarity to Marlon Brando. "How can you turn down a premium almost double what most banks receive? They wanted us, and they got us. Done deal! Sold to the high bidder!" He smacked his desk with his right hand to emphasize the closure. I'd never seen a larger smile on his face.

"Were there any other bidders?" I asked, as I continued to follow the money.

"We didn't have a FOR SALE sign up inviting offers," Chad said, leaning back in his chair. "Honestly, and just between us, you're right—we didn't have to sell now, but when Merchants offered what they did, we had no choice. It was my fiduciary duty as CEO to give the best return to our shareholders. The deal happened because Merchants wanted us—not because we wanted Merchants."

Chad appeared to be much more comfortable now, so I asked him, "What did you get out of the deal?"

"Jack, I gave up a family heritage and leading Philadelphia's best bank. How dare you ask me what I'm getting? I'm doing this for everyone else—not just me. Did you not hear what I just said? You really have a lousy attitude. If you don't like it, you should quit—now."

I couldn't believe what I just heard. Quit? The last word, "now," almost exploded out of his mouth. Usually Chad would brag about what he was getting in any transaction to me, always saying "just between us" as a way of ensuring some privacy for his greed. But I had made a mistake. I made my second error by responding without thinking.

"I am not going to quit—ever. If Merchants wants to make this work, they better hope I stay," I said.

Chad was smiling, as if he knew what I was going to say and had already scripted his response. "You're wrong. You're not going to make it, Jack. I'm disappointed." I wasn't expecting this response. "It's all about you, isn't it?" Chad continued. "You don't even appreciate what I've done for you, do you?"

I paused to put my thoughts together. A strong sense of déjà vu enveloped me. Chad had used the same line in our only other real confrontation years before—the first time he asked me to sign off on one of his stock "deals." He had walked into my office after everyone else had left the building and thrust the last page of what appeared to be a contract of some type in front of me and asked me to notarize the document for the previous day's date. When I asked him what I was signing, you would have thought I made a disparaging remark about his mother. Chad blew up. I had never seen him so angry and out of control. He asked me if I trusted him. I told him, yes, but I couldn't notarize a document for a person I didn't see in front of me. Chad told me that I should trust him or quit. He said, "Jack, working with me is working for me. Sign it or quit—it's your choice." I notarized the document. Chad told me not to worry and that I would do great working with him if I did as I was told. I found out later that he had purchased a large number of shares from an elderly client at less-than-market price. In addition, he knew the bank was getting ready to split the stock, making the date crucial. He bought 5,000 shares, but actually received 7,500 shares after the stock split, resulting in a huge profit for Chad.

With that memory playing in my head, I reminded him of what I had done for *his* benefit over the years.

"Jack, you're the one in hot water if you ever bring up that or any of those deals again. You're the one who notarized the document, swearing the person was there—right in front of you! You're the one who would lose his job, reputation, and get sued in the process. You could even go to jail. You have a choice. Get on board the Merchants ship or jump off and start swimming. Let me remind you that jobs are getting tougher to find. I want an answer . . . now." Chad nearly screamed as he hit his fist on his desk, his face turning red and veins popping out on his forehead and neck.

I tried my best to compose myself. I wanted to go through more of the dirty-laundry list of things I had done for him, including firing people because he wanted to replace them with his relatives and making loans on the most liberal terms to his friends and business partners. Somehow I controlled my tongue. He was right. I was as guilty for blindly witnessing documents and being unethical as he was for pressuring me to do so.

"I'm on board," I said.

"Good. I'll do my best to forget what was said today. I think you need to leave now. Go home, or wherever you go after you leave work, and think about what you need to do to keep your focus to stay on board. Good luck, Jack. You're going to need it."

Chad's face lit up with a smug smile of victory. I nodded my head in pitiful agreement, stood, and walked out the door.

• • •

As I lay in the hospital bed, the monitors were chirping rapidly, showing my physical response to the memory of my capitulation to Chad. Returning my thoughts to the present, I decided to take José's advice and try to calm myself down.

I remembered Tina's comments from her visit. She had been

honest; I'd created a monster—or worse. *Tina doesn't care about me. The kids don't care. They just want my money.* I did everything for them.

Or did I? The monitor started to beep faster. I tried to gain control again. *Okay, deep breaths, Jack, deep breaths,* I told myself.

I fell asleep.

19. How Do You Feel?

"HOW DO YOU FEEL?"

Feeling the effects of the drug-induced sleep, I could barely make out the voice. Opening my eyes, I saw my physician standing at the head of the hospital bed. Dr. Hall had been a client of PT&G for years, but I rarely saw him outside of business. I had met him when I was a loan officer many years ago and successfully talked him into moving his business to the bank.

Seeing me wake up while he was reviewing the chart, he continued: "Jack, what are you doing here? I need someone to stay at that new bank and take care of my money!" While I'm sure he said it for a comforting laugh, Dr. Hall was being partially sincere. He spent as much time making sure every penny of his earnings was being invested properly as he spent taking care of his patients. I knew this from experience.

"Sorry, Doc," I said trying to smile. "I'll get right back to work as soon as you unhook me. What's my problem?"

"After looking at everything, it appears you suffered what amounts to an anxiety attack. That's the only way I can describe it at this point. Have you ever experienced anything like that before?"

"No, never," I said. But even as I was saying the words I remembered getting short of breath in the elevator several days earlier. And there were other times in my life when I had felt something similar to the nausea and claustrophobic feelings. But I didn't tell him.

"Are you sure it was an anxiety attack?" I asked. "I've always handled stress very effectively."

"I'm sure you have, but stress catches up with you—you can't outrun stress. Tell me what happened. What were you doing before this happened?"

Embarrassed, I said, "I had a meeting with my boss—he wouldn't listen to me and I got angry." I didn't go into detail. "I remember trying to stand up, feeling nauseous, and sitting back down. Then I was here."

"That must have been some kind of meeting," he said, smiling and continuing to look at the charts. "The only way I would have gotten that upset would be if my accountant told me I was being audited by the IRS." He laughed, folding the cover over the clipboard. "Or if you guys were raising the interest rates on my loans." Again, he was telling a partial truth. I wished he would tell me I could leave.

"All of the tests so far appear to show nothing that would evidence a heart attack or anything else. I was shocked we found a heart in there," he said, trying to be humorous again. "However, to make sure everything is working inside I'm going to put you through a full physical today. When was the last time you had a complete physical?"

"I haven't had time to get sick or even think about being sick," I said. "I can't remember ever having a full physical. I've been busy."

"Everyone is busy, Jack," he said in a much more serious tone of voice. "You need to get focused more on your health than your job." He looked me squarely in the eyes. "We are going to poke, prod, and test to see if you have any complications we aren't finding. But even before I get any results from a physical, I'm sure of a couple of things. First, you need to lose weight. Second, you need to exercise, starting moderately but staying on a regular fitness regimen. Third, your diet is obviously poor, so what you will begin to eat starting today will probably taste different than the fried food you have been digesting on a regular basis." He smiled, looking at my huge stomach outlined below the hospital sheets.

"Will that keep me from having another attack like the one today?" I asked.

"Count this as a warning shot fired over your boat. It's time to get yourself a tune-up before something bad happens. We'll begin the tests and get your physical exam done while you're here. I want you to spend a night in the hospital so we can monitor you and complete our examination. Plus, you look like you need a good night's sleep. We can make sure of that here. Then we'll figure out a program for you to deal with your stress. Sound fair?"

"Okay, Doc," I said. "Just be sure to change the oil and rotate my tires."

Dr. Hall laughed and said, "Don't worry, we won't miss anything."

• • •

At any other time in my life, I would have been worried about what would happen at work without me being there. I would have immediately called the office and begun telling my secretary Carol all of the things she would need to do to make sure nothing slipped. But I leaned back, shut my eyes, and began taking deep breaths.

José stepped back into the room. "Thanks again for being so patient with your worst patient," I said.

"You're not my worst—but close to it," he said with a huge smile. "How did everything go with your doctor?"

"It's not good," I said, trying to appear as serious as possible. "He said you people were going to probe me and test me like a laboratory rat. Is that what you do to bankers?"

"So you're a banker," he said. "I knew you were someone important."

"Bankers aren't important," I said. "We may think we are, but we aren't."

"My banker has helped make my life better," José said. "His name is Henry—Henry Starnes. He's getting ready to retire from the credit union. I'm gonna miss him. He took a chance on me when no one else would. He helped me get loans so I could finish college. Got me a loan to buy our house. He's like one of our family. I take my kids into his office at Christmas every year and they give him a present, usually something my wife has baked."

I did everything I could not to cringe. Of course I knew Henry—I had fired him many years ago, securing my first promotion. I didn't know what to say. José continued, "Henry said he used to work for the big bank that was bought. He said he worked there over twenty years—but they didn't appreciate him. It was their loss, our gain at the credit union. Do you know Henry?"

"Yes, I know Henry. I haven't seen him for years. I always thought a lot of him. He was one of the friendliest bankers I've ever met. He's a good man."

"So you know him—small world! He's a great guy," José said as he continued checking all of the gauges and the IV. He then asked, "Which bank do you work for, Jack?"

"The wrong one," I said, turning my head away.

I was ashamed.

{
Knowing what's wrong
can help you find
what's right.
}

—BENJAMIN FRANKLIN PRICE

20. What's Wrong?

"WHAT'S WRONG?"

José's question had sparked a memory from many years earlier. I sat still, thinking about what was wrong with me. "Are you all right?" he asked again, seeing the obvious vacant look on my face.

"Yeah, I am. Could you do me a favor?" I asked.

"Sure, as long as you don't ask me to sneak you out of here," he said.

"The first thing you told me was that I was where I was supposed to be. I believe you. But I need to make a call to confirm a trip I'm supposed to go on."

"Mr. Oliver, I mean, Jack. I'm not sure you need to get on the phone right now and make business phone calls," he said.

"This isn't about work—this is about going fishing," I said.

"Fishing—that sounds like what you need."

"Could you get the number for me?" I asked, still nearly bound to the bed with gauges and tubes. "It's a yellow sticky note inside of my coat in the closet."

"Is this it?" José said, pulling out the yellow note. "Benny Price?"

"Yes, he's a new friend," I said. "He invited me to go fishing."

"You need some time away from work every now and then. Fishing is something I would prescribe," José said. He gave me a big smile and handed me the note.

After José left the room, I shut my eyes and thought about what had just happened. I hadn't heard the name Henry Starnes for years. Now, I was hearing it in a hospital. When José had asked, "What's wrong?" I had a flashback to a time Tina had posed the same question.

• • •

"*What's wrong?*" Tina asked, rolling over at three o'clock in the morning to find me flipping through TV channels.

"Nothing," I said. "I'm fine."

"I don't think so," she said. "You look like you're annoyed—or something worse."

"Nothing's wrong," I said. "I can't sleep."

"Jack, you look like you're really upset—tell me what's wrong."

The day before Chad had asked me to perform a favor for him, approving a loan to one of his close friends. "It's just a little deal," he told me. The loan didn't meet PT&G's loan policy, but I approved the deal. Only a couple of days earlier I had chewed out one of my top lenders for making a loan that bore less than 10 percent of the risk I had just approved for Chad's friend. My conscience was bothering me.

"It's just work," I said to Tina, trying to avoid any further discussion. "Sometimes you have to do things on the way up the ladder you don't agree with—but you have to do it to get ahead."

"What did you do?" Tina asked.

I explained the situation to Tina.

"How do you explain something like that to the lender you chewed out?" Tina asked.

"I don't," I said. "I don't have to explain anything; I'm her boss."

"So you're doing to her what Chad has done to you?" Tina said.

"That's why I have tried to claw my way to the top as quickly as possible," I said in one of my rare moments of honesty with Tina.

"The higher you climb the more you avoid situations like that. You reduce the amount of dirty work you have to do."

"But the higher you climb the more you get to dump on people below you," she said.

"I wouldn't call it dumping on them—that's their job," I said.

"To do Chad's dirty work?" she said.

"It's not dirty work—it's what we do. It's part of the job," I said.

"So, does that make it right?" Tina asked.

"No," I said, "but at least it won't be my problem."

"I don't understand the person you're becoming," Tina said. "It's like you can't or don't distinguish right from wrong anymore."

"I know right from wrong," I said, "but in business, there's a lot more tolerance. There are no black-and-white, right-and-wrong answers—everything in business is gray."

"I hope and pray you really don't think like that," Tina said, rolling over away from me. "You don't, do you?"

"I don't know," I said, "I really don't know."

• • •

Putting some "gray in play," as Chad referred to it, always helped. He said the act of rationalizing the pros and cons helped to cloud the issues enough to avoid a moral quandary. It allowed us to believe the ends justified the means. Seeing gray helped to remove the black-and-white, right-and-wrong ethical choices.

"What we do can't be put in the context of right and wrong," Chad reminded me over the years. "What we do is *business*. Business is survival of the most profitable—not the most moral."

I thought about moments of questionable judgment during my brief stay at Jefferson Hospital. Had I become so jaded in my life that I had actually forgotten the difference between right and wrong? Or had I simply tried to ignore the difference so I could sleep at least two or three hours a night?

I remembered a section from Benny's book about right and wrong:

Instead of asking "What's right?" and looking for the right answer, I will ask myself, "What's wrong?" This reduces the field of choices—what's wrong usually stands out. By reducing choices, I can make a better, less-confused choice. Knowing what's wrong can help you find what's right.

If I had taken that simple advice over the years, it would have limited my upward mobility at the bank. Admitting that something was unethical would have slowed my progress, so I looked for gray as Chad had told me. I had done a lot of the wrong things to find something I believed was right for me and my family. *My life was a pitiful representation of the Jack Oliver I had aspired to be,* I thought. As hard as I had tried, success was always out of reach. Going back to the Monopoly strategy and all of the strategy, plans, and hard work, one mistake was now clearly evident—my aim was wrong.

But now I had hope.

I dialed Benny's direct line and reached him on the first ring. "Good afternoon, this is Benny Price. How can I help you?"

"Benny, this is Jack Oliver," I said, trying to cover any discomfort I was having sitting in the bed. I hoped he wouldn't hear the monitors or ask where I was. "I've thought about your very gracious offer to visit you in Virginia, and I accept. I still have a lot of doubt anything will come of it, but I would like to talk with you more if you're willing to spend the time and expense to get together."

"I'm glad you decided to visit. It won't be a waste of your time or mine. You can bank on it! We'll arrange the travel itinerary for you. I don't have a private jet like your employer, but we'll get you here comfortably. Roanoke is not too far out of the mainstream."

"I appreciate your consideration," I said, and without thinking I closed with saying, "I'm looking forward to visiting." I was telling the truth.

"It will be a pleasure for us to have you visit. I'm looking forward to meeting you in person. Take care of yourself, Jack. If you don't, no one else will."

While I realized he was not able to peer through the phone line and see me lying in the hospital, it felt as though Benny somehow sensed that I needed to hear those words and to heed that message.

I believed him.

• • •

After a day in the hospital I felt as though I had had every crevice of my anatomy scoped and poked. As a rule I believed being in a health care facility was not good for your health. But I found myself more than relieved that I had a full physical at Jefferson. I felt that my time at the hospital had done me good.

I knew it was his job, but I gained a great appreciation of José's work. He had been superb both as a nurse and a positive influence, not only to me but also to the other patients. You could see and hear him talking with passion and care about each of his patients. It was unmistakable. He loved what he was doing.

"You do a great job, José," I said as he prepped me for leaving the hospital. "Don't you ever leave here? It seems like you've been here the entire time I've been here."

"We have the option to work twelve-hour shifts—basically three days on and four days off. That way I can spend more time with my family. I'm also taking two college classes, so finding the time to keep my grades up is a challenge."

It sounded like José was like me in a lot of ways. "Are you looking at moving up here in the hospital?"

"When you say 'moving up' do you mean like a promotion?" he responded.

"Yeah, it sounds like you're working hard to get ahead," I said.

"Actually I'm not really concerned about getting ahead of anyone—just being the best I can be," he said. "I love my job, but it's not perfect. I work long hours. The hospital has cut back their staff, which made things a lot tougher the past few years. I could leave and get more money at University of Pennsylvania Hospital—probably not work as hard. But I fit here. I look at my job as the way I can be part of the world. Maybe make the world a better place. If I can bring smile to a person who is in pain I'm doing my job. If I can help a person gain confidence that they will be healthy again, I feel like I have done my part. When I'm having a bad day I tell myself, 'José, you are here for the patient, they aren't here for you.' That makes the difference. I'm here to serve and to help others."

It was a new way to look at things for me. I asked, "Don't you have plans to move into a supervisor's position? You're the best I've seen here at the hospital, or any hospital for that matter."

"I'm really not here to get ahead," he said. "Most of the supervisors here never spend time with patients. All they do is paperwork. Those people seem like they aren't very happy with their lives. I have a job I love to do. I enjoy being with patients, not papers."

José's sincerity in his own unscripted purpose statement stunned me. I finally understood what he was saying. *"I'm here for the patient."* And I believed him. He definitely wasn't like me. His family came first. He worked for others—not for himself. What had happened to me? If I had prioritized my life around the core values José had chosen would I be here now? José brought the idea of service to others to life for me. If I had truly changed my values from my stay at Jefferson, the question "Why am I still at Merchants?" demanded an answer.

"I appreciate what you've done for me," I said. "You're a very unique person: someone who loves their job."

"I don't have many options. I can love it or hate it. Loving it is more fun!" he said and then laughed.

José took me in the wheelchair, hospital rules, to the main floor. Patting my shoulder as he glided me through the lobby, he said, "Jack, take care of yourself—if you don't, nobody else will."

Surprised by the almost exact quote of what I had heard from Benny, I turned and looked over my shoulder. I smiled and asked, "Have you been talking with Benny?"

"The only Benny I've ever heard of is the guy you were calling," he said, laughing. After a pause he added, "The only other Benny I've heard of is the guy who has all the statues and his name on everything here," he said, laughing. "But I don't think Ben Franklin is around to talk to you."

"Sometimes I wonder—they're similar—the two Benny's," I said.

"Then you should listen to both of them," José said, smiling. He pushed me through the automatic doors.

"Thanks," I said as I got up from the wheelchair and turned to shake his hand. "You helped me."

"That's what I'm here for, Jack," he said, returning to the fifth floor and the job he loved.

I left to go back to my apartment, alone.

· · ·

Driving back to my apartment I called the office and told Carol I would be back in the office the next day, but to change any appointments for Friday. "I'm going to take a quick weekend trip to do some fishing," I told her.

"Fishing? I never knew you liked to fish," she said.

"I didn't—but it seems like a good time to start."

"Are you sure you're okay, Jack?" she asked.

"I will be," I said. "And thanks for calling the hospital and getting me help."

"I was scared to death," she said. "If you don't mind me asking, what happened?"

I wasn't ready to confide in Carol, even though she had known me for twenty years. "Carol, I'm fine, I promise. They checked me out and I'll have to wait and see what they say. But don't worry."

"Okay," she said. "We're worried about you."

"I'm not sure *many* are worried about me there," I said, unable to hide some of the pain. "But I understand—most people don't like their supervisors."

"I've known you since you started here. I'm very proud to work for you. I always knew you were going to be a success."

"I don't feel like much of a success since we were bought," I said. Immediately I wanted to take back the words. "I shouldn't have said that. I'm sorry. I'm just tired from the last few days. I didn't expect the changes with Merchants to be so tough."

"I think you've changed—for the better—since Merchants took over," she said. "Everyone's noticed it. You listen better and have tried to help people get through it. I hope you don't get mad at me for saying this, but you're much more connected now than before." After a pause, Carol said, "Honestly, I hate Merchants, but I'll keep working here because of you. A lot of us feel that way."

I didn't know what to say. "Carol . . . that may have been one of the nicest things anyone has ever said to me about what kind of job I'm doing. Thanks."

"I mean it, Jack, now take care of yourself."

"Everyone keeps telling me that," I said.

"Maybe it's time to listen," she said.

• • •

After returning to my apartment, I knew I had to tell at least two people that I was going to visit Benny about a job: Tina and Cassie.

I decided to call Tina first.

Following a brief summary of all of the tests I had at the hospital, I told her about my plans to visit Virginia—potentially moving there as Benny's successor. Tina snarled over the phone. "So, that's your solution? Run away—again!"

I tried to explain my garbled set of emotions. I couldn't tell her about my conversation with José—it would have only validated her perspective of my life over the years. I told her a small portion of the conflict with Merchants Bank. Her response seemed driven by a sense of satisfaction, like a venomous *I told you so.*

"You spent all of your time at work, and now they don't need you as bad as you need them. I don't really feel sorry for you, Jack. You reap what you sow. Speaking of sowing, is your little friend Cassie going with you? Or is that against the law in Virginia?" she asked.

My mood of reconciliation had passed. I was angry.

"No, Cassie isn't going—and if she did, so what? That's none of your business. Besides, it's obvious you don't care anymore," I said. "Someone has to work to pay for everything you and the kids buy," I said. "You never helped bring any money in. But you sure helped to spend it. I didn't see you worried about my health while I worked sixteen-hour days. You were out having fun, enjoying life."

"I was enjoying life? You really think that's what I did all day and most evenings while you were at work or with Cassie? Go ahead, Jack. Run away from it all, if that's what you need. I really don't care," Tina said, cold and calloused. "Find a new place to work yourself to death. That sounds like something you would do."

My next call wasn't any easier.

My last conversation with Cassie had been a brief call from the hospital. I had told her not to visit me, fearing she might run into Tina or one of the kids. "I don't need any more drama right now," was what I had told her.

"I understand. The man I love is in the hospital, and he tells me to stay away because he's afraid if I visit him I'll stress him more," she said before hanging up. That brief conversation set the stage for what I knew would be her explosion when I told her I was definitely going to travel to Virginia to check out the potential new job, a topic on which she had already made her opinion known.

I decided to call her to avoid a face-to-face confrontation. She barely talked. After telling her my rationale for the trip, she said, "I expected this. You don't need to say anything else. I've told you how I feel. I love you, but that doesn't seem to be enough. I don't agree with what you're doing. I think you're running away from me as much as from your job. If you get on the plane—we're over. I mean it."

"I'm not running away."

"It certainly looks like it. I would have never expected Jack Oliver to give up a pile of money, his reputation in Philadelphia, and dump me to go off to some place in the middle of nowhere," Cassie said. I could hear she was crying. "You've never been honest before—why should I expect anything different now? Good-bye, Jack."

She hung up before I could say another word. She was right; I was giving up a lot of money if I left Merchants. And I was tossing away our relationship. But was I really running away? I decided to call John. I needed to hear something positive.

It seemed as though I could do nothing right.

21. What's Right?

"WHAT'S RIGHT?" I asked John. "I need to know because I certainly have a strong command of what's wrong."

"Most of my exes would say the same thing about me," he said. "I've got so right at being wrong, I figure I could write an advice column called, *Don't Do This—I Did and It Doesn't Work.*"

We both laughed. I had called John to let him know I was leaving the next day to visit his hiking partner. I could tell he was happy about it.

"You've done a lot right," John said in a more serious tone. "Benny will help to bring the best out of you. I'm sure of that. I think fate is guiding you there."

"You're really high on Benny and me working together."

"I believe—no—I'm for sure you'll be great for each other," John said. "Just remember who put you in the saddle there if I should fall on hard times here in the great state of Arkansas."

"I thought you said 'fate' was guiding me there, not you," I said, laughing. "Make up your mind, John."

"No, it's fate," he said. "I'm just a small part of it. Benny helped me—I know he'll help you."

"What did Benny do for you that helped you so much?" I asked.

It was a question I had asked several times, but I had never received a direct answer.

"I can't explain it," he said. "But I know you'll be a changed person after spending a weekend with him."

"You make it sound like it's a psychotherapy retreat instead of a job interview," I said. "Or one of those healing preachers—cast the demons out!" I said, trying my best to mock John's imitations of Southern evangelists. We both laughed.

"Well, ole friend, I think it's a little of both—I guess Benny helped me to focus on what's *real* in life. I guess after spending time with Benny I have a greater appreciation for reality and what I can do *now*. Not tomorrow. I no longer worry about how I screwed up yesterday, or even a minute ago, but what I'm doing right now. That's how he helped me."

"Is he like one of those Southern Baptist ministers you imitate?"

"No, Benny is much more sincere than most of them. He's into reality—they're into your pocket most of the time. I've never heard of him passing the collection plate."

"Well, if he does—I'm putting an IOU from John Helms in it," I said. "I've got to finish packing. What should I take?"

"Let's see, fishin' and hiking, something you don't do much—I would take what you're comfortable in, Jack," he said. "The only things I would guarantee you won't need are a suit and tie. Men don't wear ties at Benny's bank. So leave your two-thousand-dollar suits behind."

After hanging up, I looked at the dozen tailored suits I had in my closet, none costing less than a thousand dollars. *No ties?* I wondered. John must have been kidding me.

• • •

Focusing on what's real in life? *So that's what made Benny so unique for John,* I thought as I continued my packing, removing the best charcoal gray business suit from the travel bag and putting it back in the closet. For years I had believed in a view of the world that had little to do with the type of reality people like José and John were talking about. I was now getting a sense of my warped perspective of right and wrong. The rationalizations I had created to live with my lifestyle choices were a crutch. I used them to hobble through the moral dilemmas I faced at work and home. I fired people when told, telling myself I had no choice if I wanted a promotion. I had a life with Cassie, believing there was no way to repair my life with Tina. As I continued to sort through the clothes, I wondered if I could hide my moral ambiguity when I met Benny. I was afraid of what he would see—the real me—the conflicted me. I didn't think I was ready for that.

He wrote a lot in his book about *sincerity*. I disdained hypocrites, but now understood that I had slipped into being one for the sake of my career. I was a hypocrite, as badly as I hated to admit it.

I did not want Benjamin Franklin Price to see me as an insincere or hypocritical person. Even if I chose to stay put in Philly, I wanted to impress him.

I finished packing my two bags with every kind of clothing I imagined I would need and sat down and opened up the now well-worn copy of *Bank on It!* I reread his thoughts on sincerity.

> Sincerity is more than being honest with others. Sincerity is how you translate your true thoughts to others. Sincerity is born in our thoughts, before words and actions. Sincerity resides within your thoughts and will let you know what's right and wrong, letting you hear your conscience when it speaks to you. When in doubt listen to your conscience. Sincerity resides there.

"My conscience," I said aloud, shaking my head from side to side. "Where's my conscience—I need to pack it for the trip." I kept reading the section.

> Being sincere does not always mean you're right—you can be sincerely wrong. You may believe in what you're doing and have confidence in your abilities, but you may be aimed wrong or fail in the execution of your actions. Always begin by questioning your thoughts and intentions. Being right begins inside.

When Benny talked about sincerity, I realized that I had failed to pass the "sincerity test" as he called it because what I wanted from life was not in harmony with what I said and did. Life was all about me. My intention was selfish. But I pretended otherwise.

I stood up and walked to the window and looked out at Philadelphia. I saw my reflection, staring back. The years had aged me. I remembered when I had worked as a teller and was shocked to see men who appeared seventy years old, but were actually in their early fifties. "Is that me?"

• • •

After finishing my packing, I sat down and poured a drink of bourbon. I wasn't supposed to drink—doctor's orders—but I felt the need to have something to calm my nerves. I picked up Benny's book to look at one more section before I went to sleep. I opened it to the first section, outlining the four steps he had prescribed for "living a questionable life." While I had never been a fan of leadership or self-help books, this book was different. *It was really very simple*, I thought, as I reread the opening of the book.

Everything was "questionable" according to him. That was something I could relate to, but his application of questioning was much different from my own. I had always viewed questions as attacks on others in order to get ahead or to look good in front of my superiors. But in his approach, questions were "beacons of light—guides to keep you on the right course in life."

Like many leadership books, he had an acronym to help connect and retain the four objectives. As a banker, I had laughed when I read the acronym they formed: BANK. The four points were connected by a series of simple questions. Almost every page focused on "being in the moment" and "living in the now." "Now is a mix of the past and future," he wrote. I continued to reread the section.

The four points of BANK were Balanced, Awake, Natural, and Knowledgeable. According to Benny, by "questioning your life" a person can live with more vitality—"choosing to be." The words "to be" were the "two most important words in our language."

"*To be* is what we are doing now—in the present—the meeting point for what we've done and for all we can do."

I reread the questions posed with each objective.

Balanced—*Who am I?* and *Who do I want to be?*

Awake—*How did I get here?* and *Where do I want to be?*

Natural—*What do I value?* and *What do I want?*

Knowledgeable—*What have I learned?* and *What do I need to know?*

"To be the person you want to be requires questioning the past and the future to connect you to the present," Benny wrote. I decided to ask myself the questions.

Am I balanced? Much of what he wrote about being balanced had to do with "bringing the inside out" as he put it. *Who am I?* I thought I had the answer for that question for years, but was floundering with it now. *Who do I want to be?* I was no longer the up-and-coming bank executive, Jack Oliver. My goal was to get ahead, but I had hit a wall. I realized I had not changed my work habits—I was working longer and harder, trying to tear down any impediment that stopped my upward climb. My personal life wasn't balanced. The family was Tina's job. Now I was alone.

Awake? My eyes were open and I was responding to stimuli, but being awake meant much more to Benny than being lucid. Did I understand how I got to this point in my life? To a point, I did, but I didn't like admitting mistakes I'd made. Was I where I wanted to be? *Hell no,* I thought. Have I learned from where I've been? No—again. I evidently wasn't as awake as I thought I was.

Natural? Were my thoughts, words, actions, and intentions in harmony with the world around me? At first these questions seemed easy to answer. What I valued and wanted was easy to describe—power and money. I was at my most natural when I was at work, but being honest with myself, I knew the means I used to achieve my goals were far from natural or harmonious. They were supremely selfish. Part of being natural according to Benny was "being at peace with yourself," something I had never felt. I wasn't at peace—I was at war. I thought that was part of life.

Knowledgeable? I had excelled in academics. I was well-read, but now I feared I had failed to learn from experience and listen to others. According to Benny's interpretation, I was not the intellectual giant I thought I was—I was immature. *What do I need to know?* I had no idea. Maybe I was just going through a rough spot in my life? *I'm a survivor*, I thought.

Would living a "questionable life" make a difference at this point in my life? I wondered if it was too late to change the way I lived.

As I closed the book and sat it down on the small end table beside the recliner, I reached over and picked up the glass of bourbon. I had yet to take a drink. I lifted the glass at an angle with the lamp so I could see through the dark liquid. Slowly, I rotated my wrist to create a swirl of movement as the liquid moved rhythmically around the sides of the glass.

22. What Are You Worried About?

"WHAT ARE YOU WORRIED ABOUT?" John asked. I had called him back after thinking and drinking . . . I was worried.

"Everything," I said. I leaned back in my recliner, pouring the third glass of bourbon.

"Well, nuttin' has changed—you're still the designated worrier," he said, referring to the nickname he had given me in college. "You worry too much, Jack. You're getting ready to learn about a new opportunity, to enjoy a great weekend, and have the chance to get out of the rut you're in. Stop worrying."

"Worrying has worked pretty well for me so far," I said, taking a drink.

"To a point," John said. "I doubt if you would urge anyone to do things your way, given what's happened at Merchants. I think it's time for you to change directions."

"I need some advice," I said. "I really do."

"I'm the worst person to give advice," he said. "But I'll tell you the same thing my grandma told me, rest her soul. 'There ain't nuttin' good ever come out of worry.'"

"Yeah," I said. "But your grandma never worked in a bank!"

"Okay, Jack," John said. He was laughing at me. "That may be true. But she lived to be ninety-five—a very healthy, vigorous ninety-five years, something I hope to do. If you keep going like you're going, you won't make sixty."

"That's what I'm worried about."

"Are you drunk? Listen to yourself! Aren't you tired of worrying about everything? How can you sleep?"

"I don't," I said. I had never been so vulnerable and open with anyone. Whether it was the alcohol, stress, or the reality of what I was facing, I was finally being honest. "I'm afraid Benny won't give me a chance," I said. "I think he'll see me—the real me—someone I hate. I know it sounds crazy, but I think I do need a change. I think I may actually want to leave Philly. I don't like who I am, John. How could he be interested in me when I doubt myself?"

After a pause, I heard John sigh. "I've known you for a long time. You're like a brother to me. I know the real you. Jack Oliver is someone I respect and admire. You aren't at your best right now, but admitting to it is the best thing you can do. You need a change. Just be as open with Benny as you are with me. Don't try to hide anything or try to be something you aren't. You're right, that won't work. Be honest. Just be you—he'll be impressed. I promise."

After sitting in silence a moment digesting his words, I said, "John, you're a great friend. I'm sorry to bother you. I'll get myself together. I'll be open and honest with him. I'm going to finally take your advice."

"Glory hallelujah, miracles happen!" John said in his best evangelical imitation. "Seriously. Don't worry—be you. And quit drinking that bourbon I know you're sippin' on. Listen to your smarter, older, and much better looking de facto brother and go on to bed and get some rest. You have a big weekend ahead."

"I will," I said.

• • •

The next morning I boarded a Delta flight for Cincinnati. I had to fly to Cincinnati and switch planes to reach my destination of Roanoke, Virginia, giving me a clue to the remote nature of the area. As I settled in on the crowded 707, a plane that was surely older than the combined ages of my children, I began to think about my history as a "designated worrier." While I had always been the consummate worrier, there was only one other time I could remember when I was as worried as I was now.

• • •

"*Why am I worried?*" I said to myself leaving Chad's office.

I had just received my third promotion and felt like I deserved it. But a clear challenge was evident in the new post. I loved the opportunity but hated the idea of working for William Crabtree, or "Bill" as he was called by his friends and the PT&G executives. From the first time we met we had never gotten along. Now, I would be reporting to him directly. This would be the most difficult challenge of my career to date.

Crabtree was no stranger. In my time at Fifth Street as the office manager I had seen him on at least a couple of dozen occasions. While he typically didn't visit local PT&G offices, Crabtree frequented the Fifth Street area often to have lunch and meet with Tom Skeens, the developer of the Fifth Street reclamation project. While he was cordial in these brief encounters when he used my office to meet and close deals with Skeens, I could sense his disdain. I was sure he believed I didn't deserve my position.

The advancement opportunity had been a surprise. Almost one year to the day after firing Henry Starnes as manager of the Fifth Street office I was summoned to Chad's office to give him a progress report. After twelve months, only two people remained from Henry's original staff. I had purposefully shrunk the number of office employees—firing two and scaring off several more—replacing the departed employees with new people who were loyal to me. The process of managing the employee turnover and cost savings looked great on paper. I had rid the office of high salary/low producers and replaced them with lower salary/high producers. I had quadrupled loan production in the office and had increased the deposits by 40 percent. I was number one in almost every PT&G category. Being humble was the toughest part of sharing my report with Chad. I didn't want to come across as too cocky.

"Last to first in less than one year in most performance categories," Chad said, looking at the reports. "That's impressive. What are you going to do for an encore?"

"Better," I said.

I meant it. I knew I could climb farther and faster than anyone at PT&G. My confidence was soaring. Since moving to Fifth Street as manager I had crystallized my belief that what defined me as a person was my position at the bank. I believed that feeling good about my life required my continual, rapid rise on the PT&G corporate ladder. I had already initiated my plan for my next move. I wanted to be a business loan officer within three years.

"You're doing great as a branch manager. But now that you have the office turned around, I need you somewhere else. You're being promoted to business loan officer here in the main office. You'll be reporting directly to Bill Crabtree. Bill will help speed up your learning curve."

I couldn't believe my ears. I wouldn't need my three-year plan. "Thank you for the opportunity," I said, still in shock. "I'll do my best."

"I'm sure of that," Chad said. "If I didn't believe in you, where do you think you would be? Never let me down, Jack. Always do what I tell you to do. It's that easy."

"You can count on me," I said.

• • •

Some turbulence shook the plane, and I brought the seatback forward. The mild shaking had halted my recollection of one of the most important times in my career. I checked my watch and calculated that the plane would land in Cincinnati in less than thirty minutes. Looking out the window, all I could see were clouds far below, the same weather I had left in Philly. At over thirty thousand feet, the clouds below formed an ocean of white for the plane to glide over, with blue sky dominating the vista. If you were on the ground, all you could see would be the blanket of clouds. The scenery reminded me of a passage in Benny's book. He said much of our fear was caused by "the clutter of our thoughts."

What do you see? Is it real or just your perception of what's real? What we see is rarely reality, but a perception—a representation of what we think it is. We confuse ourselves with the clutter of what-we-think-we-see, creating our own distorted image of reality. Our fears help to create the clutter of our thoughts and the clutter in turn creates more fears causing us to suffer. There's no one to blame. We create most of our own suffering thinking what we see is real.

I was afraid of what the future held for me. "What do I see?" I asked myself, turning away from the window and shutting my eyes.

• • •

I recalled my first official day as a business loan officer. I was scheduled to meet with Bill Crabtree early in the morning. I remembered how nervous I was, similar to the way I felt about meeting Benny. But there was a huge difference between Crabtree and Benny Price.

I had been afraid of Bill Crabtree.

After keeping me waiting outside his office for almost an hour, Crabtree made things clear with me from the beginning. "Jack Oliver—my new business loan officer," he said as I sat down, looking over his huge cherry desk. His gargantuan leather chair appeared to be trying to swallow him. "You have a new assignment. At least you're not firing me on your first day like you did Henry," he said with a smirk.

"No sir, I am here to learn from you. You're the best," I said.

"Save your bullcrap for someone else, Oliver. You want to learn just enough to get ahead and move on. You have no intention of staying in this area any longer than necessary. I'm sure you'll do very well because you wouldn't have it any other way—to make yourself look good, like you have at Fifth Street. I know how you made your numbers look so good. Fear—you bullied and scared everyone to do everything they could to make *you* look better. Being a bully won't work in your new job—now you're a salesperson. And make no mistake about it, and I want this understood—

this is my department. You can go to church on Sunday, but when you're here—I'm God to you. You may think you're the apple of Chad's eye but an apple can rot, typically from the inside," he said. He nervously bounced a pen on the arm of his chair.

"That's not true," I said, struggling with a response. "I'm honestly here to learn from you."

"We'll see," he said, repeating his favorite doubt-filled expression. "We'll see."

• • •

After working in the department for six months I realized Crabtree was right about my intention. I wanted to do what I had to do as a business lender and then move on. I didn't enjoy the constant negotiations with clients. My role as a business lender focused on sales and placed me firmly as a middle man in the loan originating process. Even though I had reinvented Jack Oliver from introvert to extrovert during my teen and college years, selling loans went well beyond personality and professionalism. If borrowers were good credit risks, they could price shop and choose the best deal they could find.

I wasn't in control—and it didn't feel good.

What decided almost every deal boiled down to two issues: how much the customer repaid (the interest rate and any fees associated with the loan); and how long they had to repay the debt (the length of the term of the loan arrangement). I would have enjoyed my role a lot more, but I wasn't in control of those two key items: Crabtree was. Everything I negotiated with clients had to come back to him for approval, putting him in control of how many loans I made.

As if he were on a vendetta to ruin Jack Oliver, Crabtree was giving other lenders better rates, making their production look much better than mine. He was making my job as difficult as he could and hurting the bank in the process. I lost several excellent customers because he refused to bend on rates and terms that he willingly surrendered to other deals. I was sure he was blaming the lost business on my inability to sell the deals. I had no control over my situation. I was in very real danger of not only seeing the progress in my career slowed but actually losing my job. I finally got the nerve to ask for a meeting so I could challenge him. If that didn't work, I planned on going to Chad, my last resort, something I wanted to avoid at all costs. Just like our first meeting, Crabtree took control from the beginning.

"Mr. Crabtree, I appreciate your time," I said, but before getting another word out I was interrupted.

"If you're so concerned about my time, then why did you ask to meet with me? You're wasting it right now—get to the point." The anger and resentment in his voice validated every concern I had. I was dealing with an enemy.

"The reason I asked for this meeting is to express my concern that you're not giving me the same conditions you give to other lenders," I said quickly to avoid interruption. "You're giving better terms and rates to other lenders, making their production look much better. I have lost several large deals, hurting PT&G in the process. Why are you doing this to me?"

Crabtree leaned forward in his chair and folded his hands together. A smile began to slowly form on his face. "I could tell you that it's your imagination, but I'm sure you could pull out examples that may point to what you may view as less-than-fair treatment," Crabtree said. He kept a serpent-like smile on his face as he spoke. "I could also tell you that you're a newcomer to business lending and part of the problem is your negotiating skills," he said as he leaned forward slightly. "But again, that would not clear any doubts you may have about my support for you. So, Mr. Oliver, I'm going to cast away any doubt about my support." He lay his hands face down on the desk. "You don't have my support. You never will. You are a sham, a fake. You have no business being in the position you're in at PT&G. You should have never been promoted. You didn't have enough experience. You would've never been considered for the job except you do everything Chad tells you to do. I didn't want you in the job—Chad did—and I don't like someone telling me who to hire. I don't like you being part of my team. Do I make myself clear?"

I was stunned. I could not think clearly and somehow found the will to hold my tongue. After a few seconds, Crabtree continued.

"If you ever repeat what I just said, I promise it'll be the last act you make as an employee of this organization. I may not be Chad, but I'm number two in this company, and I can sink your ship anytime I want to. Now that we have addressed your concerns, do you have anything else to ask before you quit wasting my time?" Crabtree said without emotion.

"How do you expect me to do my job?" I asked.

"I don't," he said. "My advice to you is to get another job—quickly."

I stood up and looked down on Crabtree. "With all due respect, Mr. Crabtree, I'm not going to take your advice. I don't give up that easily."

"You can leave now, but before you do I want to remind you of something," he said as his mouth broke into a broader, even more evil smile. "I make the rules here—you don't. I control your fate. Quitting is the only option you have any control over, young man. Good luck, you'll need it."

• • •

I could still remember the feeling I had when I was leaving Crabtree's office. My legs were weak, and I was nauseous. I did my best to smile at his secretary as I left. I walked down the hall to the restroom. After splashing water on my face, I felt the nausea overcome me. I turned and ran into one of the stalls and vomited. After the nausea subsided, I stepped back to the mirror hoping that no one would enter.

Looking in the mirror I saw what Crabtree saw in me. I had finally realized the fear imbedded in me since college—that I was a fake. That fear had motivated me to prove to the world that I was not a sham; it spurred me to overachieve in academics and in my career. I thought I had outgrown that terror, leaving it behind in the wake of my achievements, but my old dread had never left me.

Not only had the fear refused to go away, it had matured.

• • •

In the small plane I felt the same way again. Beads of sweat formed on my forehead. *Is this another anxiety attack?*

I remembered José's advice and began taking slow, deep breaths. The gentleman seated beside me saw my discomfort.

"Are you all right?" he asked.

"Yeah, I'm fine," I said. "I'm not a fan of flying."

"Neither am I," he said. "We're almost there."

Leaning over to look out of the window of the jet traveling hundreds of miles per hour thousands of feet above the earth, I was not afraid. But the thoughts of that time when my career was on the line and I wasn't in control resurfaced—I was afraid then and now.

As I continued taking slow, deep breaths, I thought about how I was able to overcome the problem.

It was luck, I thought. Hopefully, I had not depleted my supply of good fortune.

I needed some now.

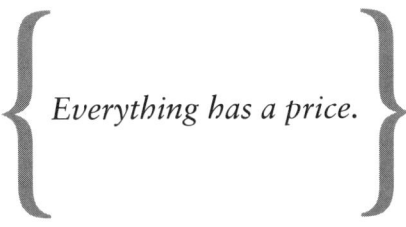

Everything has a price.

—BENJAMIN FRANKLIN PRICE

23. What's It Worth?

"WHAT'S IT WORTH?"

I had never imagined I would ask Bill Crabtree the question. It was one of the best moments in my career. The memory created a smile on my face as I considered how luck had revived my career. Whoever said, "I'd rather be lucky than good" was right.

The pilot had just announced we would be landing in Cincinnati in ten minutes. As the plane slowly began its descent, I recalled how I was able to win the war with Bill Crabtree and secure my first executive position, well ahead of even my own plans.

At the time, it had been worth everything to me.

• • •

After attending our weekly department meeting just two days after the contentious meeting with Crabtree, I had decided to work late at the office and catch up on paperwork. I was in no hurry to go home to Tina and the family. Her nagging and complaints about my work habits only made me want to stay away even more. I had bought a new home for Tina, Jessica, and our newest addition, Joshua. That didn't stop Tina's complaints. *What does she want from me?* I thought, sorting through a mass of papers on my desk.

I had not told her about Crabtree's threats. I didn't want her to worry. Even more importantly, she didn't need any more ammunition to criticize me.

If I lost my job I would lose everything, I thought. I was still trying to decide what to do. Then I got a break.

As I walked out of my office down the hall to the copier I heard Crabtree talking on the phone. The copier was located in a small room adjacent to his office, but out of sight. He evidently did not know anyone was still on the floor. After sitting for hours reviewing loans, he would go around the room and tell each person what was wrong with their efforts. He expected the team to go home after he concluded the grueling sessions, but today, I had decided to stay. He had put the phone on speaker and was talking with Thomas Skeens, a voice I recognized very well.

"Yeah, Tom, that'll be wonderful. I appreciate you letting me in on that deal. It worked out for everyone," Crabtree said.

"Bill, I'm glad you're happy. But you've never lowered the interest rates on my lines of credit. That was part of our deal. I put a quarter-of-a-million-dollar profit in your hands for doing nothing other than giving me a loan. You're costing me money. I want those rates dropped—now." Skeens nearly shouted.

"I told you I couldn't take the rates any lower. Your rate would be the lowest of any borrower in the bank. The bank examiners have classified your loans as high risk. Even Chad views you as a high-risk borrower and thinks your rates are already too low," Crabtree meekly responded.

"A deal is a deal, Bill," Skeens said. "I'm sure Chad would love to hear how you've been turning big bucks on the side using the bank as your private source of capital."

"Don't threaten me, Tom," Crabtree said in a tone I recognized. "We go back a long way. We've been doing this for almost ten years. You know I'll come through."

"Then just do it!" Skeens shouted. "Do it, or I'll find the biggest whistle I can find to blow and I'll point at you, my friend."

"Consider it done," Crabtree said in a nearly faint voice. "I'll do it."

"Good," Skeens said. "Don't ever try to go back on a deal we made—or it will be the last deal I'll let you in on—and the last deal you'll make as a banker. If Chad thinks I'm high risk, what would he think of his top loan exec making loans to himself through illegitimate corporations?"

"Good-bye, Tom," Crabtree said, hanging up the phone. I could hear him slump back in his chair and sigh as I turned and walked back to my office to avoid detection. I gently shut the door and sat down in my chair. What I had just heard could get Crabtree fired. It was my responsibility to tell Chad. But was that the best thing for the bank? Crabtree was the reason the bank was ahead of budget. On paper, he was doing a great job. While I didn't like him, he was a respected member of Philadelphia's inner circle of executives. I wondered if I could use this situation to my advantage.

On the following Monday I reviewed the interest rate change reports. The reports showed any changes in interest rates. Despite prime rate being 8.00 percent at the time, Thomas Skeens and his various corporate entities all had received a rate decrease to 7.00 percent, one full percent below prime, far and away the best rate at PT&G. I did some more background work on the loan history for Skeens and his myriad of corporations.

I had my proof. Now, I had to make a decision about what to do. After a lot of thought I settled on a course of action. It was a huge risk, but my options were limited.

Walking into Bill Crabtree's office without any notice was something no one ever did. But on that Tuesday morning, I did. I shut the door behind me and sat down.

"I hope this is important, Mr. Oliver," he said, looking over the top of his glasses at me. He was obviously surprised by my abrupt and unplanned entry. "I'm very busy."

"I'm sure you are," I said. "That is a great break Thomas Skeens got on his interest rates. Does Chad know yet?"

"That's none of a rookie's business, Mr. Oliver," he said. "You're out of line coming in here and saying anything about clients that you have zero knowledge of or connection with. Leave now."

"Okay, but before I do, I do know something," I said. "I know you made a quarter of a million dollars in a silent partnership with a classified borrower, Thomas Skeens. You put the money in accounts outside of PT&G—something that was easily traced. I have copies of all the transactions. The corporate names have nothing to do with you, but you seem to get paid a lot of money from them. You've been doing this for a long time. Your decision to drop the rates on all of Skeens' loans was part of your arrangement; one that Skeens will gladly talk about when I tell Chad and we increase the interest rates to prime plus one percent on all of his loans. Now, I'll leave." My knowledge of the situation and boldness had completely caught Crabtree off guard. As I stood up from the chair, Crabtree spoke.

"How do you know these things?" he asked. "Are you spying on me? If you are—I'll fire you."

"No, I'm not spying," I said. "But you got greedy and made a lot of mistakes. All of that money made you sloppy—you didn't cover your tracks. If I can find it, I'm sure the auditors will ultimately find it, too. You're the one with your neck on the line, Bill. You'll be fired if I make a call to Chad. I have my proof. Is that what you want, Bill?"

Using "Bill" fueled his anger. I remained standing, my heart beating at a thousand beats per minute. "If you were going to report me, you would have done so already. What do you want, Jack?" he asked.

"*What's it worth?*" I asked.

"Sit down," he asked in a much calmer tone. I sat down on the edge of the chair. "It sounds like we may have similar interests."

"All I want is to be treated fairly," I said. "No more or less, just fairly. I'll put this information away and never divulge it if you're fair to me and stop your little campaign to ruin me. And . . . you must stop using PT&G for illegal transactions. If I ever see you doing it again, I'll make sure you're out of here, even if it costs me my job."

"I was right about not trusting or liking you. I always viewed you as ruthless, someone I couldn't trust."

"Trust?" I asked. "Yeah, Bill, I can see where you have trust issues."

"No need to be a smart-ass. But that really doesn't matter, does it? You have me over the proverbial barrel, don't you?" he said. He removed his glasses and leaned back into his oversized chair. "I guess you feel good about yourself, don't you? You want money, don't you? A piece of the business."

"Yes," I said, "I have you over the barrel. Do I feel good? Hell no. If you had been fair to me, I wouldn't have been working late and heard you and your friend arguing. That was your fault. I don't want any money—none. All I want is to be treated fairly. What is wrong with that?"

"Nothing, except I must say, you know exactly what you want in life and nothing will stop you," he said. I thought I heard a hint of respect. "You have it. I'll do what I can to help you out, and you'll forget what you know about Skeens and me. The bank is still making a lot of money on Skeens. I'm not hurting the bank," he said.

"No, and you're definitely not hurting yourself either," I reminded him. "You're the greediest man I've ever met."

"Well it takes one to know one," Crabtree said. "I know you pretty well. It's like looking in a mirror, but you're much greedier than me in your own way. You want power more than money, don't you?"

"Power is money," I said.

• • •

My performance improved dramatically after this. William Crabtree treated me fairly for the remainder of his time at PT&G—a little less than four years after I confronted him with the Skeens situation. He decided to step down from his position and retire to one of his several retirement homes. He did do me a favor when he left: He recommended me for his position.

"Jack, I know we've had our differences, but I'm going to recommend you for my position," Crabtree said. His face was thin and pale. "One thing I want you to promise me. I want to know that the past is the past and you will never disclose anything you think may have happened."

"Are you doing this because I could talk about the past—or are you doing it because you think I'm the best person for the job?" I asked. After my slow start, in the nearly five years I had been making business loans I had distinguished myself as the top producer and most profitable at PT&G. This did not come at a small price. I worked 24/7 to make the deals, perform underwriting, and move in the social circles necessary to stay in touch with Philadelphia's players. It was a heavy price, but one I had been willing to pay.

"You're the best we have," he said. "I also want you to forget the past. It's the best for both of us."

"Agreed," I said. "The past is the past—it's all history."

Over the years, Chad told me about where he would like to see me as I moved through my career. "I need people like you, Jack, that I can trust," he said. "That is an absolute necessity for any executive position at PT&G; I must trust the person, without fail."

With a little over five years of experience I was promoted into Bill Crabtree's position. I was the bank's top producer. There were others more qualified in terms of years of experience, but they lacked what I had—Chad's trust.

Just like earning my reputation as a top producer, I had earned Chad's trust by putting everything on the line. I went after deals that Chad specifically wanted. Much of the risk associated with many of these deals was outside of our policy, but Chad was the person who ultimately made the call. He had a purpose in mind. "I want to make sure that everyone in Philadelphia knows that PT&G is the best bank in the city. To do that means we take risks. But life is a game, and if you don't roll the dice you'll never win." Chad had said this on many occasions, especially after deciding to approve a risky deal.

My next promotion wasn't much of a surprise—I had worked for it. I was called into his office on a Wednesday afternoon after the PT&G monthly board of director's meeting. "Today the PT&G Board of Directors approved you as the new executive vice president and senior credit officer. Congratulations, Jack, you're now a PT&G executive."

I thanked Chad for his support because I knew he was the person making the promotion happen.

"You're absolutely right," Chad said. "Never forget who pulled the strings and moved you up the ladder. I'm counting on you. Never let me down."

As customary in those moments where I was pledging part of my soul to Chad for career advancement, I said, "I'll never let you down." I meant it. I would do anything to achieve my goal. I wanted to take Chad's place when he stepped down.

But my course had changed. Instead of Philadelphia, I was in Cincinnati on my way to Roanoke, Virginia.

{
To others,
you are what you do.
}

—BENJAMIN FRANKLIN PRICE

24. What Do You Do?

"WHAT DO YOU DO?"

It was a question I used to enjoy answering. It allowed me the golden opportunity to recite the Jack Oliver story in all its glory. Career success after career success adorned my recital. But now, it was a question I would rather not answer.

With a two-hour wait before the flight to Roanoke departed, I decided to step into one of the two airport restaurants at the small Cincinnati airport terminal. My trip to Benny's was taking me far off a direct path. Making the detour worse, weather delays had created a crowd. After scanning the restaurant, I took the last available seat at the end of the eatery's L-shaped bar. As soon as I climbed onto the bar stool the person sitting next to me began to talk. He was a young man, probably in his late twenties, and well-dressed. Without talking to anyone specifically, he continued what sounded like a commentary on Barry Bonds and the use of steroids in sports. From the way he was slurring his speech, I realized he had consumed more than his fair share of scotch and water. There was a news story debating Bonds' chemical dependency on the large, flat-screen television directly in front of us. I ordered a Coke and looked for another seat, but nothing appeared to be opening soon. I was stuck beside the amateur talking head.

"I think they should leave Barry Bonds alone," he said. "I don't care if Barry hits a home run, stops at second base when he is running the bases, and sticks a needle in his ass to juice up. He's the best. He's not the only one who's shot himself up with steroids. They all do it."

Being a long-time baseball fan and still able to recite almost every major record in professional baseball from memory, I didn't agree. I couldn't keep quiet. "Hank Aaron hit more homers than the Babe without steroids," I said, looking at the video featuring Bond's huge head and no-neck profile. "Babe Ruth hit 714 home runs without steroids. Where would Barry Bonds be without steroids?"

"It's a different world now," he said. "Babe Ruth wasn't an athlete. He drank beer in the dugout. He had a gut Santa Claus would have died for. His legs looked like tooth picks. What a joke. Hank Aaron played well beyond his prime just to break the record. Those guys are just memories. Neither could play professionally now. Barry Bonds is the most feared hitter of all time—with or without drugs. You should appreciate Bonds—he's an old guy like you who's still playing."

"How can you say that when steroids are banned from baseball— they're illegal," I said, refusing to back down. I didn't appreciate his "old guy" comment. "Just because one person cheats it doesn't open the door for everybody."

"What do you do?" the stranger asked, taking a sip from his beer and looking at me for the first time.

"I'm a banker," I said, not knowing where he was coming from.

"Well, your job and your age tells me why you're so out of touch with reality," he said, laughing. He turned his attention back to the flat-screen television. "My Dad sounded a lot like you—completely out of touch—you guys live in a dream world."

"Out of touch? How could anyone say using steroids is good for baseball? It's cheating. Is cheating okay in your world?"

Hearing our voices growing louder, the bartender stepped in front of us. "Is there a problem here?" he asked, wiping the edge of the bar with a white cloth.

"No," the young man said, "the only problem is this guy has his head up his ass."

Before I could say anything, the bartender firmly told the young man, "Listen buddy, I know you're tired of waiting on your plane, but that's uncalled for—get out of here."

Without saying a word the young man slid off the stool. He bumped me with a hard pressed shoulder as he walked away. "Can you believe that?" I asked the bartender, shaking my head and readjusting myself on the stool.

"It's getting worse," he said, shaking his head. "People don't care anymore. It's like everyone's mad. It's not just here at the airport. I work two jobs to support my two wives—the ex and the current one. My other job is worse."

"What do you do?" I asked.

"I collect bad loans for a finance company. It's almost like being a policeman, without the gun and the badge."

"That's how I started out a long time ago," I said. "I collected. I'm a banker."

"A banker?" he said. "No wonder the guy thought you were a jerk—how can you people say you're doing an honest job putting people under all of that debt? I don't see how you can sleep at night."

Seeing that I was now in my second unexpected confrontation just from mentioning I was a banker, I reached in my wallet, pulled out a ten-dollar bill, and put it on the counter. "I sleep fine. Keep the change." I got up and walked back into the busy center of the airport. No seats were available. I found a small corner where I could stand and set my carry-on bag on the ground between my feet. I looked at my watch and then looked up at the flight schedule looming nearby. My plane was running thirty minutes late.

● ● ●

What seemed like the same outdated plane I had flown from Philly to Cincinnati was now in the air heading southeast toward Roanoke, Virginia. I was seated by the emergency exit. While flying didn't bother me, sitting by the exit did.

I decided to turn my attention to my weekend with Benny and the situation with his bank. Merchants had stuck to their acquisition plan. They had a target list. Most of their takeovers appeared friendly because they bought off the CEO and the controlling interest of the board. But they had failed to gain any market share in Virginia. A bank like Benny's would be a perfect fit. The bank was relatively large, but not too large to be swallowed up by a bank the size of Merchants. Benny's bank was profitable, so if Merchants could force the sale of the bank at the right price, they could afford to pay a premium. Finally, if the executive board was aging and ready to put the bank up for sale, the final obstacle would be cleared. All those factors fit with the idea that Benny's bank was a target of Merchants.

While Benny didn't discuss this with me in the early phone negotiations, I was sure I would hear about it once I was on the ground in Virginia. Immediately, the idea of getting a chance to fight Merchants appealed to me. But, at the same time, if I went to work for Benny and was then acquired by Merchants, my career was as good as over. I continued to mull over the positives and negatives as the plane moved closer to Roanoke.

This makes it even more interesting, I thought, as the plane touched down at the Roanoke Regional Airport.

I had finally arrived.

25. How Was Your Trip?

"How was your trip?"

The flight attendant had noticed my difficulty in making my way toward the exit. The basketball team for Roanoke College dominated the seats in the back. As soon as the plane landed and we got the okay to unbuckle, the team rose quickly and moved into the aisle forcing their way to the front, altering the typical row-by-row exit. Frustrated by standing hunched over waiting to step into the aisle, I gave up and sat down to wait until they all passed.

I was the last passenger leaving the plane.

"It was okay," I said, answering the flight attendant. "Other than the fact I couldn't get off the plane."

"I'm sorry you had to wait," she said. "The basketball team seemed a little anxious."

"Anxious," I said but gave her a smile, "I'm the anxious one."

The itinerary called for Benny and his wife, Ann, to meet me at the airport, and then Ann would return to their home in Salem (wherever Salem was). Benny and I would drive to Smith Mountain Lake to fish, hike, and "spend the weekend getting to know each other" as he called it. This had to be the most radical step in my career, I thought, as I walked through the narrow entry into the Roanoke Regional Airport. A job interview on a boat? A Philly banker in the woods—it seemed almost ridiculous to me.

I had told myself that regardless of what happened over the weekend, leaving Philly for even a couple of days would be a good thing for me. I had never really enjoyed leaving town—there was always so much to do at work. Philly had everything for me with the exception of NASCAR. I was satisfied staying put. But I needed a break, which my time in the hospital had made clear.

I had tried to picture what Benny was like. He had said he liked gardening, fishing, and reading. He was probably sedentary—a lot like me. He was somewhere around seventy years old, making him even less active. His wife was a great cook according to John, so he had to carry a few extra pounds. My mental image of Benny was of a short, overweight balding man with glasses; scholarly and appearing to be what people expected when they heard the term "banker." His wife probably looked like Barbara Bush.

Looking around the concourse I didn't see anyone fitting that picture. Walking slowly forward in the rope-lined area behind the line of passengers, I saw ahead a gentleman who was almost as tall and physically fit as the members of the basketball team standing near him. He was talking with each of the players as they walked by as if he knew all of them.

The gentleman stood out in the crowd. He had thick white hair and was smiling. *That's Benny,* I thought. I was completely wrong about what I expected. The woman beside him was taller than me. *Ann,* I reasoned as I moved forward closer to the couple. She was thin and athletic, complementing Benny's physique. She was very attractive and didn't appear to be retirement age. They both looked like they were ready to compete in a marathon instead of a bingo tournament at the senior citizens center.

I felt a twinge of intimidation. I had reminded myself I was one of the top Philadelphia bankers, a successful business leader in one of the most competitive arenas in the country. I was well known throughout the industry. They were lucky for me to even consider stepping away from the lucrative big-city market to come to a place as small as Roanoke. But now seeing Benny and Ann, I felt like an overweight, out-of-shape guy who needed them more than they needed me. I had stepped into a world I did not know or understand. I felt like a fat midget in a land of giants.

Benny stepped forward and beamed a bright smile, shaking my hand with a firm grip. "You must be Jack—I'm Benny Price. This is my wife, Ann. We're so glad you're here. How was your trip?"

Shaking hands with Benny made much of the self-doubt go away. The strong handshake felt genuine. Benny and Ann radiated warmth. I couldn't remember feeling this welcome anywhere in recent memory. Or had I even cared whether I was welcomed in the past? Somehow, this was different.

"The trip was fine," I said. I didn't need to tell them about my confrontations in Cincinnati. "I'm glad to be on the ground in Virginia."

"We're glad you're here," Ann said. "I wish your family had been able to make the trip."

"Well, they were tied up. You know how teenagers are," I said, already telling a lie. I did not want to talk about family.

We chatted and walked to the luggage pick-up area. The airport, while very small, was modern and one of the cleanest I had ever visited. I heard people talking. That was something you usually didn't hear in an airport terminal. Even families who were meeting after months of separation typically hugged and rapidly left the airport as if the plane would suck them back in and carry them away if they didn't get out quickly. But here it seemed very relaxed.

As we stepped outside into the bright Virginia sunshine, the air was clear and seemed to be something your body wanted to breathe. When I had left Philly early in the morning, it was raining and felt as though the heavy sky was collapsing around the tall buildings. Now, standing outside the Roanoke airport, I was viewing a landscape of sky and rolling mountains. It felt as if a weight had been lifted. It felt good.

We talked in the parking lot for a few minutes about the weekend plans. Ann told me to not let Benny wear me out hiking, fishing, or talking too much.

"You're the guest, Jack, so exert your rights!" she said, laughing. "Benny, bring Jack back in one piece." Ann turned to Benny with a sweet sincerity that I had never seen between people who had walked down the aisle together. "I have all of the food you two guys will need, just be sure to put it in the fridge when you get there.

Don't forget, I'll be fixing supper on Sunday evening, so be sure to be home on time. The food will be ready!"

"Thanks, Ann," I said. "I'll try my best to keep up with him."

"That can be a challenge," she said. She gave me a hug and told me she was happy to finally meet me. "I've heard so many good things about you. I hope you enjoy our little piece of heaven here in Virginia." She then hugged and kissed Benny and drove off in a white Honda Civic, a hybrid model. The car she drove was not what I expected—neither was Benny's. We put my gear in the back of his forest-green Jeep Grand Cherokee, a model at least ten years old. The exterior was worn and a little torn. When we both were in the vehicle I noticed the mileage reading started with a "1" with five figures after it. I tried not to be obvious as I leaned over to read the gauge. This guy was obviously frugal. *I bet he's tight,* I thought to myself, *with a capital "T."*

• • •

The winding road to the lake was something I never imagined. The road had more curves than I had ever been subjected to. Benny drove at a steady if slow pace. At first, I thought I would get car sick, but that feeling left me as we talked. He wasn't in a hurry. It still felt very strange for me to be riding along in the Jeep with Benny. If John Helms could see me now, he would get a laugh. I could hear him saying, "City boy in the country . . . you're lookin' outta place, Jack, ole boy!"

The sounds of travel were also different. Benny drove with the windows rolled down. The clean scent of the fresh, cool mountain air filtered into the Jeep. Benny waved at different people traveling on the two-lane road near the lake. They waved back using all of their fingers. I was impressed. In Philadelphia, people drove with one hand on the wheel and the other holding a cell phone or a coffee cup. Caught up in the differences I was seeing, I mentioned it to Benny. He laughed.

"Well, Jack, cell phones don't pick up a reliable signal out here," he said. "I don't have a cell phone. I did, but it was so irritating. They may be good for emergencies, but they seem to cause more problems."

"You don't have a cell phone?" I asked.

"Cell phones don't give you time to think," Benny said. "I like to have at least a few seconds of time to think before I put my foot in my mouth." A slight smile curled up on his face. "Plus, they're dangerous when you're driving, especially on a road with this many curves."

"I can see what you're talking about," I said, leaning into the next curve. "Some people send text messages—they use their cell phones to type in messages—while they're driving."

"That's taking technology a little far, isn't it?" he said. "Typing-on-the-go!" We both laughed. I then realized I was one of the idiots we were laughing at.

Still, I was surprised. A CEO of a bank, albeit a mid size bank, without a cell phone—*that's remarkable,* I thought. Without thinking I blurted out, "How do you get away with not having a cell phone handy?"

Benny laughed and seemed to enjoy the question. "I am always available when I'm outside of my Jeep. People have my phone numbers and usually know where I can be reached. I did give into technology. I have answering machines at home and at the lake cabin, just in case—but not at the bank."

"I live with my cell phone strapped to my side like a cowboy with a gun in his holster," I said smiling, using an analogy Carol had used, unabashedly prideful in my attachment to work. Then the last statement Benny made finally registered. "Wait, you don't have voice mail at the bank?"

"We have voice mail—but not during working hours. I'm sure that may surprise you, but what do people prefer? When I call a place I always want to speak to a person, a person who identifies who they are. I want to hear a person with a smile in their voice—someone inviting, not intimidating. That's part of our practice at Citizens. If the phone is ringing, we're in business! If a client isn't walking in the door or calling—we're in trouble. I don't trust allowing a machine to do business for me."

I was shocked. No voice mail. I told Benny how people invented ways to talk only to voice mail and it was an accepted method of communication. Deliberate phone tag. "Who has the time to talk?" I said, caught up in the debate.

"Who has the time to talk? Well, your clients," Benny said with vibrancy I had yet to hear in his voice. "They have time, or they wouldn't be calling. The greatest sound to me is the sound of a door opening or a phone ringing. Clients want you to take the time not to talk, but to listen. Voice mail is, at best, a catchall. I despise phone tag. Phone tag is alive and well in Virginia. We may not be Philly, but dodging a ringing phone is everywhere," Benny said. "We make our business different by answering the phone within the first three rings. We train our people to do that. We also have to keep enough people on staff to answer the phone. That is an expense I never mind paying. Call it *paying attention.*"

Paying attention. Benny was certainly inventive with his expressions, I thought. But his ideas were radical. We continued to talk about the similarities and dissimilarities of banking as we continued on the curvy road.

"People are the same everywhere," Benny said. "We're all connected. Whether they're in Philadelphia or Blacksburg, they want the same thing—service. I haven't seen anything to tell me otherwise. Don't your clients expect good service?"

I gave Benny a ten-minute perspective on Philly customers and their short-sighted demands on being served. But the more I talked, the more I kept being drawn back to the simple reality that Benny was right—customers were more similar than dissimilar in Philly and in Virginia—they expected service. But this was new to me. How we viewed our interaction with customers was totally different. Benny's focus was on giving the customer above-average service. We focused on our profit, efficiency, and sales. I couldn't remember the last time I had talked about improving customer service.

But Benny's way was more expensive, I thought. It was a dreamland of wishes that could never come true. I saw an old man reminiscing about the way it used to be. *Get real,* I thought, as he talked about his bank's simple approach.

He's out of touch, I told myself as we wound our way down the narrow highway's steep descent. Then I saw something ahead that stood out.

It was a sign.

26. How Much Is Your Time Worth?

"HOW MUCH IS YOUR TIME WORTH?"

After driving over one hour, we were nearing a community, albeit a very small one. We had reached a clearing, and I saw a small, white wooden church ahead on the right side of the road. It could have been out of a Norman Rockwell painting except for what appeared to be a portable, illuminated sign parked in front of the sanctuary. The sign's message asked, HOW MUCH IS YOUR TIME WORTH?

"What a shame to clutter up a beautiful little church with a sign like that," I said. "The only time I've seen signs like that is in front of 7-Elevens."

"We have our fair share of signs and billboards here. My favorite one was outside a church in downtown Roanoke," Benny said. "The message on it said, GOD IS LIKE ALLSTATE: YOU'RE IN GOOD HANDS!

"I believe the pastor is an insurance agent and leaves no doubt about his allegiances," Benny continued. "He obviously never misses an opportunity to get his message across. I just hope his business card isn't on the back of the hymnals."

"Whatever you do—don't tell him your idea—it sounds like he would do it!" I paused. "Religion and insurance kind of go hand in hand," I said.

"What did you think of the message on the sign we just passed?" Benny asked.

"What's my time worth? Is that meant to begin negotiations over my salary?" I asked, only partially joking.

"In some ways, I guess you could look at your salary as a part of the value of your time," Benny said. "But I thought the message was a very good one. I believe the most valuable time in your life is *right now*."

"Right now?" I asked, confused about where he was going with the conversation.

"What other moment has more value? You can't go back in time and relive the past. You don't know what's going to happen in the next second. What are your thoughts, Jack?"

I was momentarily stumped by his question. "If I could go back and redo some of my worst mistakes, that time would be the most important—much more important than now."

"But you can't go back in time," Benny said. He took a quick look at me, briefly turning his attention from the now much straighter roadway. "Or can you?"

"Time travel—that would be great; I could go back and mess up again."

"If you could go back in time, why would it be to a time when you were unhappy? Wouldn't you want to go back and revisit the best of times?" he asked.

"No, I wouldn't," I said. "I would want to fix things. That would make the future better."

"Would going back in time and trying to do something differently make you any happier?" he asked.

"No, but I wouldn't feel as guilty," I said, emitting a small laugh. "It would relieve some of the pain." I'd just met Benny, and here I was opening up to him. I wondered if John Helms had done the same.

A convenience story, Harry's Stop & Shop, was the first sign of any commerce since we left US 220 over one hour earlier. Another back-lit message sign on wheels, parked in front of the store, gave the price of milk and bread and beckoned people to visit the Bait Shop. I thought that was an odd combination. "I'll take a gallon of milk, a loaf of bread, and a dozen worms," I could hear a customer say. I'm sure that type of request was commonplace at this end-of-nowhere mini Wal-Mart. The portable, back-lit signs were everywhere, not exclusive to churches. I wanted to ask if he used them at the bank, but I was afraid to hear the answer.

I shifted the conversation back to the topics I felt much more comfortable discussing: banking in Philly and my strong resume. I talked most of the time, allowing some of my frustrations with Merchants to seep out.

I had finished my talking resume as we closed in on our destination, Smith Mountain Lake. We took a sharp turn off the two-lane paved road onto a single-lane dirt road with grass growing in the middle and wheel ruts making the Jeep bounce so hard I banged my head against the top of the interior. We were now officially in the middle of nowhere—without cell phone service.

• • •

When I thought of lakes, my impression was much different from what I saw as the Jeep climbed one last hill and began the last descent toward the shore. The lake was stunningly beautiful. I hadn't expected a body of water so large and unpopulated. Benny had said the lake was small and crowded, but I didn't see anyone. After driving through narrow, forest-lined highways, seeing the blue waters stretching out ahead was a shock to my already overloaded senses. As the Jeep made its way down the steep hill I saw a large log cabin. It had a tin roof that reflected the cracks of sunlight penetrating the deep foliage of the tall trees surrounding the cabin. It had a covered porch facing the lake. Two wooden rocking chairs and a swing were on the porch. I appreciated that they weren't chained down.

"This is beautiful," I said, as Benny pulled the Jeep beside the cabin.

"Yes, it is," he said, pausing to look out at the lake before getting out of the Jeep.

"So what do you think of our little piece of heaven, Jack?" Benny asked as we entered what appeared to be the cabin's main living room. The ceiling rose to the second story with a loft situated above the main level. A stone fireplace dominated the opposite wall.

"It's not much, but we enjoy it more and more the older we get. I can't wait to leave the city and come here."

Did he say city? If Benny thought Roanoke was a city, I needed to take him around Philly on the nontourist tour. Roanoke's tallest building was probably a dozen stories. I told Benny if he wanted a real shock to his system, he should be in my shoes. "Coming from Philly to Smith Mountain Lake seems like a world apart," I said, already smitten with the beauty of the lake. "I can see why you would want to come here so often—it's great," I said. "The fireplace must have cost a small fortune to build."

"We hauled all of the stone here," he said. "It was a lot of work. I can remember carrying every stone—getting it here and placing it—all of us working together."

A slight melancholy tone was evident in his voice. But after a pause, Benny was telling me about the history of the area. He told me how the lake had been expanded with the construction of a series of small dams, but remained similar to what the Indians had seen hundreds of years ago when they had hunted in the area.

Looking around the cabin I saw lots of photographs. A variety of pictures of the scenery of the area were on display, along with a number of what I assumed were family photos. "Is photography one of your hobbies?" I asked.

"Yes, I used to enjoy photography—I took my fair share of pictures as you can see."

I stepped over to a large sofa table. The first photograph on the left side of the table was of the sun rising over the nearby hills with the mist from the lake lifting upward, the reflection of the sun muted on the water. It looked like something right off the front of a postcard. "You're very good," I said.

"Pointing the camera and clicking the shutter requires very little real skill, at least for the purely amateur level I would claim. Aim, point, and click. Getting the right photo is all about timing— just like most things in life," he said with a smile. He stepped beside me and picked up another photo of the lake. "Being at the right place is only one part of the challenge. Having the patience and attention to be at the right place at the right time is what takes the thoughtful effort. Remaining in touch with what is going on around you requires attention to the moment. You have to be awake—in the moment."

"I would say so," I said. "I never had the patience to wait for anything—especially the sun coming up so I could take a picture of it. You must have a lot of discipline."

"The discipline is in opening up, being there—in the present. Photos should capture something. They aren't just a reminder of the moment. A great photo puts you there, so you feel the ground under your feet, smell the air, and hear the sounds. You're there experiencing the moment! That is a rare photo. I took hundreds, probably thousands of photos to come up with a couple of dozen photos that come close to capturing what it's like to be there. But a photo only takes you so far. We see everything in life through our own filters."

"This one has to be one of those rare ones," I said, looking at the photo of the sun rising.

"That one is special," he said. "For many reasons . . ."

Benny picked up a photo of a group of people crowded on the front porch of the cabin. "Every photo has a different view—just like life. After the photo is developed I usually find something I missed when I was clicking the shutter. Interesting how you can find something you overlooked—something that was there but you didn't see it at first glance. A photo is one of the few ways to give you a second look at life, isn't it?"

Benny was obviously talking about much more than photos. "I'm not so sure that would have been a good thing in my life," I said. He let my comment pass.

"To me, photos are a way for me to share a moment with others. It's a way to show a different view of the world. If a picture is worth a thousand words, then a picture helps to make the world a simpler place to live, something I love—simplicity!"

Simplicity was the farthest concept from my reality. Hearing him talk about simplicity after rereading his book only reminded me that he was out of touch. I wanted to say "Life ain't simple," but I kept the thought to myself.

"I never want to *take* a picture; my goal is to create a vivid memory of what I am seeing so I can share it with others. I would call it sharing the experience of the moment. I'm probably boring you, Jack. I apologize."

"No, you aren't the least bit boring," I said. Trying to find a way to connect to photography, I thought of the only camera I had, a digital camera I had rarely used. "Do you use a digital camera?"

"No," he said. "I have several older film cameras that I enjoy working with," he replied, softening his tone.

"Digital cameras let you see the picture instantly," I said. "Isn't that an advantage?"

"Where is that desire for something instantly coming from?" Benny asked. "It seems like a source of so many problems. Rushing to invent, package, or manipulate what you're seeing may give you something you *think* you want, but not necessarily what you really need. When you look at the photo you just took, you're paying more attention to the past, and you may miss what is happening *now*. The past becomes a distraction. For me, having a digital camera defeats my purpose."

I wasn't sure the choice of a camera was so crucial. "And that's why I would never be a photographer," I said, laughing. "I have the patience of a three-year-old for things I want." After uttering the words I realized how childish it sounded—like a three-year-old. Before I could attempt to cover up what I had said, Benny spoke.

"It depends on what you seek. It's kind of like fishing. If you're always checking to see if you're getting a bite, you'll never catch anything. Is it the catch that makes the experience memorable, or is it the effort? Remember, you don't always catch a fish when you want to," Benny said as he moved toward the kitchen. "Speaking of fish, I believe we need to put the feast Ann prepared in the fridge."

The idea of satisfying desires instantly was obviously a sore spot for Benny, and I did not agree with his viewpoint. For someone so focused on now he seemed to lack the desire to get the things he wanted—now.

"I wouldn't argue about patience being a necessity for fishing or taking pictures," I said, wading into a debate. "But I would have been put in front of the corporate firing squad for telling my supervisor or our board of directors to wait for something to happen."

"So what did you tell them?"

"I told them what I was going to do to make things happen," I said as I almost dropped a Tupperware container. "I reassured them that I was taking charge and would make it happen."

"You used an interesting word—*taking*. Instant gratification springs from the idea of taking," Benny said as he finished loading food into the refrigerator. "This need for wanting and expecting something instantly removes some of the best things in life. Instant rewards, instant gratification, instant emotions. It's like fast food— you get it fast, but it's unhealthy and can make you feel miserable. Instant is making the metabolism of our lives unnatural." Benny turned and looked at me. "Life is not a race. If you behave like it is, what do you think is waiting at the finish line?"

"If you get there first, you win," I said with confidence. "Being honest, I like getting things faster than slower," I said. "I like e-mail, laptop computers, my Blackberry, cell phones, microwaves, and even, I hate to admit it, fast food. I like to get news and information when I want it, and I don't want to wait for it. When I push a button I want a response—instantly."

"Do those devices make your life better or just faster?" Benny asked. He leaned against the cabinets.

"Of course, they make life better," I said. "I use my cell phone constantly to maintain contact with my managers. E-mail allows me to send out mass communications to my team and make sure they're on the same page I am. My Blackberry keeps me on schedule to make sure I don't miss anything. I've got my entire life wrapped up between my laptop computer, Blackberry, and cell phone."

"Your whole life, Jack? That's a lot of reliance on three machines. Is that how you really want to live—that connected to work?"

"I guess I don't know any better," I said, finding myself laughing at the words springing from my lips. Had I just exposed myself as ignorant or immature—or maybe both? But how could I survive without my machines, as he referred to them? At that point, I began to feel that life was indeed much different in the hills of Virginia and something I needed to understand. "How do you do it?"

Reaching into his back pocket he retrieved a small appointment book with a plastic cover bearing the Citizens Bank name and logo on the front. "If you're talking about scheduling, we give these out to our clients in November and December every year as part of our marketing," he said.

I had not seen a small appointment book like that in what seemed like an eternity. "I didn't realize they still made those. It looks pretty simple," I said, still marveling at the thought of a small bundle of paper holding my schedule.

"Just the way I like it, Jack, simple," Benny said.

"I doubt that I could ever get my life so uncomplicated I could write down my appointments and to-do list in a small book."

"Then maybe you're trying to do too much," he said. "You can't do everything you want to do."

The idea of "too much" was an excuse for many, I believed. "I've got too much to do" was an excuse I had heard from almost all of my team. "Too much" was just a way of giving up. "Then what do you do?" I asked.

"You do what's most important," he said, "what's right—now."

I stopped before speaking because I knew I had just driven my argument over a cliff. "I guess you're right—prioritizing is a must."

"Doing what's right goes beyond prioritizing. Let's go out on the porch, and I'll share some of my ideas and see what you think," Benny said. "I enjoy hearing your thoughts."

"Sure. What else would we talk about the entire weekend—banking?" I asked, smiling.

"Exactly," Benny said. "I'll fix some tea while you finish unpacking."

• • •

I stepped into the bedroom and looked around. The sunlight was flowing into the room at an early afternoon angle. I walked toward the window and looked outside. The light was shimmering on the calm water. The view toward the lake reminded me of Benny's photos. I remembered looking out the window in my apartment in Philly the previous evening. The view was remarkably different. The cold, dark sky of my hometown was replaced by the bright rays of the sun in Virginia. But I still felt detached.

"This is a different world," I said to myself as I stared out the window. I turned and saw my reflection in the mirror and remembered one of the questions Benny posed in his book, "Who am I?"

I turned my head to look out the window toward the lake.

—BENJAMIN FRANKLIN PRICE

27. Who Am I?

"WHO AM I?"

The question appeared simple for me to answer. I was Jack Oliver, banker. I was successful. I was one of the masters of the universe in the Philly business world. I was connected to money and power. But something had changed. The foundations I had constructed my career and life on were crumbling. I had been looking at myself through a filter, detached and disconnected. The question "Who am I?"—I was beginning to understand—had little to do with a job or career. I had avoided answering that simple question most of my life because I didn't like the answer. For some reason, being here on the edge of the lake in a place far from my home with a person I barely knew, I felt as though I might finally attempt to understand who really Jack Oliver was.

Benny was preparing a pitcher of tea. Similar to the other four bedrooms Benny had showed me when he gave me a tour, my room was chock-full of photos. The thought struck me that Benny and his wife had two homes to fill with memories, and I had an apartment filled with regrets.

I saw several photos in the room of a very youthful Benny, Ann, and a boy who looked like Benny's much younger twin. *Is that his son? It has to be,* I reasoned. While we had talked quite a bit I had never heard him talk about children. But then again, I hadn't either.

Most of the family photos filling the room were taken at the lake. But one photo stood out from the rest. It was a black-and-white picture, with Benny in military attire. He was kneeling in front of a plane—probably a jet, I guessed. Given his age, I wondered if he had been in Korea or Vietnam. He didn't seem like the military type. I walked outside to join Benny who was now sitting on the cabin's front porch.

"Jack, I hope you like sweet tea. It's actually clove tea. It has a different taste, something that you may have to acquire."

I actually wasn't a fan of tea, but I was willing to try something new. I was thirsty, and I didn't see any beer in the fridge. Before I had the tea to my lips I could smell the scent of the clove. I took a small sip. It was different, just like everything I was being exposed to in Virginia. The taste seemed to open my nasal passages and make my eyes slightly water. "It's different, but I like it."

"That's what this weekend is about, Jack. I'm going to show you why this place is so special to us," Benny said as he laughed and took a sip of the tea.

"I couldn't help but notice the photos in my room. You've had this place for quite a while," I said.

"Yes," he nodded and turned his focus toward the lake. "We've had it for a long time. It's as much our home as our home in Salem."

"I saw a picture of you in front of a plane. Were you in the military?" I asked.

"Yes. I was in the Navy. I was a pilot."

"Were you in Vietnam?"

"Yes," he said. "I served in Vietnam."

I took another sip of tea, sensing his hesitancy to talk about his time in the military. The breeze from the lake blew what little hair I had left on my head. "This is such a beautiful place. I never imagined it would be like this. Do you spend much time here?"

"We try to get here as much as possible," he said, sipping the tea. "It's our little piece of heaven here on earth."

"I saw a young man in several of the photos. Is that your son?" I asked.

"Yes."

I waited for Benny to continue. The pause was uncomfortable.

"Jack, those photos mean a lot. The young man you see in the photo is my son. He died twenty-seven years ago. He would have been close to your age now," he said as he continued to look out on the lake. He took a drink of tea and sighed deeply.

Embarrassed for being so blunt and shocked to hear his son was not alive, I said, "I'm sorry. I didn't know."

"He was a junior—Benjamin Franklin Price Jr. I was so proud to share my name with him. He went by Ben. He was an incredible person. He was intelligent, caring, and compassionate. He got all of those traits from his mother, including his good looks." Benny said this with a smile, but his face conveyed a pain I could not imagine.

From the photos I saw, Ben looked like Benny's clone. He appeared to be as tall as Benny with dark, wavy hair. He had a huge, genuine smile in every photo. I wondered what happened, waiting to see if he was going to talk about it.

"Jack, if this makes you uncomfortable, I won't talk about Ben. It's still very difficult for me to do, but I feel drawn to share his life with you," he said as he turned toward me.

"I would be honored to hear about your son," I said. I couldn't remember ever using the word "honored," but I meant it. I knew I was going to hear something that Benny had not shared with many others. I also sensed a certain strength and peace radiating from him along with the obvious pain of his loss.

• • •

"How can I go on?"

It was the same question I had asked myself after my mother had passed away.

"After Ben was gone, I asked myself 'How can I go on?'" Benny said, turning to face the lake. "I felt like I had died." I sat in silence looking at the side of his face, his gaze firmly fixed on the glistening water.

"Ben was always an athlete. He loved sports. He played baseball, football, and basketball and had a natural talent for anything competitive. But what he liked most was to run. He loved to run. When he was running it looked as if his feet were so light they didn't touch the ground. He looked like he was gliding—finding a way to defy gravity. You should have seen him, Jack."

I could imagine seeing him running. I felt connected to Benny's words—not my usual detached perspective. I realized the numbness I had cultivated to protect me from the life I was living in Philly wasn't working here.

"So many people appear to be in agony when they're running. But Ben was different. I'm not exaggerating—Ben smiled the entire time he was running. His track coach said he had never seen anything like it. He could be nearing exhaustion and somehow at the time of his harshest exertion he didn't grimace—he smiled."

I hadn't opened my heart to feelings like this for years. But now, sitting in a rocking chair at Smith Mountain Lake, my heart was suddenly exposed.

"When someone is doing something they love, people can see it. Ben won almost every track meet he competed in, even though he was competing against high school juniors and seniors three or four years older." Turning toward me, Benny said, "Winning wasn't what made Ben run so fast. It wasn't the competition—even if someone was nearby, it didn't change his pace. He ran at his own pace. It wasn't because of his physique or his technique. I had track coaches from the competing schools come up to me and tell me that Ben was the best they had ever seen at that level and age. One of the coaches from Blacksburg told me what made my son so unique. He said he was a *natural*. When he ran he was in his own world. Nothing seemed to affect him. He was purely in the moment." You could hear the pride and happiness in Benny's memories. I thought of Joshua and Jessica. I had barely been present most of their lives. Benny looked back to the lake, putting his hands on the rocking chair's arms.

"Ben loved it here at the lake. He would come here and we would fish, hike, and work on the cabin. He helped me build the deck and expand this porch. We carried every rock that went into building the fireplace." Benny paused for a moment, lightly patting both hands on the arms of his rocking chair as he slowly rocked. "When I come here, I can feel his spirit, as if he were going to bounce onto the porch, sweat pouring from a five-mile run and ask, 'When are we going fishing, Dad?'"

It was at that moment that the pain of his loss hit again—but much harder. I wasn't sure I could have tolerated being here if I was Benny, with all of those memories. I felt a tear drop down my face. I quickly wiped away the tear and took a deep, silent breath.

"One of Ben's rituals was to get up early and go on a morning run. Not a jog, but a run. He didn't do it for training purposes; he did it because he loved it. It was a Saturday morning. Ben was on the porch stretching. He rarely talked before he went on his run. It was like he was already there, out on the road, visualizing where he was going. But that morning he talked."

Benny was now struggling to keep his voice even. He was gripping the arms of the old wooden rocker with a slight tremor visible in his left hand. He continued to rock the chair in the same rhythm. I was frozen and trying to keep my emotions in check.

"Ben told me that his conscience was bothering him and he wanted to get something off his chest. I'll never forget it. He looked at me in my eyes and said, 'Dad, I lied to you and Mom about drinking at the party last weekend.' He told me everyone else was doing it and felt like he had to do it. He told me he got sick and was embarrassed. He said, 'Dad, I know you knew I'd been drinking, but you didn't say anything.' He was right—I knew. I figured he was already punishing himself enough for lying. My son was a very honest young man, Jack."

I felt another shot of guilt strike me. No one had ever accused me of being honest—it had always been the opposite.

Benny leaned forward in the rocker and continued. "Ben said to me, 'I'm sorry I lied. I learned my lesson and won't do it again. I just want you to know you're the best Dad in the world and I love you.'"

Benny had stopped rocking. Tears were streaking down my face. I was not wiping them away. I wasn't embarrassed to feel the pain. I thought of my relationship, or lack of, with my father and my son. What Benny's son said to him were words I had never spoken and would never hear.

"I told Ben I loved him, and he was the best son a father could ever hope for. We hugged. I patted his shoulder as he turned. He smiled and said he was going to run his five miles and would be back to eat pancakes with us. He bounced off the porch running toward the road. I stood and watched him go over the top of the hill, floating along like he had wings. That was the last time I saw him alive."

After a moment, as I choked back the streaming tears, I asked, "What happened?"

"We don't know. Someone struck him with a vehicle on Route 37 past Harry's store. Hardly any traffic is on the road at that time of the morning. Evidently a driver didn't see him and was going too fast and hit him. When Ben wasn't back in an hour, I got in my truck and drove out to look for him. I knew something had happened. I thought he might have sprained an ankle. I knew his route. After I went about two miles from the turnoff I saw him on the side of the road, curled up almost as if he was in the womb. He was already gone. The injuries he suffered from being hit took his life almost instantly. I held him. I didn't know what else to do."

I felt Benny's loss. I couldn't imagine losing one of my children. The pain I felt from his loss was now turning to anger. How could this man, a good man with a family, lose a son? A son who was obviously special? A son who would live a good life? A son who any man would have been proud of was taken away too early. Why? My emotions were cascading. I put my hands together and began rubbing them tightly. I didn't know what to say. We sat in silence, with only the sounds of the birds and the lake lapping against the nearby shoreline. I don't know how long we sat in silence.

Benny began talking again in a voice that helped to calm me, even though the loss was so much his. "I was angry. I wanted to find the person who killed my son and make him pay for the crime. After the police had exhausted their search, I hired a private investigator. I wanted revenge. But nothing helped heal the loss. I kept asking, why? Losing Ben wasn't the only thing I lost—I lost hope. Everything changed. Our life, which had seemed so perfect, fell apart. Ann and I rarely talked. Every time we would start to talk, we reminded each other of Ben. I couldn't stand to come here to the lake. We listed the cabin with a realtor for sale. I hated going to work. Everywhere I turned, I saw a place where Ben should be. It seemed like there was no peace to be had in living. I hated my life."

He paused and looked down, now slowly rocking. "I was lost, Jack. I didn't know what to do. Ann and I tried counseling. That didn't work. I tried everything I could do to take my mind off of life. Most of it was harmful and made the hurt worse. I wasn't myself. Ann moved to Charlottesville for several months to be with her mother. Left alone, I made terrible choices feeling like nothing mattered anymore."

Rising from a near-slumping position in his chair, he repositioned himself upright. "On a Saturday about six months after we lost Ben, I drove back here to the cabin. I don't know why I came back. I had decided I never would come here again, but that morning I got in my truck and drove here. When I got here, I parked my truck and walked around the cabin, almost afraid to look at it. The leaves were off the trees. It started to rain. I had never felt so lonely—I wanted to die. It started to rain even harder. I walked up here onto the porch to get out of the rain. I sat down in this rocker. It was facing the road. I began to replay the morning Ben left for his run."

Benny then maneuvered the rocker to face the road. I could now see the side of his face. I leaned to the side to share the same view— staring up the dirt road into the trees. He continued to talk in a calm voice. "As I sat here that morning, Jack, I remembered the last time I saw him alive. I had blamed myself for his death. I had turned my pain into a selfish pity that was killing me. I realized what I needed to do. As I remembered Ben running over the top of the hill going out of sight, I decided at that moment I would never sell this place. I vowed that I was here to live, not die. Two words were in my thoughts—honor Ben. Since that day, whenever I feel the grief and pain coming back—whenever I feel like I have no options—I remember to honor Ben. That's why I'm here, with you, right now, Jack. Otherwise, I probably would not be alive. I had given up. I know you're here this weekend to talk about a job, and that's important to you and me. But life is so much more than a job. I'm here to honor Ben. What else could I do that could mean more?"

I remained motionless staring up the road. How had I handled losing lives of people close to me? I tried to run from death, but it had finally caught up with me. I had never come to terms with my grief and anger over my father's death. The guilt I carried from not being there to help him, from being powerless to stop him from jumping from a bridge, poured over me. But my guilt didn't stop there. I had nearly frozen my mother out of my life. She died without hearing me say I was sorry. She didn't hear me say I loved her. Why did I treat her so coldly after my father died? Why? Benny's story of a life lost much too early shook out the lies I had told myself over the years. The past grasped my heart. I felt a wave of nausea, but remembered José's advice and slowed my breathing. After a moment, I told Benny, "I could never handle something like that."

"Yes you could, Jack. You never know what kind of strength you have inside until you find yourself looking down into the abyss. The choice is clear. You summon your will and strength, and do the best you can. The options are few when you reach that point. I had absolute clarity in what I needed to do. I chose to live."

• • •

"How can I get rid of my pain?" The question Benny had posed himself after the death of his son was another question I knew well.

"Even though I chose to live, it hurt," he said. "For so long, every breath I took hurt. I wondered if I was going to be able to get rid of the anger and pity. As every day passed I realized the choice was more than just to live—it was a choice of *how* I wanted to live my life. I looked at myself as honestly as possible. I was tired of the self-pity, the anger, and the hatred. To honor Ben, I had to be different. I had to change."

When he spoke those words, I listened carefully. If ever there was someone who needed to change, it was me.

"I decided I was not going to let my sorrows define me," he said as he turned facing me. "I didn't know the answers to all of the questions I was asking myself. Who am I? What is my purpose? Why did I lose my son? I decided to not run from the questions I couldn't answer but face them. We aren't supposed to know all the answers. But we have to keep asking. We have to live a questionable life—a life filled with questions. The life we have been given."

I was ashamed. The question that I asked all my life was "What else can I take?" I did something I had never allowed myself—I was honest with someone about how I felt.

"I'm the opposite of what you're talking about," I said. "I'm still running from those questions." I told Benny how I had lived: a life devoted to getting, giving only the minimum in the process. I exposed who I was to a person I barely knew. Finally I said, "I'm sure I'm not the person you would want to be your successor. I've wasted my life."

"Jack, you're still alive," Benny said, smiling. "You haven't wasted your life as long as your heart is beating. It sounds like you're a lot like I was years ago. You're out of balance. It's like a wheel that's out of kilter—it may still work, but the faster it turns the more you notice the imbalance. Balancing is a moment-by-moment effort."

"But how do you balance your life?" I said.

"I've found you have to be rebalance," he said, a huge smile lighting up his face. "You have to give more than you take."

"What do you mean?"

"What causes us the most suffering is chasing after things. You are trying to hold onto something you only think you have. The one undeniable law of the universe is that everything changes. Trying to hold on to things in order to avoid change only sets us up for disaster. We think we can be satisfied by having more or keeping the status quo. That's where the wheel goes out of kilter. We are simply taking more than giving."

"That's me," I said. "But how can you ever get ahead in life without wanting more from it?"

"Jack, you just said it—wanting more and getting more *doesn't* satisfy. To find balance, you must change your intent. If your intention is to have more, you're already aimed at the wrong target. You'll never find balance in wanting more. But we will in letting go and simply living, accepting change for what it is—part of life."

Letting go of anything was almost impossible for me. I had taught myself to hang on to everything I had worked so hard for. Now, this man was telling me to let go. I was struggling with the idea. "That sounds good if everyone is doing the same thing," I rebutted. "But that isn't reality. Most people are out for themselves. If you live like you suggest, you'll be taken advantage of."

"You have to start trusting that giving is of more value than getting. Life is an interdependent process, a process you share with everyone. To live fully, you have to let go of the attachments that drag you down and hold you back. I ask this with all respect, Jack: Is the life you've been living working for you?"

I leaned over with my head down, rubbing my hands together. Then I told Benny about my father, something I had never talked about. I told him everything I felt—the pain, the anger, the loss, the guilt. I then told him how I failed with my mother. I shared the story of how I only told her I loved her when she was in a coma in the hospital and that I was asleep as she passed away. I couldn't stop the tears. The guilt was too heavy. "No," I said. "My life isn't working—for me or anyone else."

Benny put his hand on my shoulder. "Jack, I know your mother heard you. You went to sleep holding her hand, at peace with yourself. She heard you and passed, peacefully, holding your hand. She was at peace. You did the right thing. You were there, and you were honest with her. You cannot change the past. But you can change now. You need to let go of the guilt, Jack. Just let go of it. It sounds like you have carried it too long."

Benny gripped my shoulder for a brief second. I remembered when I was in the hospital and I told my mother I loved her and I was sorry, I thought I felt her tighten her grip on my hand. Just for a split second, I felt the slight pressure of her grip. It wasn't my imagination—it did happen. She did hear me.

"Jack, you need to forgive yourself. Don't live in the past. Your parents loved you and were proud of you. You have *your* life to live. Live a life that will honor your parents. Drop the baggage you're carrying, Jack. Only you can let go."

"You're right—I'll try." But letting go seemed impossible. I did not tell him I had much more baggage. How could I drop that so simply?

"I think we forget sometimes how connected we are to everything. The rose grows out of dirt. We use garbage and waste to feed plants that help to sustain our own quality of life. The world we live in is in a fragile balance with everything. One of the wisest people I've ever met told me, 'All is all.' Beauty isn't separate from ugliness. Creating opposites is only our way of trying to lessen change. But change is life; the good comes with the bad. Everything's connected."

I had never thought about the interconnected nature of things. It was something I had avoided. Being separate made my life easier to accept. I was still feeling the lightness of a confession.

"Thanks for listening," I said. "This is the most unusual job interview I've ever heard of."

"Always expect the unexpected," he said, laughing. "I'm going to get you another glass of clove tea. It looks like you enjoyed it," he said, smiling as he stood. "See what trying something different will get you—a new favorite drink!" He laughed and stepped inside the cabin.

I looked back up the road where I had visualized Benny's son. By sharing his loss, I was able to shake loose many of the chains holding back the guilt of my own life gone wrong. I felt lighter, as though a huge boulder had been lifted from my back. I still had the baggage, but I knew what to do with it.

Let it go. But could I?

28. Who Do You Want to Be?

"WHO DO YOU WANT TO BE?"

It didn't take long for me to retreat from the ideas about change that Benny had brought up. I had stepped back inside the cabin to wash my face and prepare for my first real fishing excursion. Walking down the hallway leading to the bathroom I saw a photo from a Halloween when Benny's son was alive. Benny was dressed as a cowboy. I smiled. He looked a little bit like a much taller version of Howdy Doody.

Seeing the photo, I remembered a masquerade party of my own. Tina had twisted my arm and forced me to attend a Halloween gathering at our neighbor's home. As usual, I didn't want to go. I was too tired to put on another mask.

"I want to be a couch—with me on it," I answered from the living room.

"Who do you want to go as?" Tina asked, rephrasing the question to get a more positive response.

"Pinocchio," I shouted. "He's a wooden puppet. That sounds close."

"What are you talking about, Jack?" Tina asked as she stepped into the room.

"You've been telling me I'm unemotional," I said, referring to an argument earlier that day. "You always tell me I do whatever Chad tells me, like a puppet. Pinocchio seems like a good fit for me."

"I was thinking of a different outfit," Tina said. "Scrooge."

"That fits, too," I said. "You find the right outfit, and I'll wear it."

"There's no need to change what you have on," Tina said. "You're already him."

• • •

I had tried to change before, but failed. After finally talking about the guilt and emotions I had bottled up inside for years, I realized that this episode would be nothing more than a replay of earlier attempts to change. I'd crashed and burned in the fire of good intentions. Why would it work this time? I was the same man now as I was then. Benny's voice brought me back to the moment.

"Are you ready to go fishing, Jack?" Benny asked. I could tell Benny was anxious to get out on the lake.

"Sure, let's go," I said, still worried that I would make a complete fool of myself. "You're going to have to coach me."

"Fishing is like riding a bike—you never forget," Benny said.

"What happens if you only went fishing once and the river was so polluted there were more fish floating dead on top of the water than alive in the river?" I asked, stepping into the large main area.

"Then you're in for great fishing," Benny said. "The odds are in your favor, Jack. You might catch something."

We grabbed the tackle box and cooler and walked from the cabin down a narrow dirt path to the lake. The shrubbery was thick surrounding the thin trail. Benny reminded me to watch for snakes. I was watching, though he hadn't told me what to do if I saw one.

We came to a small dock with a metal cover. You could not see the boat and dock from the cabin, since it was tucked in a small cove, enclosed by the thick overhang of foliage. It looked as though the water level was lower than usual, with a patch of bare, brown soil outlining the rim of the lake. "The lake looks a little lower than its normal level. Have you had a drought?"

"That's observant, Jack. I'll make a fisherman out of you yet. The water level is regulated by the Corps of Engineers, but the lack of rain has brought the level down to one of the lowest for the lake since I can remember. But the low water level and cooler temperatures just might help our fishing today," he said. "Are you ready?"

Did he say "cooler temperatures?" *Benny should spend a winter in Philly,* I thought, tiptoeing my way through the brush toward the dock. "I'm ready to fish," I said. I felt like a kid. When was the last time I felt youthful? I couldn't remember. Besides snakes, I wasn't concerned about anything other than avoiding the appearance of being the city boy I obviously was.

Benny had climbed on board what he called his "bass boat." Walking the last few steps to the side of the vessel I smiled, thinking about how people named boats after the type of fish they hoped to catch. I wondered if a sign was on the bottom of the boat alerting all sea creatures: THIS IS A BASS-ONLY BOAT. I handed him the gear I was carrying and lifted my left foot to step on board the wide, flat boat as if I knew what I was doing.

"I'm okay, I don't need any help," I answered, carefully watching where I stepped. As soon as I put my foot on the boat, it started to move away from the dock. I suddenly found myself doing a split with Smith Mountain Lake under me. My mind was telling me to step back on dry land, so I quickly pushed off with my left foot to try to propel myself backward toward the dock, only making the boat move even farther away. Everything appeared to be in slow motion as I turned into a gymnast, my legs spreading as the boat continued its movement from the miniature pier. Seeing the gap widen between my feet, all I could think about was how stupid I looked.

Benny said quickly, "Jack, take my hand!" I held out my left hand and Benny pulled me onto the boat. While it wasn't pretty, I made it on board—in dry clothes.

"You're better at balancing than what you thought, aren't you?" Benny said, laughing as he settled back into his seat, the craft still rocking from my entrance.

"It wasn't pretty, but at least it worked," I said, feeling the red heat in my face. "I guess I did need a hand, didn't I?"

"Would you mind throwing off that line beside of you, Jack?"

"No problem," I said, "as long as I don't have to step back on the dock."

As I leaned over and carefully unraveled the rope holding the front of the vessel to the dock, Benny said, "No one can live their life alone, independent of everyone else."

"At least not on a boat," I said, still trying to generate some humor. As Benny started the motor and maneuvered the craft out of the cove into the wider expanse of the lake, I thought about what had just happened. While still embarrassed, what stood out about my near-fall into the lake was the fact I couldn't remember the last time someone offered to help me. Tina, Cassie, and especially people I had worked with never offered me assistance. They either did what I told them or asked them to do, or they minded their own business, without any regard for me. Why was that?

Gliding across the smooth waters of the lake, hearing the lapping of the waves I admitted to myself that I didn't want anyone to help me. I had always believed asking for help was a sign of weakness. I always did things alone. But if Benny had not stretched out his hand, I would have been wet and stupid. Yet, I only took his hand out of necessity, almost too late. He had just said that no one could live independently of others—but I had always tried my best to do so. It wasn't others failing to offer assistance; it was my resisting any help. How many times had I needed a helping hand and my ego had stopped me from asking? Even worse, how many times had someone asked for my help and I had ignored them?

Benny guided the boat down the middle of what he told me was the main channel. As we made our way into an even larger section, I began to see some large homes dotting the shoreline and several other boats. The weather was perfect. A light breeze kept the air cooled, and the sun shone brightly on the water, making it sparkle. I was glad I had sunglasses on. Benny offered me some sunscreen to put on my arms and neck, but I told him I wanted to get some tan. "Are you sure?" he asked. "You can get burned pretty quickly out here."

"No thanks," I said. "I have the skin of an alligator."

"Okay, Jack," he said. "We're closing in on what the locals call 'Catfish Corner.' That's where we'll see if we can catch something for supper." I remained quiet, waiting for Benny to tell me what to do. After placing the two reels between us, Benny broke out the bait from a small compartment near his seat. "Hellgrammites work great here," he said, lifting one of the small but menacing creatures from its container.

"They look like mini lobsters," I said, carefully reaching down to snag one of them. Actually, they looked uglier. As soon as I grabbed one, I found out it grabbed back.

"Watch out for their claws—they can put a little bite on you if you're not careful," Benny said—too late.

"Yeah," I said, jerking my hand back from my bait. "I just got a bite."

Benny took some time to show me the finer art of casting and after a couple of tries I placed my line in the water where Benny said I might get a bite. I was actually enjoying myself. It was remarkably quiet. You could hear birds chirping from the shoreline. The entire setting was like a giant amphitheater. I leaned my head back slightly to enjoy the breeze. It was tough to find a one-foot-square space of solitude in Philly. Here, privacy was available in vast quantities. I looked across the boat at Benny. He was angled to the other side of the craft, sporting a slight grin on his face. This was something he could enjoy whenever he wanted—no wonder he was smiling.

"I haven't shared the story about Ben with very many people. If you don't mind fishing and talking, I feel compelled to share what happened after we lost our son."

"I'd like to hear," I said. "I'm sorry I rattled on so long about my past and about my mother and father. I'm embarrassed. I've never talked so much about them."

"Jack, never apologize for being honest," he said. "I appreciate you trusting me enough to share it."

I had never thought about it, but I discovered I had a habit. I often apologized for telling the truth. Being honest was not the most natural thing for me. Evidently I felt the need to announce it: "Jack Oliver is telling the truth—listen up!" Tina had told me many times over the years that I had a habit of saying, "Let me be honest with you" at the beginning of statements that I was trying to accentuate. This usually came after I had told a lie. Cassie had said the same thing. Was I that obvious?

The other problem I had was trust. Somehow I trusted Benny,

even though I barely knew him. "I'm not used to being so open," I said. "Believe me—I'm usually not that way."

"It's a good habit—being honest and open," Benny said with a smile. "There are a lot worse habits."

I knew a lot about habits—bad ones. Could he see through me that easily?

• • •

"*Why am I afraid?*"

The question leaped from my mouth before I could stop myself. Benny had been telling me more about what happened after his son died. I realized how much a lack of control frightened me. Benny couldn't control what happened to his son. I was feeling fear—of the unknown. I was afraid what the future was holding for me.

"I thought I had it all, Jack. I had a great family, career, and friends. The future looked bright. I had big plans. But my life changed in a morning, and I wasn't ready for it." He paused, turning to face me. "You wonder sometimes why you remember certain things. After Ben was gone, I remembered a section from Dante's *Divine Comedy*: 'I found myself in a dark wood where the right way was lost.' Why would I recall that line? That line, from something I had read in college, was in my thoughts when Ann and I were driving to Ben's funeral. It said a lot to me. I had lost the way in my life."

Hearing a fellow banker spout off a quote from Dante in the middle of a lake in Virginia was a little surreal. Even though I had what everyone said was a photographic memory, as soon as I had finished an exam, I forgot what I had learned. Like a computer, my mind deleted the files. I had passed the test and moved on to what was next. My attention returned to Benny's story.

"Death can be life's greatest teacher," he said. "Death taught me how to live. Until we lost Ben, I thought I knew how my life would progress, the stage was ready, and the next act was in progress. And it was comforting to a certain extent. I always felt like I knew what was going to happen. But when Ben left, my world fell apart," he said. "I found that the things that worked before Ben's death had little value or meaning after he was gone.

Ann and I struggled to find peace between us. The bank I worked for was being sold. I was at a crossroads in every sense. I didn't know what I wanted out of life."

As I listened to Benny, I realized that until now I had always known what I wanted from life. Now, I was unsure.

"I was drifting along, allowing the current to take me where it wanted to take me. I was rudderless. Looking back, I see that even before Ben was killed, my life wasn't going in the right direction. I was out of kilter—I wasn't balanced."

As Benny talked he kept pulling gently on his fishing line, absent-mindedly going through the motions of fishing. I sat quietly, listening and paying no attention to my line.

"When I had my own awakening here at the lake and decided to live again, I found that what I had done before wouldn't work now. I had to acknowledge that my world had been turned upside down. I was trying to hold onto what worked before. But it didn't work. I realized I had to live life differently, more effectively. I stopped letting the current pull me. I began to keep a journal and wrote down questions that I needed answers to. The very first question I wrote down was a question I thought I had answered years earlier: Who am I?"

I had tried to answer that question recently. I didn't like the answer.

"That was a tough question for me, Jack," Benny continued, jerking his reel slightly. "I didn't know who I was. I had been Benny Price, bank president, but my bank had just been acquired. I didn't know what the future had in store for me. Obviously, the same was true away from work. I thought I was Benny Price, father, but my son was gone—I was no longer a father. I thought I was Benny Price, husband, but my marriage was falling apart. I believed I was Benny Price, community leader. But I found no joy in giving my time to anything or anyone."

I couldn't believe how much he sounded like me. How could that be? He definitely wasn't like my father. My father would never admit he was wrong. I had been wrong in my belief that the two would be alike. Benny paused and turned in his seat to look at me.

"It took total honesty to admit I wasn't the person I wanted to be. It hurts to know you're wrong, but it's even harder to convince yourself you're right when you're wrong. It was tough to acknowledge it, but I was totally out of balance. That's when I decided to make my life a life that could honor Ben. I had to change."

"But how did you answer the question—who am I?" I asked. I could tell he liked the question. He knew I was listening.

"I was trying to be the same Benny Price—with a lot of baggage. I was holding onto a fantasy, the way things had been. I understood that I couldn't change the past or dictate the future. I understood I had to change who I was and what I was doing—that instant."

I wasn't sure his past could ever touch the dark corners of greed where I had lived my life of ceaseless want. But I could see our similarities. "I set out on a new question—a leading question: *Who do I want to be?* That was the beginning of a new chapter in my life, a second chance. I decided I wasn't going to fail; fear wasn't going to stop me. I wanted to have the courage to accept change as part of life."

"So you decided what you wanted in the future?" I asked.

"No, actually it was almost the opposite," he said. "I decided who I wanted to be in the present. I changed my intention and attention to the present. Now is where the past and future meet. We only have this moment to engage. Now is the only moment we have to become who we want to be."

"But you still had goals, didn't you?"

"They were goals of the moment. Not something I waited for, like a promotion. The biggest challenge I faced was change. The person I wanted to be was going to be fearless of change," he said. "A person who learned from his mistakes and shared the knowledge he gained from his experiences. I wanted to be mindful of what I had learned—good and bad—to remember to be *awake*." He paused and looked at me, as if to see if I understood what he was saying. "The past repeats itself when we choose to let it. Ignorance is ignoring what you know and making the same mistake over and over. I did not want to be ignorant."

"I'm at the same point in my life," I said, still not comprehending everything he was saying. "I know I need to change but I'm afraid to change. Why am I afraid?"

"Because you're human, Jack," Benny said as he turned to look at his fishing line, his smile lighting up the face shadowed under the bill of his baseball hat.

"I hate my job with Merchants, but I loved my job before my bank was bought," I said, the tempo of my words much more rapid than normal. "I spent too much time at work and not enough with my family." I told Benny what I was sure he already knew. My marriage was over, my kids were strangers, and I needed to answer the two questions he posed—honestly. "But I know I could never change like you have—I'm not you."

"You and I are not so different," he said. "We're all unique and the same—all one. We want peace and happiness. We believe it is something we need to search for. Sometimes we even think we can buy it. But in reality, it's inside of us, now." After pausing, Benny leaned forward. "Happiness isn't a destination, Jack. It's a choice that resides inside of you, not outside of you. Happiness and peace are there for the choosing—a selection that you alone can make. I am responsible for who I am and what I do. Happy or sad, it's my preference. There's no one to blame but me. The same is true for you. The only way to understand your choice is to question your life."

●　●　●

"*Why ask questions?*" I understood part of what Benny was saying. But I believed life was a search for answers, not questions. "I want answers that make sense—something I can count on," I said.

"Questions lead," he said. "When I question my life, I find its purpose. The purpose is to transform my life—so I can be the best person I want to be. Asking the right questions is more important than having the right answer, if there *is* a right answer. Choosing the right way to live each moment—to be—requires constant questioning."

He held up his hand and pointed in a slow, circular motion around the lake. "Imagine being in the ocean, surrounded by nothing but water. You're thirsty. You see what's all around—it's water! You drink it. But instead of satisfying your thirst, it only exaggerates your thirst. If you drink more of the salt water, you'll be sick.

Wanting does that to all of us. More isn't the answer. Neither is the act of simply wanting answers. Asking questions allows us to think in a less concrete manner. It's the ultimate reality check. Anyone can recite answers, but will the answers that work now be right tomorrow—or even in the next moment? Questions let us reexamine life closely and continually. Do you understand what I'm saying?"

"I like answers," I said, still debating the old guy. I was growing agitated with the idea of questioning how I live. I had already revealed enough to feel better about myself.

"We all do," he said. "But without questioning your life, how can you change? You can't rely on following in the footsteps of others—you'll end up trying to apply their answers to your unique life. Each person must find their own way at a pace and place that is right for them. You can only find your own way in questioning."

Without taking any time to absorb what he had just told me, I asked about something that was troubling me. "What happens when someone does something harmful to you that you didn't ask for or anticipate? It's like you said about the person who killed your son. That wasn't your choice. How do you deal with things like that?" Before he could answer, I continued, "If finding happiness is inside me, it must be deep inside because I haven't found it."

"No one is immune to pain. Most people view themselves as immortal. I was no different. I felt in control of my life. That was the problem. I had put so much attention on things that would happen in the future I had forgotten to live in the now. When Ben was taken away, instead of dealing with the pain, I masked it with revenge. Blame and self-pity took over my thoughts. I fueled it. You can't control what others do, but you can choose how you respond. That day at the lake house, I realized I need to change."

I thought about what he was saying. "In my entire life, I have never admitted so many failures and faults to anyone. I always believed that telling someone else about a weakness made you weaker, vulnerable to attack. That person would then have power over you—something they could use if they wished. But I trust you, Benny," I said. "Honestly—I don't understand why I'm being so open."

Suddenly, I felt a strong jerk against my arm. "I think I've got a bite!" I said to Benny with the glee of a child. Benny coached me on how to reel the fish in. Once it was beside the boat, Benny reached down with a large net and lifted the fish upward. "That's a great catch, Jack," he said.

We fished and talked for several more hours, catching four more keepers, as Benny called them. As the day wound down, I noticed a sensation on the back of my neck and arms that I could not remember having for years. I had a sunburn—a really bad one.

"Jack, I think you got a little too much sun," he said. "We have some ointment in the cabin. You need to put some on when we get back."

"I should have listened," I said, acknowledging my stubbornness. "I didn't think I was getting that much sun."

"It's a little different here compared to Philadelphia," he said, guiding the boat through the cove leading to the dock. "Tomorrow we'll be in the woods. All you have to do is watch for snakes and make sure you don't fall off a cliff."

I laughed. Despite the sunburn, I had enjoyed the fishing. "I'll try to avoid snakes, and I'm sure I'll avoid any and all cliffs—I'm afraid of heights."

"You'll overcome that fear," he said, laughing. "The view is incredible—from the edge."

We made our way back to the cabin.

29. To Be or Not to Be?

"TO BE OR NOT TO BE?" Benny said as he sat down in the living room. "That is *the* question." After pausing for a moment, he smiled, patting his stomach, and said, "Or is the question, 'Dessert or no dessert?' One thing is for sure, I ate too much. That's one of my bad habits."

We had returned to the cabin with the fish we had pulled from the waters of Smith Mountain Lake. It was almost dark as we entered the cabin. Benny started a fire in the huge stone fireplace while I got out the containers from the refrigerator to start preparing dinner. Benny took the time to show me the fine art of cleaning fish. He then used a batter Ann had premixed to coat the fish fillets before frying them. "Everything's fried in the South, Jack," he said, using what appeared to be a very old iron skillet to cook the fish.

While he was busy with the fish, I methodically pieced together the rest of the dinner following the directions Ann had taped to each Tupperware container, on how to use the microwave. We devoured the catch with Ann's mashed potatoes, creamy corn, green beans, and homemade rolls. And, of course, my new favorite drink, clove tea. I couldn't remember the last time I had eaten a home-cooked meal.

After dinner, we put the food away and loaded the dishwasher. "I think the dishwasher is probably one of the great achievements of mankind," Benny said. "Dishwashers have probably saved many a marriage! More than all of the marriage counselors, self-help books, and advice columns combined."

I wanted to say that the dishwasher hadn't helped my marriage. Of course, in my case I had simply ignored the dishes after a meal. "I have some work to do," was familiar after-dinner talk I shared with Tina. Or in the later years, I remembered, I wasn't even home for dinner. I was hiding out at Cassie's. It was no wonder Tina did not want to be with me. *I was a fool to live so selfishly,* I thought, as we finished our chores.

Now finished with the kitchen cleanup, we ate Ann's delicious peach cobbler. Wanting to pull the conversation back to an area in which I felt more certainty, I brought up an issue we hadn't discussed all day—Benny's bank. *I was here about a job,* I thought, *so maybe now was the time to discuss it.* I had hundreds of questions for this self-professed questioner. I thought I had the silver bullet to shoot down his simplistic approach to life, and I was prepared to fire off a round to bring him back to reality. "You said that you were upset that your bank had been bought and your job changed years ago. Is that when you formed Citizens Bank?" I asked. "Surely that was a time that put work before home."

"After Ben passed and I needed to find balance in my life, I focused on answering the question, who do I want to be? Knowing I would spend a large part of my life at work, I wanted to find the right livelihood that didn't conflict with the person I wanted to be and the life I wanted to live. I found that I no longer had a desire for money, titles, and power. The loss of Ben changed me. My intention had changed. The question boiled down to simply, what can I do to help others? The new organization wasn't right for me. So, with the help of a small group of people, we began a new bank, Citizens Bank of Virginia, the same bank I work for now."

"But wasn't the purpose of the bank to make money?" I asked.

"If you're attentive to what you're supposed to do, what you intend to do, everything else takes care of itself, including profits."

"That sounds too simplistic for a start-up business," I said.

"It may sound simplistic, but that's why we've been successful, Jack. We kept it simple, on purpose. We formed the bank with the intent of supplying the necessary banking services to clients who were left without banks in many small communities. This market niche was available to us. When the big banks bought the smaller banks, they generally closed and consolidated offices, especially in small towns. That's where we stepped in to fill the void."

"You formed a community bank," I said.

"Most people would call it a community bank, but we viewed it as a service organization. We were a group of people with a common goal: We existed to serve. We started off small and kept growing, finding communities with needs we could fill. We never bought another bank. We never tried to go toe to toe with the large banks on their turf. We served the small businesses and average-size client accounts they discarded. The profits were a natural result of our purpose. We have minimal fees—most of our services don't even have charges associated with them. We have low loan rates because our expenses are minimal. We don't spend money trying to get business we can't afford. We've been successful, and I know it's because of our intention—to serve."

"I've gone over the financial results of your bank, and they are incredible. You keep growing, despite more competition."

"That's the secret to our success, if you can call it a secret," Benny said. "We're not competing with anyone—just doing the best we can to serve our clients."

"How does that translate into growth?"

"The best advertisement is a happy client. Word of mouth serves as the best way to market our service," he said.

"Then why are you being pressured to sell?"

"We had never discussed selling the bank, until recently. We have a few of our board of directors who forgot our purpose and are a little greedy. That is why I need some assistance. I need a successor. I'm getting old, Jack."

I knew the bank's successes. Benny was a near-legend in banking circles. But was this his swan song? Had greed finally got the best of his organization? "What do you think is going to happen?" I asked.

"I would have never spent the time and energy to start Citizens Bank if I planned to sell it. I'm going to do my best to ensure that the bank is still there serving clients long after I leave the planet."

"My bank was bought," I said, entering into a territory I felt more comfort discussing. "We're similar in that respect—I don't like what happened after we sold to Merchants. A bank like Merchants does many of the same things you mentioned. They gut it and turn it into a profit center. Everything changed after we sold to them." I was hoping my comments would allow an opening to explore the idea that Merchants was one of the suitors vying to buy Benny's bank. The ploy didn't work.

"Who the buyer ultimately may be is not the issue," he said. "If the bank is sold, its purpose will change. I haven't seen another owner who could do better than what we're already doing. If there were such a bank, I wouldn't have a problem selling to them. But I don't see such a bank on the horizon—anywhere."

"I understand," I said. "I'm shocked your board wants to sell."

"Never be shocked by what greed can do, Jack."

"No, I understand greed," I said.

"Citizens Bank is more than just a job to me. It's part of my purpose, my giving. It has helped thousands of people. I don't want that to die after I leave. I've examined my intention. I'm not motivated by selfishness, pride, or greed. I'm not motivated by trying to avoid change. Our success was the result of change!" Benny rose up in his chair. Leaning forward and folding his hands together, he said, "I would have never formed Citizens Bank if it wasn't for Ben. It's one of the ways I've honored his life. That is why I called on you. To see if you want *to be* part of helping all of the people we touch with our organization—helping the bank change and improve what we do. To live on—to be."

After sharing some stories about our friend John Helms and my ignorance of all things South, Benny said we needed to get an early start the next morning. "This is a late night for me," Benny said. It was just about 10:30. "I'm usually asleep for almost two hours by now. See what happens to you when you get old, Jack."

"I don't sleep much," I said, thinking about the sleepless nights I had for most of my life. "I wish I could figure out how to get a good night's sleep."

"It's easy," Benny said. "Let everything go—sleep will come naturally. I used to have the same problem. Thinking I was in control kept me up at night worrying about how I could hold it all together. When I let go, I slept much better."

I thanked Benny for the fishing trip and the excellent dinner. While I had more questions than answers, I had enjoyed the day, something new for me.

"We have to get up pretty early tomorrow," he said. "How does leaving around 5:30 sound to you?"

"That's great," I said. "I'm used to getting up early."

"Good night, Jack. Sleep well," Benny said as he stepped into his bedroom.

• • •

I couldn't sleep. Benny's ideas about balance were making me recall the countless moments I had been taking instead of giving.

The first person I thought about was Tina. She had trusted me, and I had let her down. I had ruined our marriage trying to enrich my ego instead of sharing my life. I wondered if I could ever find a way to make things work out. *It's too late*, I thought, in the stillness of the cabin.

I then thought about my kids. The emotions I had felt from hearing about the tragedy of Benny losing his son were fueled by guilt for not being present while my children had grown up. Some of the very things I blamed on my old man I had done to my children. What did they think of me?

Finally, my thoughts turned to my father. I had assumed Benny was like him. As an assembly line of thoughts carried my exhausted mind to sleep, I knew that my assumption was wrong.

Benny wasn't like my father.

I was.

—BENJAMIN FRANKLIN PRICE

30. How Did I Get Here?

"How did I get here?"

Just like the previous twenty-four hours, waking up was different. Opening my eyes, I did not see an alarm clock. There was none in the room. I was momentarily confused.

As I adjusted my focus, I saw a photo of a very youthful Benny lifting his son on his shoulders, serving as a springboard for a dive into the lake. All it took was one moment to destroy Benny and Ann's world. *How different the world would be had he lived,* I thought. The idea of a different world took hold. "How did I get here?" I asked again. Maybe the death of Benny's son brought me here. How could the accidental death of a young man in Virginia, far from Philadelphia, many years ago with no apparent connection to me, now affect my life so dramatically and everyone linked to me? His death changed a lot of worlds.

Still focusing on the photo, I recalled Benny saying, "Everything's connected." *Maybe he's right* . . . I let go of the thought, tired of trying to answer a question that appeared to have no finite answer.

Benny knocked on the door. "It's your wake-up call, Mr. Oliver," he said in his best impression of a British butler's accent. After putting on what I thought would be the most functional clothes for hiking, I stepped out to the scents of a breakfast in the making. "How do you like your eggs cooked?" Benny asked.

"Uh, scrambled," I said, walking into the kitchen. Benny had prepared bacon, home fries, and a large pot of coffee. "I think you could give Ann a run for her money as a cook."

"You'll need some nourishment today. The hike is a little challenging," he said, smiling as he pulled a tray of biscuits from the oven. "What you'll see today will impress you—even if you're out of breath from the climb."

We were going to travel on the Blue Ridge Parkway to a place called the Peaks. After finishing breakfast and cleaning up in the kitchen, we put the gear Benny had assembled for the hike in the well-worn Jeep and pulled out into a heavy fog. Sunrise was still an hour away, which made the drive even more harrowing. I was glad Benny was behind the wheel. I could not see ten feet in front of the vehicle for most of the hour-and-thirty-minute drive.

As we drove through the fog I began to think about Benny's stint in the military. There was no mention of Benny's military experiences in his book. He had barely mentioned it to me. I decided to ask him about it.

"You said you were in Vietnam," I said. "I say this very respectfully, but you don't seem like the military type."

Benny laughed. "What type of person would you characterize me as, Jack?"

I had already thought about it. I said, "You're a Peace Corps kind of guy. I could see you going to some remote village in South America and rebuilding huts, helping people who want help. It's a compliment."

"I'll take it as one," he said. He gave one of the heartiest laughs I had heard from him. "You don't mind me telling Ann about that, do you? She would probably faint from laughing."

"I'm not that far off, am I? I really can't picture you in combat."

"The experience changed me forever. I had graduated from Virginia Tech with a business degree. My father had already made up his mind about my future. He wanted me to be a lawyer. He pulled strings so I was accepted at the University of Virginia, one of the top law schools in the country. It looked like everything was set—my life was neatly laid out in front of me. There was one problem. I hated the idea of being a lawyer. I didn't know exactly what I wanted to be, but it definitely wasn't a lawyer."

I understood his lack of desire for a legal profession. "I couldn't see you as a lawyer," I said.

"The summer after I graduated, I backpacked all across Europe by myself. I thought I would find my calling in life—my purpose. After three months of living by a thread, I returned home more confused than ever."

"Traveling across Europe in the early 1960s—that must have been an experience," I said. "Communism was at its peak. The war in Vietnam was building."

"I assumed a lot before the trip. I pictured the world differently. My perception at the time was wrong. I had an immature view of the world. We had helped Europe in World War II, not that long before my backpacking excursion. We had helped to rebuild much of the continent. I thought people would view Americans in a certain way. I thought I would be viewed differently. I was wrong, and it hurt."

"They were ungrateful?" I asked.

"No, just not what I expected. Everyone had a different point of view. The Italians had a different viewpoint than the French. The French were much different than the Germans. But in each country, each region, each town, and even each neighborhood, they all had their own built-in prejudices and beliefs. I realized it was down to individual choices. After hiking across Europe, I realized *everyone* was different.

"When I returned home, I had a strong desire to do missionary work; I wanted to help people. I wasn't a religious person. I never have been and doubt if I ever will be. But being a missionary was a way to help people. That was my idea as I made my way back to Virginia."

"A missionary?" I asked.

"But on my first day back in the States, I was told my best friend from high school had been killed in Vietnam. While I was bumming my way around Europe trying to find myself, he was killed protecting others. I felt guilty. I had a lot of anger over his loss. But I also felt an obligation to serve my country. I had flown small planes since I was sixteen. It was one of the youthful passions I had. Flying was the only time my father and I ever spent together. The Navy wanted pilots. So, as part of my rebellion to break out from under the life my father had fashioned for me, I decided to join the Navy. It broke my father's heart. After I told him I enlisted—well . . ." He paused. "My father was very strong willed—but so was I. My mother understood my rebellion but hated the idea of her son killing another human."

I still could not picture Benny in the military. Benny appeared to be one of the kindest and gentlest people I had met in my life. "I can see you as a pilot, but I can't see you as a military pilot," I said. "You just don't seem the type."

"I was different. The world was different. After joining I went straight to Pensacola and trained as a pilot. When I finished my training, I went straight to Vietnam."

From the sheer luck of the date of my birth I had avoided the Vietnam experience. But I was old enough to remember the newscasts and how the war split much of the country apart. I asked, "How long were you in Vietnam?"

"Four years, nine months, and three days, a total of 1,736 days," he said as he continued to maneuver through the fog.

Not knowing anything about the military, this seemed like a long time for a noncareer soldier. "Did you sign up for more than one tour of duty?"

"No, Jack. I was a prisoner of war for 1,548 of those days," Benny said without emotion.

I was stunned. I asked, "How were you captured?"

"I was flying an A-4 Skyhawk. We were based on an aircraft carrier, the USS *Oriskany*. On a mission no more or less dangerous than any other, my plane was hit by anti-aircraft fire. I ejected from the plane and was almost immediately captured after landing. After being in several different prison camps, I was finally housed at the Hoa Lo Prison. You may have heard it called the Hanoi Hilton."

Again, the experience was something I couldn't imagine. "How did you survive that long?" I asked.

"I was lucky, in a sense. The North Vietnamese dragged me half-alive to their camp. I had broken my leg when I was ejected. I was an officer, so my value to them was worth the effort. They saw me as a potential part of their propaganda. Vietnam changed me forever. I never understood what freedom was until I was a prisoner of war." After a pause, he said, "There's a lot more to the experience, but I would rather not talk about it now."

We went back to banking. Benny talked about how Citizens had grown and changed over the years. He talked about the successes and some of their failures. Citizens had won the Medallion Service Award, the most prominent national service award of its kind. It was the only bank that had ever won the award. But other than the award, his pride in the bank's accomplishments focused on people. He rattled off name after name and the person's achievements. He always mentioned how the person "made a difference" and that "everyone had the same purpose—to serve." Benny's voice brightened.

We arrived at a small park entrance and drove on a tight, two-lane road up to what appeared to be a picnic area. "We'll park here and start our hike. We'll be going about twelve miles up and back. Are you up for this, Jack?" Benny said with a smile. "I can't carry you out if you give out on me!"

"If I drop over, just leave me for the wolves," I said, pulling my backpack from the back of the Jeep.

I twisted the backpack over my shoulder, feeling the weight for the first time. "This is kind of heavy," I said.

"I tried to go light," he said. "On a twelve-mile hike, you want to be prepared. Here's your snake stick." He handed me one of two long pieces of what looked like tree limbs that had been tucked in the side of the Jeep's storage area.

"Snake sticks?" I asked.

"When we see a snake today, I'll show you how useful it is," he said with no hint of humor in his voice.

I had dealt with snakes most of my life, but that was at work. *At least the kind I worked with didn't bite,* I thought, trying to smile as we prepared to start up the trail.

We began the hike up a less-than-obvious dirt path that wound its way up the steep slope. The fog was still providing a dense cover, hiding the early morning sunlight from us. The thick shroud of trees and foliage made the side-to-side winding trail upward seem like something in a *Dracula* movie.

The fog appeared to be getting a little less ominous. Rays of light were breaking through. "Is the fog always this heavy?" I asked.

"Fog is fairly common in these mountains at this time of the year. We should walk out of it in about thirty minutes," he said. "I think we timed it perfectly. Some of the people who grew up in the hills believe that the number of heavy fogs—like this one—will predict how many big snowfalls they'll get in the winter."

"Is it true?" I asked, now panting from the climb.

"Only if you believe in Santa Claus and the Tooth Fairy," he said.

As we walked up the narrow path, I was nearly out of breath. The years of tobacco, liquor, and inactivity were creeping up on me. I started to sweat heavily, despite the cool morning air. Benny was walking ahead, almost thirty years older than me, without breaking a sweat or even showing any signs of difficulty in breathing.

We finally reached a clearing in the trees and the fog. We had walked for almost two hours with only two short breaks for me to catch my breath and get a drink of water. As we came to what he called a ridge, I saw a large outcropping of rocks ahead. The path forked with one path continuing a steep vertical ascent and the other leveling out near the rocks. "We're going to take a slight detour—this is the first scenic view of the day," he said. We walked back down a slight decline through an even thicker overhang of trees and leaves. It looked like a green tunnel, but there was a light ahead.

Stepping out into a clearing, I found myself standing on a huge rock. I realized what a scenic view was now.

I had never seen anything like it in my life.

{ *You're already who you*
need to be—be yourself. }

31. Where Are You Going?

"Where are you going?" I asked.

"To the edge," Benny said. "The view is much better."

"Be careful—you could fall," I said with an air of urgency. He seemed to be one step away from a deadly plunge into the mountain canyon.

"I love the view from here, Jack. You need to step closer to really appreciate it."

"I don't think so. I'm afraid of heights."

"You are?" he asked, still looking down into the gorge.

"Yeah," I said, stepping closer, but still leaving at least three feet of rock between me and the edge. "I've always had a fear of heights." As I peered over the brink I immediately stepped back.

"Is it heights you're afraid of," he said, turning toward me with a mischievous grin, "or falling?"

I had never thought about the difference. Still nervous, peering at an angle into the deep chasm, I began to chatter. "No—I'm afraid of heights. That's what I'm afraid of. I've always been afraid of heights. I don't know why. I'm even afraid of ladders. Anything that takes me off the ground makes me nervous."

"So you aren't afraid of falling—just being off the ground?"

"Yeah, I guess so," I said, taking another half-step backward.

"Does flying in a plane bother you? You're really off the ground when you fly."

"Well, not really, only when I look down."

"You're still on the ground here. This rock has been here a lot longer than you and me," he said, stomping his right foot down as if proving the worthiness of the rock's strength. "It'll probably be around a lot longer. The only bad thing that can happen to you would be if you fell off the rock . . . or a snake bit you."

I turned and looked slowly around to make sure a snake hadn't joined us. "Maybe you're right. Maybe I'm afraid of falling. I hadn't thought about the difference."

"Why don't you sit down on that rock," he said, pointing toward a large boulder to the right of the ledge. "You can get a good view without looking straight down—and you're still on solid ground. I want you to enjoy the view. It's changing every second."

The vista looked like something from an IMAX movie. The fog surrounded us. As it was lifting skyward, it allowed cracks of sunlight to shine into the deep canyon below. From my new vantage point I could get a sense of how steep the drop was into the crevice hundreds of feet below. A narrow, winding river was at the bottom, barely visible through the slowly breaking fog. I felt a wave of dizziness come over me.

"Amazing, isn't it?" Benny said, looking directly down into the canyon. "That's why getting here early is important. The fog rises quickly. You don't get this view very long. Everything appears to be changing, right in front of our eyes."

It was. You could see the fog lifting gradually and dissipating as it moved leisurely upward, vanishing as we watched. "I've never seen anything like this," I said.

"I've been here many times looking down into the same gorge at the same time of the morning yet it's always different. The gorge hasn't appreciably changed—it's a canyon, rocks, and a river—but the view is different. But you have to be awake to notice the difference."

Awake? *Being awake wasn't a problem,* I thought. My fears and worries kept me awake. I looked down into the gorge at the fog's methodical rise. I felt more comfortable perched on the rock, but I wondered what Benny's view, peering from the edge, was like.

Benny turned away, facing the gorge less than a foot from the edge. "Thirty minutes ago, you couldn't see anything except the fog. You wouldn't have been able to realize the depth of the canyon or that a river cut its way through at the bottom. If you wait another thirty minutes you'll be able to see the railroad track that runs along the rim of the river. You can even see the white water the river churns out from pouring through the slim channel. But as the day passes, the sun will start to set behind the mountains, darkening the gorge. The view changes again."

"If you came over here and stood with your eyes closed, so you couldn't see down into the gorge, would it get rid of your fear of falling?" he asked. A smile started to form on his face.

"No," I said with a definitive tone. "I would still know the cliff edge is there."

"What if you didn't know you were close to the edge? Would that change how you felt?"

"Yeah, but I *do* know. I can see the drop-off!"

"Well, unless you make a foolish error in walking or you choose to jump off, a fall is very unlikely."

"That's why I'm not going near the edge," I said. "I'm playing it safe."

"But you're missing out on a great view," he said, looking back over the ledge.

"I'll take your word for it," I said, laughing.

• • •

"What's the worst thing that can happen?" Benny asked, still standing near the edge.

It was another question that I had never spent time thinking about. "Dying," I said. "What could be worse?"

"Is that the worst thing that can happen to you, Jack?" Benny asked. His back was turned toward me.

I thought for a moment before responding. "No, there are things worse than my own death. The death of one of my children or seeing them injured or suffering would be worse." I paused again. "If I were paralyzed and unable to move—that would be worse than death to me. You know, Benny, I had never thought about some of the things we've talked about."

"That's one of the challenges of living a fast-paced life. We don't have time to be meditative, to think calmly. We surrender our lives to our schedule and don't leave time to consider what we've done and what we intend to do—now. But open spaces and a slower life can bring you that."

"The only time I had to think was when I was driving. But my cell phone rings constantly," I said, laughing.

"We all need time to think," he said. "Thinking is a choice. You have to be awake, present, to think the right thoughts."

I thought about the thoughts that kept me awake at night. "My problem is turning off my brain—it seems like it just keeps churning," I said, "even when I don't want it to."

"I was the same, but I learned to discipline my thoughts. At one point in my life I was faced with having little to do except think."

"In Vietnam?" I asked.

"Yes. It's almost funny that I had to go half way around the world and be kept in a cage to find some time to think," he said. He turned and walked back to the rock I was sitting on and leaned against an adjacent boulder. "When I was a POW, I came face to face with a lot of my fears. I asked myself a lot of questions. While it was an experience that could not be termed as good by any means, I learned from my time there."

"I could've never survived something like that," I said, trying to picture myself in a POW camp. "Being trapped and held captive against your will had to be something that was worse than death."

"In many ways it was. But I discovered what freedom was," he said.

"That's something only a POW could probably appreciate."

"No, I think there are a lot of people who are prisoners and don't realize it."

I wasn't sure where Benny was going with this.

"People build their own prisons. I've met a lot of people who are trapped in a prison of their own making—a prisoner of their mind. They refuse to change. Their fears blind them. They may not be in a jail cell, but in many ways it's worse. They're never fully awake to reality. It's almost like they're sleepwalking. I was one of those people before I was a POW," he said.

Worried that he saw me as a sleepwalker, I brought the subject back to his experience as a POW. "What kind of prison did they keep you in?"

"It wasn't anything like a prison or jail here—I spent most of my time in a bamboo cage."

"Did they ever let you out?"

"No, there were a limited number of jailers, so they kept us locked down in the cages."

"How did you survive?"

"I survived because I remained *awake*," he said. I realized being awake was more than having your eyes opened.

"I knew I couldn't leave. Being rescued wasn't a reality. So I had to find a way to live as a prisoner and keep my hope alive."

"Did they try to brainwash you?"

"That's an interesting term—brainwash. Actually, they were trying to clutter my mind, not clean it. A confused mind is a fearful mind."

"But weren't you afraid?"

"Yes!" he said, smiling at the question. "That's what I fought every moment I was there. My worst enemy wasn't my captors—it was fear. It can paralyze you—it can stop your mind from being awake and alert. You stop seeing things as they are. You're blinded by horrors real and imagined. Doubt destroys your hope.

"But a Buddhist monk named Chi Mai helped save me. He helped me learn to stay awake."

"Was he a supporter of the North Vietnamese?" I asked.

"I asked him the same question. His response was, 'I'm human.' I trusted him after I heard him say that. The NVA accepted him as he was, detached from the war, and allowed him to bring some food to us POWs. As a Buddhist monk, he didn't present any challenge to them, but they watched him. His visits were brief and didn't allow much time to talk. He spoke fluent English, but because the North Vietnamese were suspicious that he was a spy, talking with him was limited. Conversations that you and I could have in two minutes took us months. I listened closely to everything he said. I also thought about what I would say. Words were precious between us, and I didn't want to waste any."

"How did he guide you with so little time to talk?"

"He asked questions."

32. What Is Freedom?

"WHAT IS FREEDOM?" Benny asked.

"Being able to do what I want, when I want to," I answered. "No one having control over me." It was an honest answer, something I had been thinking about during our conversation.

"That was probably how I would have answered before I was a POW. But there's much more to being free than being free from someone else's oppression. It was the first question Chi Mai asked me. Imagine having nothing else to do or think about for weeks except that simple question. That gave me some focus."

It was difficult for me to imagine the agony of being locked in a cage—that loss of freedom. With nothing else to do but think, fear could take over your thoughts.

"I thought about what made people free. I concluded it was the power to choose what they thought," he said. "It was almost a month before I could tell him my answer. I knew I would only have a couple of seconds, so when I had my chance I said, 'My choice.' I expected him to say 'That's right' or at least nod his head to acknowledge the answer. Instead, he asked, 'What binds you?' He left, leaving me with another question to ponder. At first, I thought of being caged in the prison. I thought about my captors. Then, I thought of what I had lost. I realized that the desire to go where

I pleased remained inside of me. I directed my thoughts. I found I could adapt them and find my own motivation and will. These were all choices I made—not someone else."

"That's amazing," I said, soaking up every word.

"On his next visit one of the jailers was standing nearby. When Chi Mai handed me a piece of bread, I looked at him and said as quietly as I could, 'Nothing binds me.' He smiled and said, 'You're awake.' It was a wonderful moment—I still had my freedom, but I had to exercise it and keep my mind active. Knowing I could choose my thoughts and responses kept me free inside, even though I was sitting in a cage that didn't allow me to stand up straight. Freedom is seeing things as they are. As long as I was awake, I was free."

"Why wouldn't seeing things as they are depress you and make you more fearful?"

"Being awake meant that I still had a choice to make in life. By having a choice, change was possible. Change gave me hope, Jack. We create our own destinies. The reason I survived as a POW was because I never surrendered my mind, never turned my destiny over to my captors. The other person who helped me was my jailer."

"Your jailer?" I was stunned.

"I learned to understand the world from his point of view. Everyone has a different view. Everything a person sees goes through filters of prejudice, hopes, and dreams, and, of course, fears, jealousy, and desires. We think we see the world as it is. But really, what we see is the world as we want to see it. His view was much different from mine. When he looked at me, he saw a man who came uninvited to his country to harm him and his world. It was easy for him to be a jailer. I was being punished because I was his enemy."

"So how did he help you?" I asked.

"We learned to understand each other and had a deep respect for each other. We understood each other's roles. We also realized that we were similar in more ways than we were different. Saying we were friends wouldn't be correct—we respected each other's differences."

"But how did that help you survive?"

"It helped to remove the hate. Other than fear, hatred toward the North Vietnamese was slowly killing me. The hate made me irrational and took away my ability to discipline my thoughts. They tortured me. I saw them torture and kill other prisoners like me. Hate was easy. I couldn't change what they did while I was in a cage. But respecting my jailer's perspective took away some of the hate."

"I doubt if I could ever feel that way toward someone who was holding me captive. I could never stop hating someone who was my jailer."

"It wasn't his fault that I was a POW. He had a job to do. He was harsh in his treatment—but after some time, he changed his view of prisoners. Then, he changed his practices."

"You learned so much in some of the worst conditions a human could be subjected to," I said. "I'm sure those were things you could never forget."

"But I did forget," he said.

• • •

Benny paused, shaking his head slowly from side to side. "I learned so many lessons there. You would think that an experience like that would always remain with you, but somehow I forgot what I learned. Once I returned home and the years wore down my memory, it seemed like a dream. It took the loss of my son to rediscover those truths. Ben's death reawakened me from my sleepwalking."

"I've learned a lot in the past couple of days about myself. I hope I won't forget."

"We lose what we fail to use," he said. "We're going to have to start back up the mountain to stay on our schedule. Are you ready?"

"Sure, I'm ready. The break was good. I just might make it to the top."

"Before we go, do you want to see the gorge from the edge?" he asked. "The view is really something you should see."

"I'll pass right now—maybe some other day. But I'll watch for snakes," I said, smiling as I slid off my rock seat. We walked past the fork in the path where we had detoured to visit the rock ledge. The climb became much steeper. I was out of breath, but had more questions about his time in Vietnam. "You said they kept you as a prisoner to use you for propaganda. How did they use you?" I asked when I had enough breath available.

"After I was shot down, I was in bad shape. I had broken my leg when I ejected from the plane and parachuted into the jungle. In the camp, they spent some time and effort keeping me alive. The treatment wasn't humanitarian. There was a reason. They wanted to use POWs in video tapes to talk about the war. It was their way of trying to turn the American public against the war effort. The North Vietnamese were well schooled in propaganda. All they had to do was break us down to the point where we would read their scripts and talk on camera. Having an officer in captivity also gave them a bargaining chip in negotiations. They viewed me as having some relative value in this context. So they kept me alive."

Benny paused and took a sip of water, seeing my struggle to keep up with his pace. I had noticed he had a slight limp. *The injuries from Vietnam had never left him,* I thought.

"After giving me enough medical care to ensure I would live, the guards kept me in solitary confinement for over two months, almost totally in the dark," Benny continued. "They pulled me out one day, and I thought they were going to kill me. That was my low point as a POW. Looking back, it was part of their tactics to wear a person down."

"After taking me out of the pen—as we called solitary—they changed their ploy. One guard spoke very good English. He told us to call him Tom. They were playing good cop, bad cop. He was the good cop. Having us call him Tom was a ploy to Americanize him. He had lived in the U.S. for several years. He had spent time in American schools. He knew what was going on in the States. He would tell us his interpretation of bits of news that gave the impression of an America in disarray. Every now and then, he would show us newspaper clippings to try to validate his point. 'They don't support you at home,' he would say. He would also remind us of the good life we were missing. Of course, the main objective was to make us feel that we were forgotten. You could tell he enjoyed telling us, 'No one cares about you—you're on your own.'

"Tom was very war hardened. He lived for revenge. He had evidently lost his family in a bombing raid early in the war. Even though he knew more about Americans than any of the other jailers he hated us. The dehumanizing process he led continued for months. Several of my comrades in the camp broke down and gave the North Vietnamese a tape. They would get much more favorable treatment— for a time. Then, suddenly they would disappear. Tom would tell us they were transferred to a better camp, with running water and the freedom to walk in a park. This miracle camp was waiting for us if we complied. He kept reminding us, 'All we had to do was talk.'"

As Benny spoke I pictured myself in the same conditions. I would have been one of the first to break. "Who could blame a solider for breaking?" I asked.

"That's true. How could you blame a solider that was alone and under this type of pressure for breaking? You can't. What we were being subjected to was mind games of the most extreme order. However, for me, I decided not to break. I was not going to surrender the only things I had left that kept me alive and gave me hope— my mind and my actions."

You could hear a resolve I hadn't heard in his voice. It was not pride. Benny stated it as a fact; it was something indisputable to him. I listened closely.

"We had little contact with other POWs. They kept us separated as much as possible. In one brief interchange with one of my fellow prisoners, I was told there was no magical prison camp. He told me once the North Vietnamese got what they wanted the POW was executed."

The tone of his voice was hardening, just as he had been hardened by his experience years ago.

"I knew it was true. It made more sense to me than the story Tom was telling. I had already seen what they did in villages to people who they thought opposed them. If they killed their own people so thoughtlessly, why should an American POW expect to be treated any better? This was the beginning of my time there, when I spent much time thinking about being awake. I was determined to be free, to live on my terms."

When I heard him say the word "free," I thought I knew what happened. Benny found a way to escape. The jailer probably helped him. "So you were planning an escape?" I asked.

"Getting out of the camp alive didn't look possible," he said. "That was the reality of the situation. I accepted the fact I was probably going to die in the camp for refusing to give them what they wanted. I accepted that they were in control of me physically—but I wasn't going to let them govern my mind. That was mine. If I was going to die there, it would be on my terms, not theirs."

Hearing him say that he accepted his own death was chilling. I thought about how I had been afraid to simply look over a ledge a few minutes earlier. Falling wasn't likely, yet I had been so afraid I missed out on seeing what I knew was something special. Here was a man who had summoned the courage to face his own death. I was embarrassed.

As we resumed walking after scaling a near-vertical slope, he stopped to give me a chance to catch my breath. As he spoke, I envied his bravery.

"The first thing I did was look at the conditions I was living under. Almost all POWs in the camp were counting the number of days till a holiday or a birthday. It was a way of coping, but I could see what it was doing to them. They would place their hopes and dreams on being freed by that date, visualizing reuniting with family and friends. Almost every brief conversation I had with any of my fellow POWs had a date in it. 'We'll be out of here by Christmas in sixty-six days,' they would say. Tom made it more difficult, reminding everyone of what was happening in the States on holidays, bringing press clippings to us showing couples enjoying the Fourth of July or a family gathered around a Christmas tree. He told us that our wives or girlfriends had likely moved on and had new lovers. He would ask, 'Do you think they remember you?' The date a person chose to believe was the date they would be freed would come and go. Nothing changed."

"A calendar as part of a psychological ploy . . . " I said.

"I realized projecting hopes on a calendar was what killed most of my comrades. Every time one of the dates passed, you could see their heart break. To me it was a test of how long I could last—testing the strength of my will. Every moment I was alive was a victory. My purpose was to survive and live another second, not just another day. I silently celebrated the passing of time."

We resumed walking up another severe grade. Of all the pain a POW endured, I never thought about the agony of a broken heart. But something was very different, or indifferent, about Benny's approach. It sounded as though he had hardened himself so his heart would not break. It was a tactic I had used for years, so I understood it. The path widened enough so I could walk beside him. I asked, "Did you try to get rid of your emotions—so your heart couldn't be broken?"

"My heart was very much alive. It was part of me. But I wasn't going to tell myself that happiness was just around the corner. I found ways to be happy. I would make sure I smiled, especially in front of Tom."

"Smiling?"

"Chi Mai, on one of his brief visits, said to me, 'Smile.' I asked him how? He said, 'Be you.' I thought about it. The only people who ever smiled were the more hostile jailers who enjoyed seeing us tortured. It was difficult at first. But then I remembered that if I was awake and free, I should be able to show it outwardly. Smiling was a choice—my choice. It wasn't controlled by the conditions I faced on the outside, but what I felt inside. I practiced finding something to smile about, as often as possible. I would see a flower blooming or the sun rising and setting and remind myself beauty still surrounded me, even in a cage. It cost me dearly—I was tortured for smiling. But it was worth it."

"You were tortured for smiling."

"Yeah, hard to imagine, but it drove my captors crazy. I'm sure they thought I was crazy, but smiling was something I chose to do. My heart, just like my mind, was mine. They weren't going to take it from me. As they carried me back into the cage after they tortured me I would smile the biggest smile I could. That is when I connected with the jailer. He knew I wasn't going to break. I had a purpose, just like him."

The rigidity and coldness in Benny's tone was a sharp contrast to our talk on the lake. "How could you maintain that level of concentration?"

"I had my moments. But I knew one thing was a certainty. The POWs who failed to survive died of a broken heart and spirit. They allowed fear to rule them and misguided hope to betray them. Doubt smothered them. Unrealistic expectations can kill. I saw it happen—every day."

"But I thought you said hope kept you alive?"

"I did, but it was a realistic hope. To survive, I pictured the worst. I visualized my own death. I came to terms with dying. I decided what I would be thinking when I died. How I would shut my eyes and exhale my last breath with a smile on my face. By practicing how to die, I found I was able to live in the moment. Once I stopped fearing death, I was able to live."

This was so different from the Benny I thought I knew. He sounded cold and calculating.

"You had lost all hope of living?" I asked.

"No! That's not what I said," Benny spoke quickly and loudly, "I never gave up hope. I was living moment by moment to keep hope alive. Coming to terms with the reality of the situation meant having a living hope, a hope that wasn't unrealistic, and a hope that wouldn't break my heart. I asked myself, *Who am I?* I was alive and changing. Then, *Where am I?* I was in a place I couldn't control or change. I then asked myself, *Where was I going?* Nowhere at that moment, but I didn't need to leave to be alive. As long as I could choose my thoughts, I was still in charge of my life. That gave me hope."

In that moment I saw something move on the path ahead of us—it was a snake. Without saying a word, Benny held out his right hand to stop. He stepped forward holding his stick in his right hand, keeping a distance from the reptile. Without touching the snake, he made several brief raps on the ground with the stick. The snake moved quickly, slithering through the dirt in an *S* pattern off of the path. Looking back at me he said, "Okay, the snake is gone" and stepped forward past the place the snake had been. I was still frozen. "It's okay, Jack. It's more afraid of us than we are of it."

"I doubt that," I said, moving cautiously on the far side of the path from where the snake had disappeared.

• • •

After trudging up the hill for what seemed like an eternity, Benny asked if I wanted to take a break. "Sure," I said, "if you need one."

Benny laughed at my out-of-breath humor and said, "There's a level patch not too far ahead."

The path, or what you could call a path, was rutted from runoff pouring down the slope. *We are climbing more than walking,* I thought, making my way upward to what I hoped would be the last break before we reached the peak.

I was simply trying to keep up with Benny and take part in the intermittent conversation we were having as we hiked the mountain. But now, I was intently focused on looking for a snake. I was exhausted mentally and physically. "We'll stop up here," he said. A slight opening in the foliage allowed some light in. The level area Benny had referred to was barely more than ten feet square. A rock jutted out directly above us.

"How close are we to the top?" I asked, after finding enough breath to speak.

"Not too far," he said. "Are you okay?"

"Yeah," I said, trying to keep from panting.

"That's good," he said. "What do you think of the hike so far?"

"I've enjoyed it," I said, looking toward the winding path we had just navigated. "This hike has definitely inspired me to get back in the gym." After another pause to get enough wind, I said, "There's nothing like this in Philly—for sure." Turning around as I spoke, I saw something on the edge of the rock directly behind us. Trying not to show how scared I was, I asked in a near-whisper, "Is that what I think it is?" Almost directly at my eye level, a snake was hanging over the edge of the rock overhang. It was only a couple of feet away from Benny.

"I see what you're talking about," Benny said in a soft, calm tone. His height allowed him to get a much better view but also put him in a stare down with the creature. "Don't worry," he said, turning to look back at me.

"What do you mean, don't worry?" I asked, puzzled that he wasn't moving away.

Smiling, he said, "It isn't what you think it is, Jack."

33. What Is It?

"WHAT IS IT?" I asked, still in a state of panic. I could see a snake within striking distance of Benny's head.

"It's a piece of rope," he said, smiling from ear to ear.

"A piece of rope?" I asked, stepping carefully toward the object. "How stupid am I?"

"It's probably something another hiker dropped," he said, reaching over and picking up the cord.

"I thought it was a snake," I said.

"Our minds will do that," he said.

"I'm sorry. Seeing the snake down the trail scared me more than I thought it did.

"It takes some getting used to—being here in the woods is a lot different than Philadelphia," he said.

"That it is," I said.

"You did say something that fits in with what we've been talking about, Jack. You asked me, 'What is it?' That's one of the most important questions you can ask."

"I thought it was a snake," I said, still trying to cover my embarrassment.

"You were looking for a snake, and your mind told you, 'I see a snake.' When you question your thoughts and ask, 'What is it?'

you begin a process of searching for the truth—for reality. It's part of living a life of questions."

As he was speaking, my mind was busily searching for the last time I had asked the question "What is it?" I couldn't remember.

• • •

We continued to trek what Benny said was the last portion of our climb to the peak. I was irritated. I was tired of hearing everything that was wrong with me. As we walked the now winding but much-less-strenuous passage, I asked about something that disturbed me the most—the idea that everything changes. I wanted to prove him wrong.

"What about time and space?" I asked. "How do they change?"

"That's a great question," Benny said, slowing his pace to allow me to walk closer. "Time and space change because of what fills them. I'm not a scientist by any means, but from what I understand even the space between us has a presence. It's like radio waves beamed around us—because you can't see them doesn't mean they aren't there. And they change, just like us!"

"Change is what makes living so difficult," I said. I was feeling sensitive because Benny knew I had trouble with impermanence.

"What makes life difficult is avoiding change. But it's unavoidable. If we don't accept change, we're not acknowledging reality. I know the dilemma, Jack. We want things to stay the same. We want to hold on to what we have. We seek happiness in having more— more money, more power, more status. We reduce life to a competition and spend our time building sand castles, thinking they are made of stone. We're killing time—the time of our lives. Go back to the question 'What's your intention?' What are you working for? If it's having more than you could possibly need, then you'll never be happy. You'll always want more."

"What's wrong with having more?" I asked, feeling bruised and argumentative. "Having more makes you more secure. I still can't see why trying to give your family more is not a good thing?"

"What's your intention, Jack? To give your family more than what's necessary? Is that the right intention?"

"Having more is better!" I nearly exclaimed, using the reserve energy my frustration supplied. "You can have some bad luck and lose everything. Someone can come along and take away what you've earned." My frustration was turning into anger. I was mad at myself for not being able to defend my life better than this with an old man.

"But if your family doesn't need the added things you're bringing them, how will they understand what it is truly essential in life? They'll never be satisfied."

Before I responded I thought about my major grievances against Tina, Jessica, and Joshua. I had said to them repeatedly, "You don't appreciate what you have, what I've given you." I could see now it was my fault. I had tried to impart my lust for more onto them. I never talked to them about *their* needs or wants. "I've never thought about it that way," I said, still thinking about how I had inflicted my world on theirs. My anger was squelched. I felt defeated.

"It's what we all face. We create our destiny. We're the authors of our own book of life. We're responsible, each of us, for what we do. It's the only thing we really own in life—our thoughts, our actions, and what we've done."

Hearing "what we've done" reminded me of something Chad had said. "How do you *deal* with greed?" I asked, careful to not indict myself with any more comment.

"I remember there are a lot worse poisons than a snake bite!" he said, poking his stick ahead on the path. "Greed is a vice best left to itself. It's part of a circle of suffering. I try to be aware of its power so I won't slip into it."

"What's a circle of suffering?"

"The worst mistakes we make in our lives are typically when we refuse to change course, even when we know we're going in the wrong direction. We repeat the same mistakes, even though we know better. We're going in circles. That's where we create our own suffering. The worst pains in life are the ones we inflict on ourselves."

"How can you say that?" I asked. "You didn't ask to be captured and held as a POW? I didn't create most of the bad things in my life."

"When I was in Vietnam, I had the same thoughts. One day Chi Mai told me the story of his escape from China. He walked hundreds of miles through some of the highest mountains in the world with only his cloak and a pair of sandals. I asked how he could walk so far in such extreme conditions. He said, 'One step at a time.' It finally dawned on me: We create our own destiny. I owned my life and what I would do in that moment. My purpose wasn't outside of me—it was inside of me. Looking outside of myself for answers had given me nothing but pain. But once I got home I forgot that. Until Ben died. I had tried to find answers in my career, possessions, lovers, or any other thing I could find that distracted me. I hated others for having more and myself for failing to get what they had. I know from experience, it's a very real circle. Yet, I stayed in the same rut, fearing that my pain would intensify if I tried to change."

"How did you break out of the circle and change?" I asked.

"I let go."

• • •

"*How can I let go?*" I asked. I was growing agitated by the idea of a life of less instead of my life of more. *It's easy for him being old and rich to tell me to be satisfied with less,* I thought to myself. "Letting go goes against reason," I said. "Everyone wants more."

"And that makes it reasonable?" he asked.

"Maybe I haven't got enough yet," I said, tired of the climb and the turn of the conversation.

"That, my friend, is the problem. Until you let go, you're never going to be satisfied. Letting go of our attachments is the only way to find any real peace." He stopped in his tracks and looked at me. "You can't escape from life, no matter how hard you try, Jack."

"I'm not trying to escape," I said angrily, hearing the personalization of his comments. Now I was tired and angry. I personalized my retort. "You don't know everything about me."

"I wouldn't assume I do. I'm sharing my experience. But you and I aren't so different," he said.

"You and I are completely different," I said assuredly, keeping my head down as I walked, not wanting him to see my expression. I was mad, and I knew I couldn't disguise it very well.

"In some ways we are different, but in more ways we're similar," he said in a reassuring tone. "I wouldn't dare to try to impose my life on yours, but I'll tell you what I've learned. The problems in *my* life sprang from wanting more of things I didn't need. Nothing worked for me. This was even after spending years as a POW and losing my son. You would think those events would have been incredibly loud wake-up calls for me—they weren't. I dug myself deeper and deeper into a rut, doing the same thing over and over again."

"How did you get out of the rut? Just letting go doesn't sound reasonable to me," I asked, trying to calm my obvious frustration.

"I remembered," he said. "I remembered the lessons I had learned from Chi Mai. He said, 'If you fight life, you lose. Just be.' Living is a miracle, not to be wasted, but to be lived. Even in a prison camp or after you lose a child. I had a choice—to be or not to be. I let go. I let go of the hate, anger, and self-pity. I chose *to be*."

"You aren't me," I said. "That's for sure."

"Be yourself. If you aren't being yourself, you aren't being natural—life won't seem to fit you. Your life will always have friction and a lack of balance, and that can destroy a person."

"You really believe that?" I asked.

"No, I don't believe it—I know it."

• • •

"Where do I want to be?"

The path up the hill had now narrowed, and it was harder to talk, which gave me time to think. The exchanges between the two of us had helped to bring me back to a question I had not been able to answer. *Where* was always important to me; location was always part of my plans. If I was able to remove some of the attachments the question wasn't as difficult.

"We're almost there," Benny said as we moved to a much more open expanse of the mountainside that allowed the sun to slice down through the thick woods, splashing light on the trail. I was happy to hear those words. The tree cover that had blanketed our passage up the mountain was claustrophobic. The physical exertion was taking its toll on my thought processing. The more I thought about my attachments, the more I realized that they were not going to be that easy to disconnect. The attachments helped me, I rationalized. They kept me on course and made me feel secure. Walking further, I asked myself, *What if he's right?* I looked up from the dirt path. As my mind mulled over my inner quarrel, the very real weight of my lifestyle was taking its toll. I was doing my best to keep up with this much older man and failing. He was like a machine. No heavy breathing—he appeared to be enjoying every step. The only time I was able to stay close to his pace was when he slowed, allowing me to catch up. His mind was equal to his physical condition. I knew I was smart—always a step ahead of others. But his thoughts appeared to always be a step ahead of mine, as though he knew what I was going to say before I could speak. *This was not a job interview,* I thought. We had passed that many words ago. Whether I got the job or not mattered less to me now as I struggled to walk the last sharp incline before entering the clearing ahead—this was about survival. Who would live to tell the tale—the old Jack or the new Jack? I was beginning to understand that I could not go much farther in my life with the baggage I was carrying. I had to let go.

My life depended on it.

· · ·

The clearing in the trees allowed a cascade of light to shine onto a field of grass on the peak of the mountain. *I made it,* I thought, enjoying the victory over the mountain. The path had now leveled completely. I noticed the difference in the appearance of the trees and the foliage. "How high up are we?" I asked.

"We're closing in on almost 4,000 feet above sea level. The temperature is much nicer here on top, don't you think?"

A breeze helped cool down the physical and emotional duress fanning my frustration. A tall wooden structure loomed ahead.

"This is the old fire tower. They don't use it anymore, but you can get a great view from the top. Let's put our gear down and make a climb to the top of the tower while we have the energy," Benny said.

After placing our backpacks at the base of the structure, we started to climb up the steep, narrow stairs. The condition of the stairway didn't help my fear of heights. The planks of wood on the steps were in poor condition. Hearing the creak of each step, I wondered if the next one would be my last. I visualized the local newspaper running a story on my death: Fat Philly Banker Dies in Fall from Fire Tower.

I walked as lightly as I could and joined Benny, who was waiting on me at the top. The view was stunning. The sky was perfectly blue, resting on top of the rolling mountains. The tower had a walkway around all four sides, enclosed by a railing. Benny described the direction and points of interest from each side as we circled the deck. Stopping at each vantage point, I made sure I was standing back safely from the railing.

"I'm sorry I was so harsh when we were talking earlier," I said, after he had finished telling me about the surroundings. "It really is tough to teach old dogs new tricks. I'm living proof."

"No need to apologize, Jack. I appreciate you putting up with an old guy who talks too much."

"Please, keep talking. I'm learning a lot about myself," I said. "I'm struggling with some of the ideas you've shared. Honestly, it hurts to look at myself from a different viewpoint. I'm not a happy person."

"You know who can change that, don't you?" he asked, comfortably leaning over the rickety railing.

Benny looked out in the distance. "Things are clearer, now that the fog has lifted."

"Yeah, they are. But I have a question," I said, preparing to open a part of my past that I kept buried.

It was a question I had never asked before.

34. Why Do I Hate Who I Am?

"Why do I hate who I am?" I asked, remaining a safe distance from the rail. I was feeling the same nervous tension I had experienced earlier at the cliff. "I think we can both come to the same conclusion—I hate me."

"It's what you've done that you hate," he said. "It's guilt. I was the same way."

"I really don't believe that—you can't imagine what I've done. You're just saying that trying to make a fat boy from Philly feel better about himself. I feel like I can't change."

"Jack, look around. You're still seeing fog! From my vantage point the world looks big to me—full of opportunity," he said looking out at the vista of green mountains and blue sky. "You can change," he said, pausing and standing erect as if to gain an even better viewpoint. "But there's really only one right path for you to choose—your path."

"I'm not the same as you. I could've never done the things you've done, been as strong as you've been."

"We all have a different life—a different path to walk. I could never have lived your life either. My guilt about things that I had done—or not done—smoldered inside for years, burning me alive from the inside out. I couldn't sleep. I did reprehensible things.

I wasn't on the right path—and I knew it. But I was afraid to change."

"That sounds like me—but whatever mistakes you've made could never top mine," I said.

"Jack, let's not compete to see who's a bigger jerk," he said, chuckling and patting me on the back. "Let's go down and get some lunch. We still have quite a hike back down the mountain. We're only halfway there!"

• • •

We unpacked our food and sat at the bottom of the tower on an outcropping of rocks, looking westward. We ate in a comfortable quiet—something I couldn't recall experiencing. I enjoyed the food, and following Benny's lead, I took my time eating. Even though it was just sandwiches, chips, and water, it tasted better than anything I had recently tasted. It was even better than Ann's peach cobbler. Meals had been obstacles for me. They took up valuable time, and I felt guilty piling more calories onto an already bloated body. To make up for the thousands of calories my drive-thru trips to McDonald's cost me during the day, I changed my tactic after work. Instead of eating I focused on drinking—another poor choice in my unhealthy life.

Benny reached in one of the pockets of his backpack and said, "Look what I found!" It was a small sandwich bag holding several cookies. "These are homemade—we have to eat them—or Ann will get upset." He slid open the clear packet and held them in front of me.

I shook my head and said, "No thanks," but he smiled and kept the cookies in front of me.

"You deserve a reward—you've done a lot of hiking," he said.

"Okay, you twisted my arm." I pulled a cookie from the bag and took a small bite, instead of putting the entire cookie in my mouth, as usual.

"How do you like it here?" he asked.

"It's really nice," I said, looking up at the trees encircling the clear area near the tower. A breeze kept the leaves and limbs moving. "Is the climb down as difficult as the climb up?" I asked.

"No, but we want to take our time. You can miss a lot letting your momentum carry you."

"I know what you're saying," I said, smiling, taking the last bite of my dessert. Everything Benny said seemed to have a purpose. Knowing this, I reminded myself to listen more intently and think about what he was saying. "Momentum" was a force in my life. Stopping was difficult once I was rolling.

"We still have a few minutes before we need to head back down. I've been thinking about what you said." He paused and turned toward me. "I learned the hard way that we can't fake our way through life, pretending to be someone else. It was a tough lesson, but I finally understood the idea of being comfortable in my own skin."

Those words fit me perfectly. I never felt comfortable being me. I wanted to tell him but stopped myself. I could tell he had a more direct point for me to consider.

"My father was very successful in business. He owned a lumber mill and was very wealthy. But he was never happy. I saw it from an early age. He was happiest when he stayed in his own element—by himself—hiding away from life. But he rarely allowed himself that privilege."

"My father was like that," I said. I thought about how I lived. I was so confused I couldn't remember who the real Jack Oliver was.

Benny said, "My father wasn't aggressive, but he felt the need to be tough in his business dealings. He was quiet, but he believed he had to be outspoken to demand respect. He was peaceful, but his inner conflict made him angry and frustrated. So he drank to try to find some peace within. Of course, that wasn't an answer. It made his worst traits more evident. Some people get docile when they're drunk. My father became violent, wanting to fight. We had several scuffles, especially once I grew tall enough to look him in the eye. I tried to avoid confronting him, but that was impossible. He wanted a fight, fueled it with alcohol, and went down the wrong path."

"My father was an alcoholic," I said, remembering my own confrontations. I paused and continued, "You said your father had your life planned out and wanted you to be an attorney."

"Yes, he felt like it was his duty as a father. And when I rebelled, he wouldn't speak to me anymore," he said.

"The same kind of thing happened with me," I said. "My father was a plumber. He owned his own business and wanted me to be his apprentice and take over for him when he quit."

"I can't see you as a plumber," Benny said with a huge smile.

"And I can't see you as a lawyer," I said, now sharing a smile for the first time in several hours.

"But he could," Benny said, slowly repositioning his view toward the westward mountains. "He died while I was a POW. The North Vietnamese looked for those things to take advantage of. Tom enjoyed telling me the news. He said, 'Your father's dead. He shot himself. He was a coward—disgraced by you.'"

"The bastard," I said. It struck me that Benny's father had committed suicide. How could someone rich and successful do something like that? He had it all.

"At first, his death had the opposite effect on me. Instead of being mad at the North Vietnamese, I piled all of the blame on myself. I wanted to die. I thought it was my fault."

The memories of the pain I had endured trying to understand my own father's death seeped back in. "My father committed suicide," I said, breathing life into a past I had buried. "He jumped off the Ben Franklin Bridge. He was depressed. Nothing seemed to go right for him. He gave up on living."

"I'm sorry, Jack," he said.

"It made me change. I became more career oriented. It really fueled my career—it gave me motivation to be a success. I never wanted to be like him," I said with a grim reverence for my past. A weight seemed to be lifted from my shoulders as I told Benny of my experience.

"It's usually those points in time that cause us to change—cause and effect," he said. "But even if you change course, if you aim in the wrong direction, you're on the wrong path, and everything starts repeating itself. That was me."

"What do you mean?"

"At first, I was depressed, blaming myself for my father's death. Then, I turned the anger outward. I started to feel better—I had a purpose. I wanted to find a way to kill every North Vietnamese I could, especially Tom. I valued my life very little. I plotted and planned. I looked for opportunities. Over time, without any prospect to make my fantasy a reality, I became depressed. Those were dark days as a prisoner. The anger turned inward. The hate began to destroy me."

"What did you do?"

"If I hadn't had the help of Chi Mai, I would have died. I was ready to give up. He told me, 'Father—not you. You're alive—live now.'"

"So you were mad at your father?" I asked.

"I was until I realized my anger wouldn't change anything. All those emotions did little except to deepen my depression. What I did have was an opportunity—to learn from his life and death."

"What did you learn?"

"To live my life, not someone else's," he said.

The life I had planned was built around goals, I thought. The goals were part of my attempt to bury the past, especially my father. "I don't know how to do that," I said.

"You can't plan it, because the world will keep changing. If you're on the right path, you'll still have challenges, but you'll know you're on course even when the winds of change blow you off course. You won't look in the mirror and see a hypocrite."

Those words were like a bomb going off inside my head. How many times had I looked in the mirror and not recognized the person I saw? "I understand that," I said. "But how do you find that right path?"

"There's no map. It's always inside of us. We have to look inside to connect to who we really are."

"What if you're afraid to look?"

"Then you know you must look deeper—past your fears," he said. After allowing me to think for a moment about his response, he said, "Let's start back down the mountain. There's another place I want you to see."

35. What Are You Waiting For?

"WHAT ARE YOU WAITING FOR?" Benny yelled. I could barely hear him.

We had hiked downward for over one hour at a much faster pace than our ascent. I heard what I thought was rushing water.

It was a waterfall.

"C'mon, Jack, I'm getting wet!" he shouted at the top of his lungs. The path led us to what appeared to be a partial cavelike walkway that went under the waterfall. I was uncomfortable again.

"Okay, give me a minute," I said, doing my best to summon the courage to walk under the crashing water. I leaned over to avoid hitting my head on the rocks. Benny was almost doubled over, making his way in front of me to the other side. I carefully planted each foot on the wet, slippery rocks, afraid I would slip and spill toward the bottom of the falls.

"See, it wasn't so bad," he said as I made my last few steps away from the falls.

"You didn't tell me I was going to hike under Niagara Falls today," I said, taking off my backpack and wiping the water from my face and neck. The water actually felt refreshing after the brisk hike.

"I told you it was different than the cliff," he said. "You should see it after a hard rain. That's even more fun."

"I'll take your word on it," I said. "That may be more fun than I could handle."

"Let's walk over here, and you'll have a better view of what you walked under," he said. I followed him through some brush and suddenly found myself at the edge of the minigorge looking straight down into the churning pool of water at the base of the fall.

"There is a cliff—I should've known," I said, moving back from the edge slowly.

"We used to jump off this when I was in college," he said smiling, able to speak in a more normal tone. "As you can see, it's a little ways down."

"That's more than a little way," I said. "I want to know who had the bright idea of jumping off in the first place."

"That was me," he said, appearing proud of his youthful risk taking. "Someone had to go first—I guess it was up to me."

Looking at the falls I saw a small rainbow formed from the water's mist as it struck the rocky slope of its vertical channel. I remembered seeing something like this. "You have a photograph of the falls in the cabin," I said.

"Yes, but I think right now would be an ever better picture," he said. The backdrop of the blue sky and miniature rainbow looked like something from a Hollywood special effects studio.

I had been thinking for the entire trek down the mountain about who I really was. But there was a part of Benny's story I hadn't heard yet. I thought it might help me understand where I had gone wrong. "I was wondering. How did you get out of Vietnam?"

"They traded me. I was fortunate."

It couldn't have been that simple, I thought to myself. There had to be more. "You never gave them any confessions?" I asked.

"No, but they did their best to persuade me."

"Torture."

"Yes, but I was already free at that point—at least inside," he said. "I also tried some torture of my own." Benny stopped and picked up a rock and tossed it down into the pool below. "When I understood they were going to photograph me, even without a confessional for propaganda, I decided to make myself a little less photogenic."

"What did you do?"

"I beat my head on the side of the cell and scratched my face. I'm sure I looked worse than anything they had done to me. It worked. I was never photographed."

"Why did they let you go?"

"I was part of a prisoner swap, but I don't know for sure why I was included. They may have thought I was crazy," he said, allowing himself to chuckle after he spoke. "It may have been they realized I was very determined. But years later, I think I may have found the real reason. It was Chi Mai."

"Did he talk them into letting you go?"

"No, but they knew we were friends. He had moved along with our group from one camp to the next. Once we were in Hanoi, he joined a protest against the North Vietnamese treatment of war prisoners." Suddenly, he leaned his head forward. From my side angle, I could see his eyes were closed. "His only protest was his last, from what I learned."

"They killed him?"

"No, he set himself on fire in front of the military headquarters. He read a brief statement of protest, recited a poem, and then struck a match and burned himself alive in front of hundreds of people in the city square." As he spoke I saw several tears fall from his eyes. "His death was probably why I'm here. I'll never know, but it had to play a part in my release."

"My God," I said aloud. "Why did he do that?"

"He wasn't the only monk to immolate himself as a protest to both the North and South Vietnamese. I would've never guessed that was what he was going to do, but he did tell me he was going to get their attention. He was the bravest man I've ever met."

"I would say so—dying like that for a cause."

"It wasn't the way he died. It was the way he lived. He never held back! He risked everything to live his life. His last words to me were, 'Live with no regrets. Forgive yourself.' It takes more courage to live your own life, Jack. Chi Mai did."

His voice changed when he spoke of Chi Mai's bravery. The thoughtful words and careful phrasing disappeared. His voice crackled with a youthful tenor. Even though the memory of the loss of his friend hurt, talking about him seemed to rejuvenate Benny.

"I owe my life to a lot of people, some I've never even met," he said. "You're no different. You don't have to be a POW to understand bravery and living a free life."

We stood on the precipice of the falls for a few moments in silence, and then we turned to walk back toward the trail. The path was wide and allowed me to walk at his side. As we continued our descent of the mountain, I thought about how Benny's life appeared to be filled with major victories and terrible losses. "I hope you don't mind me saying this, but you've had some of the worst luck any person could ever have."

"There's no luck, Jack. Everything has a purpose—a cause and effect. If you try to blame luck for things happening, it takes away what life is. Life is never going to be perfect. "

"Maybe luck isn't the best word. But you've had more than your share of bad experiences," I said.

"I'm here because I was there." Benny said. "Everything in the world is connected. Everything is important. I learned that from experience—painful as it was, but I learned. You've learned the same way."

Thinking before I spoke, I told Benny about how I had ruined my marriage because of another woman. "I chose her over my children. I was selfish, thinking only of myself," I said—frustration and self-pity shrouding my words.

"I understand. I did the same thing."

Benny had already told me many things that surprised me, but nothing did more than this. "You didn't . . ." I started to say that I had misinterpreted what he had said.

"I told you we shared a lot of the same experiences," he said. "I was living a life that wasn't mine. I hated being me. There was no one to blame but me. I made bad choices. But I've learned from the experience."

Remaining in shock over his confession, I paid little attention to his words. How could he do that to Ann? But how could I do what I had done to Tina? "Does Ann know?" I asked.

"Yes, I told her."

"Why?"

"I had to, Jack. I loved her more than my pride and ego. We stayed together, stronger than before."

"That's a miracle," I said, thinking about my experience with Cassie and how it helped end my marriage.

"No, it wasn't a miracle. We loved each other enough to forgive."

• • •

"What do you want?" The question was bouncing inside of my head as we walked down a steep and winding portion of the path. We were now far enough away from the din of the waterfall that all I could hear was the sound of our feet moving along the path. We were deep in the forest. I was deep in thought about my past.

I was recalling my last effort to reconnect with Tina. That evening, we had decided to visit all of the places in Philly that were special to us. We had walked through the town square, looking in at the shops littered with memorabilia for tourists. We ate at our favorite restaurant on the edge of the old district. We had always held hands in college, and as if by habit, Tina grasped mine as we walked back to the car. It felt uncomfortable for me. Tina sensed it, and released my hand at the corner before we crossed the street. I was doing my best to be as natural as possible, but the conditions felt wrong.

The evening had been my idea, and now it was slipping away. We talked little while driving. The kids were staying with their friends. We were going to be home alone. After walking inside, we went upstairs. I had talked up the evening as a night for us to reconnect. She had believed me. When we entered the bedroom, she told me to wait while she changed. As I sat on the bed, I started to think about Cassie. I wondered what she was doing. I was with my wife but felt as though I were cheating. As I rubbed my hands over my face and through my thinning hair, the bathroom door opened. While it was Tina, it didn't look like the woman I had fallen in love with. "I can't do this," I said, my honesty making a brief appearance.

"What do you want?" Tina said. Tears poured down her face. "I thought you wanted to try and make it work?"

"I don't feel comfortable. It doesn't feel right. I'm sorry."

Her words were intelligible. She threw a glass intended for champagne at me. I left, still hearing her angry cries. "How could I fix that?" I asked myself silently.

Since that night Tina had lost the weight she had gained and she was prepping to run a marathon. I was fat and out of shape. I looked over at Benny and saw a man who could outrun me, even on his seventy-plus-year frame.

Benny broke the silence with his own question.

• • •

"What motivates you?"

"Is this part of the job interview?" I asked.

"Would it make any difference if it was?"

"No, you're right," I said laughing. "I want to be happy."

"That sounds simple enough," he said. "What makes you happy?"

The question should have been easy to answer. My pause was noticeable. He knew I was having trouble giving an honest answer. Earlier he had asked me what made a person successful, and I had recited my resume—obviously not the answer to his question.

"Can I give you an answer later?"

"Sure, I wasn't trying to impose—I was curious."

"What makes you happy?" I asked, hoping to find a light at the end of the tunnel of confusion I had built.

"Being," he said.

"Huh?"

"Being awake, being alive. Being me, at my best. That makes me happy," he said.

"That's a large amount of territory you're covering. It sounds like you could be happy almost anywhere."

"That's the way life should be," he said.

"I thought you meant happy—like really happy," I said, trying to clarify what *happy* meant to me. "I've reached goals, and that made me happy. Some of my accomplishments made me happy. But I'm still waiting."

"Waiting for what?" he asked.

"To be happy," I said, repeating my earlier response. "I still have some things to do first."

"Don't wait to be happy, Jack."

"Happy never really fit me," I said, failing to hold back some rare honesty. "But I have learned this in the past couple of days—there is hope for me. I'll get back with you on this, too."

"Okay, Jack," he said laughing, "You'll figure it out. Just keep on asking yourself the question."

36. What Have I Learned?

"WHAT HAVE I LEARNED?" Benny asked. Benny had asked me a lot of questions. "I've learned to not answer a question without thinking," I said.

Benny laughed. We were nearing the cabin at the lake. The hike had been an incredible experience. I was exhausted from both the physical and mental challenges the hours on the mountain had inflicted on me, and the drive back had been filled mostly with talk about banking and my background. "I ask myself that question constantly, so I was curious what you've learned today," he said, smiling as he drove.

"I'm serious," I said. "I've learned to think before I dive in and start talking. I had never realized how programmed I was for a quick response."

"That's a great point," he said with enthusiasm. "Programmed! I used to call it autopilot but I like your term better."

"I like it here," I said, looking out the window as the sun was beginning its final drop behind the mountains. The red tint of the sky on the clouds was something I rarely saw in Philly. Or was it that I hadn't taken the time to look up at sunsets?

"That's good," he said. "That's why I wanted you to visit in a less-structured manner. If we had had a normal job interview, what would we have really seen or learned?"

"It's been a great experience," I said, leaning forward to look again at the fading sunset.

"Knowing something without feeling it is worthless," he said. "Knowledge must be felt for it to have value."

"How do you separate your emotions?" I asked.

"You can't," he said. "It's foolish to believe that you can think your way through life and keep your emotions at arm's length. Knowing something without feeling is dead knowledge."

I thought back to his story about the POW camp. I asked, "Fear is an emotion. Didn't Chi Mai try to teach you to remove your emotions so you wouldn't be afraid?"

"Fear is real if it's real," he said. "Fear without knowledge is the same as knowledge without feeling. You assume something without understanding. Chi Mai told me, 'See it, feel it, know it.' He was right. Reality is knowledge felt, not just understood."

Seeing the cabin ahead as we made our way down the dirt road I began to think about the possibilities and choices we both had in front of us. Would he offer me the job? If he did, what should I do?

After pulling the Jeep in front of the cabin, we carried our backpacks inside and began to prepare the second of Ann's preplanned meals. As we ate dinner, I commented on the freshness of the tomatoes. Benny told me about the care and attention he gave his garden.

"You can't plant cabbage seeds and expect a tomato to pop out," he said smiling, looking over at me. "When they say you reap what you sow, that's true. Gardening is a process. Even if you get the intention right, planting the right seeds at the right time with the right nutrients, it still takes work to bring it to harvest."

"I guess I forgot to pay attention to what I was planting and nurturing."

"We all do, Jack," he said.

• • •

We had settled in by the fireplace to eat more peach cobbler. I wanted to know how I could prepare for the changes I needed to make to put my life in order. "Something's missing in my life," I said.

"Jack, after spending time with you I know you're a very intelligent, capable person. I say this in all honesty. There's no secret to success or to living a remarkable life. Life all comes down to *right now*—this second. I know you read it in my book, and now you've heard me say it more than once. It's a choice to be or not to be awake in the moment. If you're living now, what's more important?"

"It's easier said than done."

"Is it?" he asked. "Doesn't it make more sense to live now instead of later?"

"I know what you're saying . . ." I said, but before I could finish my thought he interjected.

"But do you feel it?" he said. "Once you feel the necessity to change you'll see what you need to do to come alive. But that's a choice you make. You create your destiny."

● ● ●

That night I barely slept. Although I was exhausted from the hike, I could not take my mind off of what was ahead of me. I was a planner. I knew better than to plant something that wouldn't grow.

My inner demons were well fed that night. After hearing how I could discard them all day, I couldn't ignore them while I was lying awake.

There were many things I needed to know. But there were also many things I wished I could forget.

Soon after taking her first steps, Jessica displayed a natural physical ability. She loved to dance. Hearing music made her face light up. I couldn't help but remember how Benny had described how his son looked when he was running.

It was the same when Jessica danced.

With Tina as the primary motivator, we enrolled Jessica in dance classes when she was three years old. Her first recital was a year later. It was held in a large high school auditorium filled to capacity with parents who sat through four long hours of seeing someone else's children perform for the few brief moments their own child would take the stage. Although the youngest and the smallest in her troupe, Jessica stole the show. Even in the darkness of the cabin, alone with the memory, the feelings of pride and happiness in her accomplishment made me smile. But that was her first recital.

I never made it to her second or any subsequent performances. My career was in full-blown glory, and taking time out three times a year to watch her perform was too much for me to schedule.

I made my choice.

I failed Jessica.

I thought about a fight I had with Tina when Jessica was about twelve. One night, arriving back home after staying out until after midnight at the hotel bar with several of the attendees of a conference, I was surprised to see most of the lights on in my home. Tina was sitting in the den.

"What's wrong?" I asked, trying to mask the fact that I had driven home with a blood-alcohol level well above the legal limit.

"You know what's wrong," she said.

"I'm sorry, but I don't," I said, sitting down in my recliner, pulling my tie off, and tossing it on top of the nearby desk. "I'm not a mind reader. Tell me what's wrong."

"You broke your daughter's heart. Before she went onstage, she asked where you were. I told her you had an emergency, but she knew. She's not a baby anymore, Jack. She had heard us arguing. She knew you chose your job over her."

"And I guess you fed that with some of your own issues," I said. I knew Tina said some pretty harsh things about me to our daughter. "Did you tell her I didn't care? I'm sure you did."

"No, I didn't have to say anything. Your actions said it all. You weren't there. She was so upset. She forgot part of the routine. She hasn't quit crying."

"Listen, I'm tired of being blamed for everything that doesn't go right in this family! Why is it up to me? She's good, but she needs to learn from her mistakes. She's a good dancer, but there's always someone better. That's life."

"You and your life-is-a-competition crap!" Tina shouted in response. "You've never told her she was the best or how proud you were of her. Congratulations, Jack, you've turned into your father!"

"It made me tough!" I said, now turning in the chair to face Tina.

"That's what made me get ahead! She'll never be a great dancer as long as you're afraid to tell her she's not the best." I had not seen Jessica step inside of the room until I saw Tina's face. As I turned to follow her gaze, I saw my daughter running away.

She never danced again.

How had I become such a horrible father—the type of father I swore I would never be?

There were other things I knew, but I had failed to accept in my life. I would have to accept them now.

I had not only failed in planting the wrong seeds—I was a weed, worthless to everyone. I needed to change.

I hated myself.

> *Never think what you*
> *do doesn't have*
> *consequences—every*
> *action has an effect.*

—BENJAMIN FRANKLIN PRICE

37. How Can I Go Back?

"WHAT AM I GOING BACK TO?" I asked myself.

I was sitting in the cramped seat of the plane returning me to Philly. Even though it had been less than thirty minutes since I had left the ground in Virginia, the place felt as though it was a lifetime away. I looked down to the ground far below. Through the clouds I could see mountains, a view I had failed to afford myself on the edge of a ledge out of fear.

Despite seeing more than a glimpse of the real me, as we drove to the airport Benny had offered me the job of president and chief administrative officer at Citizens Bank. "You're the right person to join our team," he had said. "But you need to be sure this is what you need."

My response was habitual. "What can you offer me?" I asked, failing to thank him for the opportunity. The money was excellent—more than my pay at Merchants. I would also have a seat on the bank's board of directors. It was a better deal than I had imagined and more than I needed. Now that the money was taken care of, I had to deal with the question that was foremost in my thoughts: "Do I want to leave Philly?" But a different question came to mind as I was approaching my hometown: "*Could* I leave Philly?" I remembered what Benny said about attachments. I had a lot.

There was so much to consider. First, I considered my children. I would have never put them first before, but this was a new Jack Oliver. I wanted to play a more prominent role in the lives of my children, but how could I do that if I was in Virginia and they were in Philadelphia? How could I ever be a better father and mend the broken relationship from hundreds of miles away?

Then there was Tina. I had been living apart from her for almost a year. Reconciliation seemed out of the question. Or was it? I missed her more than ever, but I still had another attachment to solve.

Cassie. She was like a habit I couldn't quit. I wanted to understand why she held such a strong grip on my thoughts. My last conversation with her had left little doubt she was not interested in joining me in Virginia. But I could not envision us together, even if she had been interested in moving with me. We only shared a couple of things in common. The more time we spent together, the more we got on each other's nerves, a condition that was not likely to improve. I stared again out of the plane's window.

Last but not least was my attachment to Merchants Bank. If I left, I would be leaving a job that I had sworn I would never quit. My recent weak performance and the threat of being fired were realities, but I had never failed before and wasn't ready to start now. Thinking of Merchants, I felt my anger stirring. Were they setting me up to get rid of me? What would happen if I stayed and tried to conform to their system? They needed me, but did they realize it? Finally, how could I walk away from a quarter-of-a-million-dollar bonus? Cassie was right—it was a lot of money.

My attention moved from Philly to Virginia. Moving to Virginia carried a lot of questions. Would I be happy at the new job? Could I adapt? Would the bank's staff accept me? Would the emotions I felt over the weekend still be there when I was working at the bank every day? Was Benny for real? Was this what I really wanted? Then I remembered the question he had asked after offering me the position. Was this what I needed?

As the plane circled the airport and began its final descent into Philadelphia, I could see through cracks in the cloud cover. The view was distorted, but it was recognizable. It was the place where I had spent my entire life. I felt at home seeing the skyline. But something was different, and I knew what it was. I was different. The harsh thud of the plane's tires hitting the runway shook me. I knew my life was out of balance. I knew I needed to change. I no longer liked the dishonest person I had become. I felt the rapid braking of the plane. I was home. It was time to choose.

"How can I choose to turn away from reality?" I asked myself as I watched the airport workers remove the baggage as I waited to leave the plane.

• • •

Driving my car out of the airport parking lot, I felt something I hadn't missed during my four days in Virginia: stress. Being back in the congested, slow-moving traffic and knowing it would take me forty-five minutes to drive five miles filled me with frustration. By habit, I pulled my cell phone from the side pocket of my briefcase to call Cassie—she was on my mind. I had not spoken to her since she had hung up on me almost two weeks earlier. It was the longest stretch of time we'd not talked in over a year. I lifted it from the leather bag, where it had remained buried for the entire trip, and changed my mind. "No, not yet," I said to myself, dropping it on the passenger seat.

The idea of going back to the cramped apartment gave me claustrophobia. I started to breathe deep breaths as José had taught me at the hospital. "Now isn't the time for an anxiety attack," I said to myself. I was amazed it had taken so little time for my body to respond to the stress. I decided to call Tina. No one answered the phone, but I decided to not leave a message. Instead, I decided to drop in since it was not far off of the route to my apartment. Going home felt like a stop I needed to make. We would have at least two hours to talk before the kids returned home from school, enough time to talk about my dilemma. Maybe I could take them out to dinner? I started to feel better with a plan in place.

I was feeling a different me, at least a different opportunity for a new me. I decided I would end my relationship with Cassie. I felt at ease with the decision. She brought out the greedier manifestations of Jack Oliver. I didn't need any help being greedy. But I was tired of being alone. Still stuck in traffic, I rolled down the window hoping to get some air. Instead of making me less claustrophobic, the odor of the exhaust reminded me that I'd left the mountains of Virginia behind. The idea of being with Tina continued to surface—I could not put away the thought. I would tell Tina how wrong I had been in the past. I wanted to show her there was a better me. I had finally found a way to climb out of the ditch I had lived in for years. I wanted her to see the real Jack. Most of all I wanted to say I was sorry, something I had always failed to do.

Driving into the narrow streets of our neighborhood, I grew more determined. If Tina would forgive me and insisted that I stay in Philadelphia I would stay. Everything Benny had shared with me made me different, but I could not leave my family behind in Philly. This was the destiny he had talked about. I could find another job after my stint with Merchants was over. The world was looking brighter. "I can tough it out here," I said, turning onto Oak Street and taking a deep breath.

Pulling into the driveway I saw Tina's black Lexus parked under the canopy by the kitchen entrance. There was another car in the driveway, a light gray BMW. The kids had told me she had found a workout partner at the gym who she hung out with regularly. They had never said anything about her. It might be awkward to introduce me. "This is my ex" I imagined her saying. I wondered what she had told the woman as I got out of the car and stepped up on the small back porch.

After knocking on the door I turned the door knob. It was unlocked. I stepped into the kitchen. "Hello, is anyone home?" I asked in a moderate tone. It felt like home. No one responded. I picked up the stack of mail: bills. Usually this would set my stomach churning and shoot up my heart rate. Along with the bills we usually shared an argument over money. *But this was a new Jack,* I told myself as I dropped the stack of mail and walked into the living room. I heard movement upstairs. I stepped through the living room into the entryway and looked up the stairs. I could see part of the second floor hallway from my angle. I called out, "Hello!"

A sudden rustle of activity followed. Something dropped on the floor upstairs. I started to walk up the stairs but stopped halfway up the wide flight and looked back toward the opposite end of the open hallway. Tina stepped out of our bedroom in only a shirt; a light blue dress shirt, much too large for her. Her hair looked mussed, as though she had been lying down. *It must be one of my old shirts,* I thought.

"Jack, what are you doing here?" she said with a hiss.

"What's wrong?" I asked, now feeling waves of discomfort bearing down on me. "How come you've got one of my shirts on?" Where was her friend? Another wave hit. It wasn't my shirt. Her friend wasn't a woman.

"You need to leave, Jack, now!" Tina said. "This isn't your home anymore. You can't just come barging in."

"What's going on? Who's here?" My thoughts were scattered.

"Jack, leave now, I don't want to have a scene," she said. She glanced quickly back toward the bedroom.

My blood began to boil. Tina had another man in our bedroom. I was stunned, angry, mortified, and furious, all at once. I felt deceived and hurt, and I wanted to break down and cry. But most of all I was mad. I leaned forward ready to march up the steps and confront the man in *my* bedroom. But I stopped. I dropped my head and paused as I stood awkwardly on the steps. This wasn't my home anymore, I realized. Tina had let go.

I turned and walked back down the steps without speaking. As I walked through the living room, I heard Tina running down the hallway barefoot and coming down the steps. I did not want to talk to her. I picked up my pace and was opening the kitchen door to exit when she caught up with me.

"Jack, stop!" she demanded. "Stop, I want to talk."

I turned with one foot out of what used to be my home on the small porch. "This isn't a good time to talk," I said looking into her eyes. I had to look away, afraid she would see the pain of my broken heart.

"Jack, I'm sorry. I really didn't want you to see something like this."

"Tina, you're right," I said, looking down at the "Welcome" mat. "This is your home, and I won't come over again unless I'm invited or expected." I turned and continued walking away.

"Jack, I'm sorry," Tina said, sobbing tears of both anger and guilt. "I've been so lonely."

Gripping the wooden handrail for support, I stopped on the last step and turned to face Tina. She looked so different. She looked like she did when we first met, with just a little wear and tear of the years I had imposed on her. She was beautiful. I felt sick to my stomach.

"Tina," I said, "I'm the one who is sorry. This is my fault—not yours. Don't apologize. Forgive me."

"Jack, please—stop—you aren't—you don't sound like yourself," Tina asked.

"I'm not," I said as I walked away, my mind already moving away. Reality had struck me solidly, awakening me to what I needed to do. Backing out of the driveway I decided I was going to call Benny and tell him I accepted his offer. I battled the impulse to look back at the home we had bought with hopes of living our life together. I turned the corner without looking back—it was history.

"It's time to leave," I said, driving away.

38. What Now?

"WHAT NOW?" I asked myself as I drove back to my apartment. The inspired plan I had pieced together for a family reunion had been laid to waste. The idea of being with Tina had seemed so real and perfect, but was now shattered. I had to face my new reality.

I waited for the sweat to form on my brow along with the short-ened breathing and tightness in my chest. At least I now recognized I was a time bomb, I thought, as I stayed in the right lane driving at a snail's pace, ready to pull off the road when the anxiety attack struck me. I waited.

Nothing happened.

Remaining cautious, I thought about what had just happened. For once in my life, I realized, I had dealt with pain in a much differ-ent and clear manner. I experienced the pain, but it was more akin to waking up from a bad dream, understanding it was a nightmare and nothing more. This was a different Jack Oliver.

While I was more alone in the world than I had ever imagined, I somehow felt at peace. I sensed a new empowerment. The world felt lighter. Tina had let go. I needed to do the same. The strings that had been holding me back were gone. My soul was no longer owned by a company named Merchants. I was no longer a bus carrying the guilt of a selfish life. I was free.

Now I had a real option. My time with Benny had changed me. As soon as I walked into the apartment I called Benny and told him I accepted the job offer. He was surprised to hear from me so soon.

"Jack, I'm glad you accept, but I thought you were going to talk it over with your family."

"I did."

"Okay, Jack, whatever I can do to make your transition work for you, let me know," he said. "Ann and I enjoyed having you with us and look forward to you being part of our family here in Virginia."

I thanked Benny and told him I would call him after I spoke with the Merchants people the next day. The circle had been broken, but there was something I needed to do. I opened up the cabinet holding my liquor. Facing me were almost a dozen bottles—some opened, awaiting my thirst. As I took one bottle at a time and poured all of the contents into the sink I knew there was no going back.

I was on a new path.

• • •

"Have you lost your mind?" Rex asked. In answer to his question, I handed him the brief resignation letter I had written the night before.

I had struggled with what to write, but began to think about what Benny had said about letting go.

"Anger is an attachment. Why give anger any roots? Why cultivate something that can harm you? Let it go," he had said in my visit to the mountains of Virginia. At the time, I couldn't imagine letting go of an emotion that had fueled much of my success. But I was now heeding excellent advice.

My resignation letter thanked Merchants for trusting me and allowing me to work for them. "I have decided to accept another opportunity," was the only reason I noted for leaving. *The truth without anger,* I thought to myself as Rex continued his verbal onslaught.

"You can't leave . . . I mean, you've got contract provisions. We could sue you."

"I'm not breaking any provisions of the contract," I said.

"You can't work for a competitor here," he nearly shouted.

"Don't worry. I'm leaving Philly," I said without any emotion. My mind was clear.

"You're going to tell me that you're leaving behind a quarter of a million dollars that's less than a year away?" he asked. "For what?"

"I simply decided to make a change."

"Jack, if it's the written warning you got I can get that cleared up. We need you here for at least another eight months." Merchants needed me—but then I would be history. I felt even better about my decision hearing him say what I knew was true. Realizing his verbal faux pas, Rex tried to change the focus of his comments. "Read your contract, it's not just Philadelphia. You're contractually bound. You can't work in Pennsylvania or any contiguous state," Rex said in his best legal tone. He sneered. "You're stuck, Jack, unless you won the lottery."

"You're right," I said. "If I was going to stay around here, I would be stuck. But I'm not."

"I knew I shouldn't trust you," he said. The sneer had turned into a scowl on the young exec's face.

"Then you should feel good about yourself," I said. "I don't trust you either, but I did something about it. Now, we're both free to do what we want to do. It sounds like a win-win solution to me."

"This is upsetting," Rex said with his jaws clinched tightly. "You can't leave me here to deal with this mess. What am I going to do? How am I going to explain this?"

"Rex," I said, "that's easy. Just do your job." As I stood and turned to leave the office, I saw the photo of Ben Hogan with the handwritten reminder from the great golfer written on the photo. "Now it's time for you to take this advice—never give up." I paused. "It helped me."

"Clean your desk out and be out of here today," Rex said as I turned to exit.

"Don't worry—I will."

• • •

Instead of making calls to tell people I was leaving, I had already sketched out a brief e-mail thanking everyone for their efforts. It may not have seemed like the best way to leave, but it was the best option. I was expected to leave promptly, and I was determined to do so. There was only one person other than Rex I wanted to talk to directly about my departure from Merchants.

I called Carol into my office. I sat down beside her. She had been my most trusted ally over the years. I noticed she had a folded letter in her hand. I knew what it was before she could say a word.

"So you're going to leave, too?" I asked.

"Yes," Carol said with tears forming in her eyes. "Too?" she asked.

"I just gave Rex my resignation," I said. "You're not the only one leaving."

"Jack, where are you going? I didn't want to leave you, but this place is driving me crazy."

"Me too," I said. "We may be a little crazy, but we're much better for it."

"I knew something was going on," Carol said, wiping away her tears with a tissue. "I never thought you would leave here. I thought we would have to carry you out. I didn't want to see that."

"That's why I'm leaving," I said. "I wasn't ready to give my life away—for this," I said pointing around the office.

"Where are you going?" she asked.

"I'm going to Virginia," I said. "I'm going to change—for the better."

"Jack, I've so worried about you," she said with new tears of happiness and relief. "I'm happy for you."

"Where are you going?" I asked.

"Home," Carol said—a smile forming as she responded. "My husband and I decided we want to spend time with our grandchildren before we get too old. We've both spent too much time on our careers. It was time for a change. The entire Merchants situation woke me up." So it wasn't just me. Carol looked as though a ton of dread had fallen from her shoulders. I was happy for her.

"Carol, I want you to know how much I appreciated everything you've done for me over the years," I said. "I let you down plenty of times, but you never gave up on me. I'll never forget it."

"Do you remember the only advice I ever gave to you?"

"You told me to never forget where I came from. That was my problem—I did. But I'm going to change that."

With more tears filling her eyes Carol said, "You've changed. I can hear it in your voice. You sound like the Jack Oliver I knew who was a part-time teller. I'm proud of you." The very words I had worked so hard to hear from my father were now being said by a person I never expected to tell me. "Being a good person is much better than being a good boss. You've tried so hard to be something you're not. You're a natural-born leader. Just be yourself, Jack."

"I promise you I will," I said. "Thank you, Carol." We stood and hugged.

"You're almost like a son to me," Carol said, now able to laugh. "The only problem was I could never discipline you and take away your toys when you were doing something wrong."

I laughed. If Carol only knew how exactly right she was.

It was time to put away the old Jack Oliver.

39. How Long Has It Been?

"HOW LONG HAS IT BEEN?" Benny asked. He already knew the answer. It was an anniversary. I had been in Virginia for one year. Benny remembered and had commemorated the date by bringing me one of Ann's freshly baked cinnamon rolls.

"One year, Jack." He sat down at the small conference table in my office for our regular morning chat, as he referred to it. "You made it. You're now officially a Virginian!"

"You've thinned me down in one year, so now you're going to fatten me up?" I asked, looking at the monstrous roll.

"You've got to eat it or Ann will get upset," he said laughing, part of our ongoing reasoning to never say no to Ann's culinary efforts.

"How come you're not eating?" I asked. "You look like you've lost weight. You're not trying to look like those models, are you?" While getting a chuckle, my question highlighted a very real concern. Benny, already fit and thin by most standards, had lost quite a bit of weight the past couple of months, making him look almost frail.

"I've had my fill," he said. "I'm lucky enough to live with the chef!" As he laughed, his newly persistent cough surfaced again.

"Are you okay?"

"I'm just changing—getting older. Nothing to worry about, Jack," he said. He turned and looked at some of the daily operating reports.

My life had changed in every way possible. I moved to Virginia within a month of resigning from Merchants. Tina still seemed to blame herself for my departure, though I assured her that no one was to blame—it was simply meant to be. We had agreed amicably to a divorce. The kids were struggling. They thought that I had run away to Virginia. Jessica blamed Tina, and Joshua blamed me for the divorce and my leaving. I had tried my best to get closer to them, but they were not ready, and had refused to visit me in Virginia.

The year had been three hundred sixty-five days of self-discovery. The year had been devoted to trimming my excesses. Sitting across from the man who had helped guide me through my transformation, I knew where the most significant change had occurred. I was much more honest. The challenge had been to be truthful first with myself and then with others. I talked to Benny about it as he continued to look at the reports. "I've changed a lot," I said. "I've got a long way to go but I think the biggest change is that I'm a more honest person. It was tough to admit how dishonest I'd been."

"Being honest with yourself can be difficult, especially when the truth hurts. But I've always trusted you," he said without looking up. "Except when it comes to saying you're ready to leave work in the evening. You still need a helping hand to drag you out of this place." While I had spent considerable time at work acclimating myself to my new role in a totally different environment, I was spending much less time than ever on the job. Benny pushed me out of the office in the evening.

I wasn't ready to give up on asking about his health. "I believe you," I said, pausing, "but are you really all right?"

"How so? I'm not showing any signs of senility, am I?" he asked, looking up with his trademark partial smile. He had aged considerably in the year I had worked with him, his skin now loose on his cheekbones, making him look twenty years older than the first time I saw him at the airport. "Are you afraid I'm going to imitate Ms. Fitzgerald and walk into the bank in my underwear?" he asked, referring to one of our more elderly large depositors who visited the bank half-clothed. "You would tell me, wouldn't you, Jack?"

"Seriously, Benny, I wouldn't be honest if I didn't ask," I said. "I'm concerned."

"I'm changing. I'm getting older. But I'm fine with it," he said. That wasn't a full answer. I wanted to probe more but stopped. He added almost as an afterthought, "Change is part of life."

Change, something that I had fought against most of my life, had been a positive aspect of my life since moving to Virginia. Benny and I, while different in almost every way imaginable, had forged a strong partnership that blended seamlessly from my first day in Roanoke. I had spent a lot of my time away from work with him, hiking, riding mountain bikes, and fishing. With Ann's prompting I had also joined the gym, hired a trainer, and started a program to regain a better level of fitness. I had lost forty-five pounds in my first six months and was keeping the weight off.

After pouring out my supply of alcohol in Philly, I had refused to take another drink. It had been incredibly difficult, especially with the move and struggling to gain my footing in the new world, as Benny was fond of calling it. I was making progress. There was only one thing missing. I realized I loved Tina and wanted to be with her and the kids.

"Change has been good," I said, "but I would like for things to even out now. I miss the kids."

"Fate works in strange ways, Jack," Benny said putting down the reports. "What you want rarely just happens. It's part of a process. You may never realize everything you want. But that doesn't mean you quit hoping and trying. Ann and I pray you'll find peace and happiness. That is something in your reach now. It's all inside of you."

"Thanks," I said. "I'm doing my best."

"I know," he said. "Never give up hope—that's not all we have, but without it nothing else matters."

• • •

Work remained important. Especially after I saw what type of organization Benny had constructed. Citizens Bank was like nothing I had seen before. People were actually happy to come to work. The turnover rate was the lowest of any bank for which I could find comparative information. It was not perfect, because people are not perfect. But the effort to serve employees and clients was a reality.

The way I interacted with people in a leadership role at work had evolved over my twelve months. Heeding Benny's advice, I had viewed my job as a serving position. I could serve from behind, in the middle, or in front. It depended on what the situation called for. I was aware of my oversized ego and refused to allow it to control me. I could see why Benny was fighting to keep the bank independent. I felt part of a family almost immediately. Because of Merchants, I knew what would happen if someone bought Citizens Bank. They would ruin it.

There would be a layoff, a large one. The number of employees at the bank was much higher than banks of a similar size. An acquiring bank would view it as over-staffed and immediately target layoffs to add efficiency and more bottom-line profits. But they didn't understand that the reason Citizens made one of the highest profits of any bank in the country relative to size was the fact that the bank had more people. It was Benny's commitment to service. He paid people a higher rate of pay, gave them much better benefits, promoted from within, and spread the wealth-effect of the profits among employees and shareholders. I would have never believed it possible: The bank's success was found in giving instead of taking.

"It's all cause and effect," he reminded me on many occasions. "A layoff would do what? Save money? And what else would it do? The effect has more harm connected to it than good. There are more important things in a business than saving a buck—it's creating the right effects. Cutting jobs and laying off staff will trigger a response—and I have rarely seen it be a positive one. You can never slash, burn, and cut your way to prosperity."

I understood now—he was right—but it took a constant effort for me to learn how to *lead* a business instead of trying to manage one. As part of this process, Benny and I met every morning to discuss what was occurring at the bank. Benny started each of these brief meetings with the same question.

Today was no different, at least I thought so.

• • •

"*Are we making progress?*" he asked, ready to begin our brief review of where we were going.

"Absolutely," I said. "We're growing despite the new credit union opening in three of the towns we have large branches in. We're making progress despite competition."

Progress? It was a word that was left out of conversations at Merchants. "I was just thinking," I continued, "that I had never really used the word *progress* until I came here."

"Progress allows us to measure every step," Benny said. "Knowing your progress allows you to celebrate the right steps now instead of waiting for some distant goal. Waiting kills a business."

But I could tell Benny had something on his mind other than progress. I waited for him to broach the subject.

"When I asked you to join us, we knew there were challenges ahead for Citizens Bank," Benny said taking off his reading glasses and placing the reports neatly down on the table. "The challenge was competing with our own success. We've been competing against ourselves as much as our competition. That's the way it should be, but our success has brought the attention of larger banks who want to buy us."

From the monthly board meetings I attended, I knew what he was talking about. Ron Landreau, a local attorney and member of the bank's board, wanted to find a way to market and sell Citizens Bank at a significant premium. In every meeting, Ron would challenge Benny to make the return better for shareholders. It was difficult to imagine how much better the shareholders could benefit, unless they decided to sell out for an above-average price. Public trading of the stock was something new—it had remained privately held until five years earlier. Because the original shareholders were aging, the stock was taken public and listed on NASDAQ to allow shareholders an option to liquidate their holdings. The original shareholders had realized over a thousand percent increase on their initial investment. In addition, the corporation's profitability allowed a quarterly dividend to be paid to shareholders, adding to their wealth. Almost all employees were shareholders, including people in nonmanagement positions. Shareholders should have been very happy, but Ron wasn't.

Unlike PT&G and especially Merchants Bank, the attention to shareholders was the culmination of the bank's purpose of helping clients and employees. Focusing on service instead of profits was something special to Citizens, but it appeared that several members of the board didn't understand how unique the business was compared to others. I had shared my thoughts with these members in one-on-one discussions. But this small group of directors still viewed me as an outsider, unlike the bank's staff who had welcomed me with open arms. Ron Landreau and his followers wanted more. I had seen this before.

"Jack, staying independent is a real challenge," Benny continued. "And that challenge is coming from someone you know."

I could feel the presence of Merchants Bank.

"Merchants Bank, again?" I asked with a brief smile. "I know them well."

"Never discount fate," Benny said.

"We can beat them. This is something we won't lose."

"I appreciate your belief and commitment. But the first thing we need to consider is the worst-case situation. What happens if Merchants buys the bank?"

It was unusual for Benny to start with the worst situation. I asked him why.

"Starting with the worst removes the fear. It's like death; removing the fear of what could happen allows us to be more rational."

"Okay."

"The worst thing that can happen is what, Jack?"

"If they buy us, they will gut the bank, in every way," I said. "Nothing will be left the same."

"Nothing?" Benny asked.

"Nothing," I said.

"Then we have some work to do. They've offered me a lot of money," he said.

This was part of the Merchants' strategy. I reminded him that John Helms and I had seen this happen up close and personal. "Where the board goes, the business follows," I said. "The battle ground is in the boardroom."

"Well, we have one advantage," he said. "I'm not interested in having more money."

"That could be enough to stop them," I said.

"But probably not, Jack," Benny said. "As you know, we have a small number of shareholders who own a significant amount of stock. They are interested in selling. Unlike at bigger banks in this situation, all Merchants has to do is convince about two dozen individuals or families to sell. That is the challenge for us—showing them the effects of the choice."

"We can educate the shareholders on what they've received over the years," I said. "Maybe they don't understand what they have."

"People seldom do until they lose it," he said with the concern. "But we could do a better job of that. I failed in impressing on the shareholders the real value of their investment. I assumed they understood; I was wrong. And greed is not rational and loves assumptions. It may be too late."

"How so?" I asked.

"The CEO of Merchants has asked to speak at our next board meeting. Ron and several of the board members have asked me to agree to it."

"Andrew Ledger," I said.

"I'm sure you've met him," Benny said.

"Only once, but I'll never forget."

• • •

The memory of my first and only meeting with Andrew Ledger remained clear. Two turbulent weeks had passed since the announcement PT&G was being sold to Merchants. I had received a memo from Chad that our executive team would be flying to Charlotte to meet the Merchants Bank executive team.

We were shuttled from the airport to the bank's forty-four–floor headquarters in the heart of Charlotte. The football stadium figured prominently in the downtown area, with the Merchants building almost shadowing it.

When I saw the building, I remembered something John Helms had told me about their home office. When Merchants Bank was planning on constructing their new tower in Charlotte, one of the most famous architects in the country was brought in to design a building that would stand out from all the others.

We were ushered up to the thirty-fifth floor into a large meeting room. Ledger, a tall, scholarly gentleman whom I had seen numerous times in banking newspapers and magazines, asked us to take a seat after shaking each of our hands.

"Good afternoon! It's my privilege to give you a brief overview of your new employer, Merchants Bank," Mr. Ledger beamed and began his PowerPoint presentation. What followed was two-hours of oratory showing the growth of Merchants Bank during his tenure. The growth was impressive, but two items stuck out.

Large layoffs followed every merger. And with each merger came a "state president." This job was the top leadership position in each state Merchants operated. All of the state presidents had started at Merchants in North Carolina. It made me wonder what would happen to Chad and, of course, me. *That should be my job,* I thought as Ledger continued to talk about the history of the bank.

"After sixty-five mergers in twenty-five years, we know what makes a merger work," he said with a huge smile. "We need to take care of each of you. You're the most important people to us in the purchase, I mean merger."

He began to describe what taking care of us meant. "You'll each be paid a bonus of $250,000 to stay on board with us for two years following the purchase. In addition, you'll each receive a pay increase of 15 percent immediately, and you'll be part of our generous stock option plan.

"What happens after two years?" one of our executive team members asked.

Andrew casually smiled and stated in an almost matter-of-fact tone, "After two years, to be honest, you'll probably take your bonus and leave. Since we have been making this offer an option, no one has stayed past two years."

At that point, I knew exactly what we were dealing with. We had truly in every sense of the word been sold—not merged. I never saw a "compassionate purchaser" as Chad termed Merchants; just a purchaser. It would be their way or the highway.

Sadly, I had been right. Now, I had a chance to prevent Merchants from destroying another bank.

• • •

"Are you going to allow him to speak?" I asked Benny.

"Part of our job is to represent shareholders. It is our fiduciary duty to listen. We may have only one opportunity to present a case for staying independent," Benny said. "Everything will likely be settled in a two-hour meeting."

"If Andrew Ledger is talking, it will be a four-hour meeting," I said. "He'll probably have a slide show."

"I've done some research on Merchants," Benny said. "I need your help to do some more."

"Benny, I'll do whatever it takes," I said.

"Just like in everything else we've done, we will do our best and let fate work," Benny said. "Cause and effect."

I began researching each of the Merchants' purchases dating back over the past five years. The bank was consistent in its post-acquisition tactics. After acquiring a bank, they would gut it of its operations and bring in several of their people for leadership roles, including the state president. They would then begin to downsize the bank's staff while changing all of the products and services.

I calculated that on average after each purchase they lost 15 percent of their customers. Comparing profitability before and after was lost in the murkiness of their accounting. What I could find was a shrinking market share, a loss of employees, and lower profits.

Merchants had covered their losses by continuing to buy. John Helms had likened the bank to being on a perpetual treadmill of buying. "They can't stop buying. Once they stop, the lower profits will show. The more they buy, the faster the treadmill speeds up. At some point they won't be able to keep up the pace. But they only know one speed—faster—a crash just waiting to happen."

I had lived my life with a similar philosophy and pace. I crashed. I knew they would. I shared this view along with my findings with Benny.

"That is an interesting analogy," Benny said. "How did their shareholders fare after each of these banks sold?"

"They received an immediate premium, but it was quickly lost. Most of the banks that sold to Merchants had problems in earnings, growth, or increasing shareholder value. None of those problems exist here or at my ex-employer, PT&G."

"Why did PT&G sell?" Benny asked.

"Executive greed," I said.

"That is what we are battling, Jack—greed," Benny said.

At least it was an enemy I knew and understood.

40. What Do We Want to Be Remembered For?

"WHAT DO WE WANT TO BE REMEMBERED FOR?" Benny asked the board members, taking time to make eye contact with each person in the room, including Andrew Ledger. The question wasn't open ended. The directors sitting in the room were in the process of making a choice that would affect more than me and the hundreds of employees of the bank and the thousands of clients.

Their decision would change their world.

The Citizens Bank board meetings were held in one of the oldest buildings in Salem, Virginia, above a restaurant called The Dixie Tavern. While it had been expanded over the years, the original two-story stone building had remained remarkably intact.

I always thought it was odd that the bank held its board of directors meeting on the second floor of a restaurant. Wood paneling covered the walls, probably a remodeling attempt made in the 1970s. The carpet was now a faded gold with well-worn tracks and stains reflecting the age and traffic in the large room. In the middle of the room were four foldable metal tables placed tightly together and covered with thin white tablecloths. Citizens Bank had ample options for meeting space, but the directors chose to continue to meet where they had formed the bank. It was an unspoken homage to what they viewed as a good luck charm, a way to stay in touch with the bank's roots. Or maybe, as Benny was fond of saying, it was because they loved the food.

The restaurant had served as the first site where Benny, Ron Landreau, Sherry Carter (the owner of The Dixie Tavern), and a few other investors met to discuss starting a new bank twenty years earlier. All of the people involved in those initial meetings had been associated with Valley Bank & Trust. Benny was the president and Ron and Sherry were directors. Valley was one of the oldest banks in Virginia and had close ties to the community, supporting many arts and nonprofit organizations. Possessing a good portion of the Roanoke Valley's banking business, it became a target for larger banks in the late 1970s. The bank's directors had finally decided to sell it to the largest bank in Virginia. After it had been sold, the hometown atmosphere was lost, according to Sherry Carter. Sherry had become one of my closest friends since moving to Virginia, taking care of "keeping Jack fed" as she liked to remind me.

"The big bank ruined what was special about our little bank—it took away its heart," she had told me. "We sold the bank because we thought we were doing the right thing for everyone, primarily the shareholders. The new owners promised they would keep everything pretty much as it was, but they lied. People got laid off. They stopped donating to the community. I was afraid to go out in public for months. Every time I went out someone would start fussing at me about us selling the bank. Looking back I know what happened. We got greedy and hoped things would work out. I think deep down we knew they wouldn't."

"What do you think about Merchants?" I had asked.

"Merchants Bank sounds a lot like the bank that bought Valley Bank but much bigger. But they're supposed to be different than most. I'm going to wait and make up my mind after I hear this Mr. Ledger talk. I don't want to make the same mistake again. But I do have to look out for my grandchildren. I'm not getting any younger."

I looked around the room filled with directors talking quietly in small groups. In a few moments, Andrew Ledger, chairman and CEO of one of the largest banks in the country, would visit The Dixie Tavern and speak to the group trying to convince them to sell. I had as much at stake as anyone in the room. My career was hanging in the balance.

Benny and I had put together a brief but clear presentation to refute the value offered by Merchants Bank. History did not lie. Merchants were scavengers. Typically they bought weaker banks that had little potential. But this was different. Citizens was an extremely profitable and growing organization. As a result Merchants had been forced to offer a huge premium, but the premium would be worth little unless Merchants improved all of Citizens operations, which was unlikely. That was our area of focus. How could Citizens be better off for selling? I felt great about the information. But as Benny said while we were driving to the tavern, "You never know what will happen when a lot of money is involved. Anytime you're dealing with greed, rationality can make a quick exit," he said.

"I'm sure you'll block the exit today," I said, trying to show as much confidence as possible.

"I'll do my best," he said, "but money talks much louder than I can."

As a ritual before the board meetings Sherry served a Southern feast of biscuits with gravy, sausage, bacon, and grits. Standing beside Benny and speaking to each board member as they entered, I could sense the tension.

Ron Landreau had been politicking the idea of selling and had visited most of the directors and large shareholders at their homes in an attempt to convince them to vote to sell to Merchants. Ron, a local politician who had held several publicly elected county positions, was using packaged information prepared by Merchants to show the value of joining a larger bank.

With almost all of the board members in the cramped upstairs meeting room, Ron Landreau entered with Andrew Ledger. While Ledger appeared more scholarly than political, he knew how to work the room. He shook hands with every director and took his time making his way around the room, leaving Benny and me for last. Finally Ledger stepped toward Benny.

"Benny, good to see you again," Ledger said. "I hope you're doing well."

"Thank you, Andrew, and I hope you're doing well," Benny said.

"Well, you can make my day a lot better by agreeing to sell to us," Ledger said.

"Andrew, I can't say it's good to see you here," Benny said calmly. "I'm going to do my best to keep Citizens Bank independent."

I was surprised. I hadn't expected Benny to challenge Ledger so strongly this early.

"Well, I understand," Andrew said. "If I was in your shoes I would feel the same way."

"You'll be in my shoes someday, and you'll know how I feel," Benny said. "*Bank on it!*"

I was ready to hit the floor. I held back a belly laugh. Benny was pulling out all the stops.

Benny started the meeting. "Our board meetings are held under *Robert's Rules of Order*, and I am the chairman. You have been given forty-five minutes to make your presentation. I'll have the opportunity to speak after you. Understood?"

"That is hardly fair," he said. "I have a computer presentation that will take at least two hours."

"You're being treated more than fairly," Benny said. "No one can listen for more than an hour to even the best of speakers without getting a numb rear end. I would urge you to use your forty-five minutes wisely. I control the clock. Understood?"

"Benny, I don't appreciate being treated like this. When we buy your bank, I'll have the watch," Andrew said, almost spitting out the words.

"You may buy Citizens Bank, but you're not buying me," Benny said.

After that tense exchange, Benny asked Ron Landreau to introduce "his special guest."

Weighing in at over three hundred pounds and standing less than six feet tall, Ron Landreau appeared to be a shorter, younger version of Andy Griffith's *Matlock* character. Dressed in a beige three-piece suit that must have been ordered from somewhere in South America, Ron began his introduction.

"Greetings lady and gentlemen," he began, "it is my distinguished pleasure to introduce one of the top bankers in the world. He is a man who has engineered almost seventy mergers and has grown his bank into one of the largest banks in the good ole US of A. He is a man who knows how to turn losing banks into winners and winners into champions. It is my honor and privilege to welcome him to our Citizens Bank directors' meeting. Please join with me in welcoming the chairman, president, and chief executive officer of Merchants Bank, Mr. Andrew Conner Ledger."

The board politely applauded as Ledger walked to the front of the room, the old boards in the floor cracking and popping. Ledger stood to the left of Benny, who was seated at the head of the board table.

"Thank you for allowing me to visit today," Andrew began. "I'll not be able to give you all of the material I hoped to give you because of the time limitation. But I think in my brief time with you I will convey the value Merchants Bank can offer you as shareholders of Citizens Bank."

For forty-five minutes an agitated and obviously frustrated Andrew Ledger fought with himself to shorten his usual two-hour slide presentation. As he raced through the one hundred twenty-six slides he realized he was only one-third of the way through his presentation with less than fifteen minutes remaining in his allotted time. Benny knew what he was doing when he cut Ledger's time. Ledger's presentation was at its weakest when it came to shareholder value. Other than showing that the stock was traded on the New York Stock Exchange, every chart depicted a stock that languished in the same trading range for years. There appeared to be very little upside to Merchants stock after getting an initial premium. The facts he hoped would be forgotten in a much longer presentation were now left visible. The deal was only good if Merchants stock could climb higher after the purchase. You could see the sweat starting to drip off his temples as he tried to gain control of his thoughts.

"Sometimes these slides aren't as pretty as they really should be," he said. "You know how accountants are."

Benny spoke up and said, "You have five minutes left." This only made Ledger angrier, raising the tension in the room as his voice rose in volume.

"I don't believe I have been given the adequate amount of time to show all of the information that would portray the value of joining

Merchants Bank," he said looking at Benny. "If you allow me, I would appreciate having at least another half hour. I would like to go back and review some slides I had to skip."

Benny knew his audience. While greed had been at play, Ledger's angry tone and failure to show any real value left the majority of the board with doubts. Surprisingly, Benny called for a vote.

"Even though Mr. Ledger gave us the same information for our review over two weeks ago, to be fair to our guest, I will call for a vote on his request for more time by raise of hands. All those in favor of allowing Mr. Ledger another thirty minutes to explain why it is a good idea for Merchants to buy Citizens Bank, please raise your right hand."

Only three of the fifteen members raised their hands.

"All opposed, please signify by raising your right hand," Benny said.

The rest of the board members raised their hands.

"Mr. Ledger, as a result of the board vote, your time is now down to three minutes," he said looking at his watch.

"I have an incredible offer for you; I am willing to sweeten that offer right now, if you give me thirty more minutes," Ledger said. "I will increase the stock premium we have offered to you by 15 percent." Everyone sat stunned for a moment. Ron Landreau raised himself from his snug-fitting chair and asked for permission to speak. Benny granted him the floor.

"I believe we owe more to Mr. Ledger than a paltry forty-five minutes. He has come all the way from Charlotte, North Carolina. He has taken time to prepare a beautiful package of information. It even has pictures." Most of the board members laughed aloud, but Ron continued. "Mr. Chairman, with a different offer now on the table I make a motion that we allow Mr. Ledger the opportunity to speak for another thirty minutes." Mitch Gannon, one of Ron's allies, seconded the motion.

Ledger, now feeling in control, put his remote control down and began to speak off the cuff. "I say this not to dishonor your fine chairman, but I have seen this many times. You all have played a part of building a great organization. But time takes its toll. You are at your peak. I am offering a deal that will be unmatched. Every stock analyst will say that I'm foolish for making an offer like this for a little bank in Virginia. But I'm not. While each of you stands to make a lot of money from this offer, I speak not just to you but also to your children and their children and their children. What you'll make from this transaction will help your family for generations. It'll keep your bank operating as you see it operating now." Hearing those words Benny looked over toward me and allowed a slight grin. "I appeal to you to consider my offer. It is the best thing for you, your family, and your community."

Ledger then stepped into uncharted territory.

"Your chairman is one of the most liked bankers in the Southeast United States. But he is ready to retire. I also understand he is sick— even though he isn't willing to share that information. If Benny is not around to lead your bank, who will? I know Jack Oliver. He is a great banker . . . in Philadelphia. You have one question to ask yourself. Where will you be tomorrow without Merchants?"

My face was now crimson. Benny looked pale; almost defeated. Ledger thanked the board for their time, smiling at Benny and patting him on the shoulder.

Benny stood. His frailty was exposed as he struggled to lift himself from his chair. If I perceived him like this, I thought, I wonder how everyone else perceived him. Ledger may have won.

"Mr. Ledger, we are glad we're such a prized catch," Benny said. "We must have been doing something right all of these years." There was some nervous laughter before he continued. "All of you know how much I enjoy questions. I'm glad Mr. Ledger asked a question. It's a simple question. How we answer may very well determine whether we will agree to sell our company to Merchants Bank. 'Where will we be tomorrow without Merchants?'" Benny leaned forward and unclasped his hands, placing his outstretched fingers on the wobbly metal table in front of him.

"Let me address where we will be tomorrow, and the day after tomorrow; next month; and even next year. We will still be here without Merchants as long as we choose to be. We choose our destiny. I have not told anyone about my health. How Mr. Ledger has discovered confidential information and then chose to use it to gain leverage is something each of you will judge as to whether it was ethical or not." Ledger squirmed in his chair and crossed his arms, looking in the direction of Ron Landreau. Landreau had his head down with his arms crossed on the table.

"I brought in a great banker," Benny said as he pointed toward me. "He's not just great in Philadelphia but also here in Virginia. Jack Oliver will not do as well as me as a leader; he will do better than me. Jack is doing a wonderful job and is part of our family." With each word Benny's voice sounded fuller. His frail frame appeared to transform in front of us into a younger and energetic man.

"While I don't believe it is proper or necessary to talk about my illness in this setting, I will do so because it now stands as an issue. I was diagnosed over six months ago with cancer. I had planned on stepping down soon and handing over the reins to Jack. I will die, but all of us in this room will do the same at some time in the future. None of us are graced with a body that will not degenerate and finally give out. Mine may do so sooner than I would like, but that is not what this meeting is about." My eyes were filling with tears. I heard Sherry quietly sob as Benny continued.

"Since Mr. Ledger wanted to link the two as a cause and effect, I will do so, too. Here is my question. What do we want to be remembered for? Is it how much money we made? Are we going to stamp our financial statement, audited, of course, on our tombstone?" he asked, smiling and standing straight. He reached down with his right hand and lightly struck the tabletop. I could see everyone had now lifted their heads and was looking at him.

"I'm not saying this in sarcasm or anger. I'm asking a very valid question. When we started this bank we said we were doing it to replace a bank that we all lost—or should I say—sold. We sold a part of the Salem and Roanoke history. We turned over control to someone far removed from our community." The words were coming quicker. He opened his arms wide and continued. "We were greedy, and we agreed that to make up for that greed, we would establish a new financial institution that was based on service, not profits." Bringing his hands back together he smiled and paused. "We created a bank that would never ignore someone because of a lack of zeros behind a number tied to their name. We created a place where people would want to work and people would feel safe putting their money. We accomplished what we set out to do and more. Citizens Bank is at its strongest, not at its weakest as Mr. Ledger has said. We made a promise; a promise I'm keeping," he said. He nodded his head affirmatively and stepped back, looking at the projection screen with a slide entitled "Return on Investment."

"If you want to sell this bank, I will not fight the transaction. I just want you to answer the question I posed. What do you want to be remembered for? Speaking for myself, I don't want to be remembered for breaking my promise and my commitment to everyone who works at Citizens and who are clients of Citizens." Benny positioned himself so he was looking directly at Landreau and Ledger. "But I'll give you one chance to have my approval and consent, Mr. Ledger," he said gazing at the slumping figure.

"Can you promise me, Mr. Ledger, that all of our people will be working here, with the same salaries and opportunities they now possess, in six months? In one year? In two years? Do you promise to keep our local management team intact? Will you promise me there will be no layoffs? Will you promise that you will treat every client with the same respect and dignity they now receive? Will you promise me that our community will continue to receive the same support?" He paused. "Mr. Ledger, if you will promise me those things—on your word—in front of these people, I will make the motion to approve the sale of Citizens Bank. Will you promise, Mr. Ledger?"

Ledger was stunned. He looked around the room and stood. I knew he would agree, lying to get what he wanted. Benny had given away the bank, I thought.

"You want a promise? That's not part of doing business. There's no room for promises. There's a price you pay for getting a huge premium: your control. If you sell Citizens it will then be Merchants Bank's. You want honesty, there it is. No promises! This is not about promises. This is not about how you or I will be remembered. This is not about service. This is about profits. That's what doing business is all about—the bottom line." He couldn't seem to stop talking.

"I am offering each of you more money than you would have ever dreamt of. You'll never get another chance to make this much money. That's why I am here. Call me greedy, call me arrogant, but you can call yourself richer if you agree to sell your bank. That's your choice." Pausing, he looked at Benny. "I agree with your chairman. We're all going to die someday and we better get what we can now. The choice is yours." He sat back down, tall and straight in his chair staring at Benny, a smile now stretching across his face.

"You were honest, I'll give you that," Benny said. "You answered the questions."

Sherry Carter stood up. Sherry, as one of the largest shareholders, had the most to gain. She had worked for years, twelve-hour-plus days doing every job in the restaurant. If anyone would be interested in the large premium offered by Ledger, she would be the one, I thought.

"Benny, I'm with you," she said with traces of tears in her eyes. "Mr. Ledger, you could not be more wrong. We did not set out to get rich from starting Citizens Bank. We set out to help our community and make a positive difference in people's lives. I don't want your money, and I don't want your bank in my town."

Jerry Culver, the owner of a car dealership in Roanoke and the oldest member of the board, stood as soon as Sherry finished speaking. Jerry was part of Ron's group of pro-Merchants directors. "Mr. Ledger, you are greed personified. You'll never get my vote. I don't want your money."

Ron Landreau interrupted the mumbling and undercurrent of sound. Squeezing himself upward from his chair and hushing the mumbling with his loud, southern twang, Ron Landreau said, "My dear friends, I'm the person who was responsible for bringing this offer to the table today. Mr. Ledger, I apologize for taking up your valuable time." Ron dropped his head and looked down at the package of Merchants information. "I've learned something in the past few minutes. I remembered why I am here." Visibly struggling to speak with emotion crackling every syllable of every word, he continued. "I'm not as eloquent as Sherry, Jerry, and Benny about why we formed Citizens, but I do have something to say. I am to blame. I am at fault. I owe each of you an apology from the bottom of my heart. I don't want to be remembered for selling Citizens Bank. I don't want to be remembered for breaking the same promise Benny and all of us made twenty years ago. That promise is what binds us.

It created our purpose, the purpose that made our bank great and unique." Wiping away tears from his eyes and pausing to gain his composure, Ron spoke in a loud booming voice. "Mr. Chairman, I make a motion to reject the offer made by Merchants Bank!"

Jerry seconded the motion without a pause. The board passed the vote unanimously. A loud applause erupted. Tears were in almost everyone's eyes. Ron walked to the front of the room and hugged Benny. I could see his lips say, "I'm sorry, friend."

I do not know how Ledger got out of the room, but he disappeared.

We had won. But Benny was sick.

My best friend was going to die.

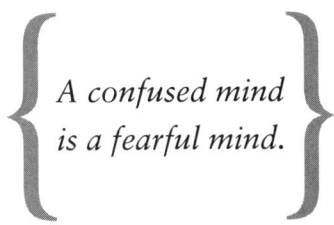

{ *A confused mind*
is a fearful mind. }

—BENJAMIN FRANKLIN PRICE

41. How Could You Say No?

"HOW COULD YOU SAY NO?" The question illuminated the shock in the community. The story of how greed lost spread rapidly. News of the failed attempt to buy Citizens Bank hit the financial reporting news wires. DAVID DEFEATS GOLIATH was the headline in the *Wall Street Journal*. For a few days the bank that said no was famous. But Benny refused to do interviews.

While the celebration of our fight to survive continued locally, I was more concerned about my friend. I didn't say anything to him driving back to the office after the board meeting. I was going to let Benny bring it up when he wanted to.

On Thursday morning in our usual start-of-the-day progress meeting, Benny was ready to talk. "Jack, I didn't want to keep my illness a secret from you. I simply felt like it was not time to talk about it. I didn't want it to be an issue in the board's decision process," he said. "I'm sorry if you think I deceived you in any way."

"Benny, I never thought anything like that, I understand. But I'm concerned. Not about the bank, but about you."

"The doctors never gave me a good outlook. They said I would be lucky to be around in six months, but I'm still here. Now, it does look like things have slid somewhat."

"You're tough," I said. "If anyone can beat an illness you can."

"Jack, I appreciate your good cheer," Benny said contemplatively. "But we're all going to die someday. I will soon."

Tears began to swell in my eyes. Benny could see I was struggling.

"I'm not gone yet, though. We have some fishing to do. What about this weekend?"

"I would enjoy that," I said.

As I stood to walk out of the office, Benny said, "Jack, one thing before you go."

I stopped and turned to face him. "Yes, Benny, what is it?"

"I'm proud of you."

I walked from his office. I walked into my office and shut the door.

I cried.

• • •

I called Tina that evening. I didn't know what to say. I had not spoken to her since the board meeting.

"Hello, Jack," Tina said. "I saw your bank's name on the news in Philadelphia. Can you believe it? It sounds like you won," she said.

"This wasn't about winning. I've changed, Tina," I said.

"Yeah, Jack, I can tell a lot from four hundred miles away," she said. "Life has always been a game to you—congratulations, you won this round."

Avoiding her sarcasm, I told her about Benny's illness. "I wish you and the kids would come down here to meet him," I said. "I would really appreciate it."

"I don't think we can swing that," she said. "Joshua is driving me nuts. He won't listen to me. Jessica is involved with some guy and talking about marriage. But you don't know anything about those things, do you?"

"I love you, Tina" fell from my lips without any thought. I couldn't contain the words anymore. I could count the number of times I had said "I love you" to Tina on one hand. Sadly, the count would include our wedding day.

"Why do you say that now?" Tina asked. "If you had said that years ago and meant it, we would not be where we're at today." I was familiar with her angry tone.

"That's the point," I said. "I had to go through this to change. It was fate. I am different. You've got to believe me. I'm not the Jack Oliver that you despise. I am the real me—the one you loved. Can you forgive me?" I asked through tears of regret.

"No!" she said with a definitive tone. "I'm not going to forgive you for what you have done to me and the kids. You didn't appreciate what you had until you lost it. I don't know why you're saying this now. I'm sure you have a plan and are trying to trick me to get something. It won't work! Suffer the consequences, Jack."

She hung up.

Tina was right about the damage I'd done. But I had changed. All I wanted was a chance to show her. *Just one chance,* I thought wiping tears from my face. I was frustrated and angry. My best friend was dying. At the time when I should have been happiest, I was back where I had started—feeling depressed. "Why can't she see that I've changed?" I asked myself as I walked out to my car. I had to get outside. It felt as though the walls were closing in and ready to crush me.

I left my condo in Salem and drove to the 19th Hole. I had heard it was a hangout for young professionals in the town. As I stepped inside, I felt more at ease. *One drink can't hurt,* I thought to myself. I hadn't touched alcohol since leaving Philadelphia. The server stepped over to my table. "What would you like to drink?" she asked as I had my head down in the menu pretending to look at the choices of hamburgers and sandwiches.

I paused and lifted my head to look around. I made my decision.

"I'll have a glass of sweet tea," I said.

"Would you like something from the bar?" she asked, almost seeing the challenge I was enduring at that moment.

"No, I'll stick with the tea," I said.

As the server walked away, I felt a sense of accomplishment greater than I had achieved in my entire career. No one was there to congratulate me or even understand. How could ordering a glass of tea be such a great accomplishment? But it was. Whether Tina realized it or not, I knew I was different—I had changed.

On Friday mornings it was a custom at Citizens Bank to have a Sweet Day—a day when each office would enjoy a breakfast celebration at the bank's expense. Benny had created the events as a way to celebrate progress. While technically the get-togethers could be called a staff meeting, it was structured as a way for employees to relax together. As part of his ritual, Benny and I would visit a different office every Friday morning. Everyone enjoyed a visit from Benny. It was fun.

We were scheduled to visit the Shawsville office. I enjoyed the drive to the sleepy little community that was lodged between a mountain on one side and a river on the other. A railroad track split the village into two sides. Taking my time, I drove down US 11 avoiding the heavy traffic on Interstate 81. I was expecting to meet Benny at seven-thirty at the office. But when I arrived he wasn't there. It wasn't like him to miss one of the Friday breakfasts. At eight o'clock, I stepped into the small conference room to call the main office to see what happened. *He's probably stuck in traffic, or something has come up,* I thought. But before I could finish dialing the number, one of the employees told me Ann was holding on line one for me.

"Jack, I'm sorry to call you like this, but Benny's at Roanoke Memorial Hospital," she said in a calm voice. "He's not doing very well."

"I'll leave right now and be there in thirty minutes," I said, knowingly shortening the drive by fifteen minutes.

"Drive safely," she said hearing the urgency in my voice.

I drove like the old Jack, making my way onto Interstate 81 heading north toward Roanoke. As I whipped my way through a maze of tractor trailers, I couldn't take my mind off the person who had played such a defining role in my life. We had planned on going fishing tomorrow, and now Benny was struggling to live.

I arrived at the hospital in exactly thirty minutes and made my way to Benny's room. Ann met me at the door and hugged me.

"Thank you for coming, Jack," she said. "Benny is doing a little better. He had a terrible night."

"I'm here anytime you need me," I said, trying to control my emotions as we stepped inside the room.

Benny saw me entering the room and smiled a half-smile. "Well, Jack Oliver, what are you doing leaving the bank this early?" he said barely audible, but trying to laugh. He coughed and appeared to almost choke. I stepped forward beside Ann.

"I think it's in good hands," I said trying to smile, "much better hands than my own."

"That's right," Benny said, squinting his eyes and slowly nodding his head to show his approval. "After I'm gone, don't forget that it's just a job and you have a life to live."

"Rubbish," Ann said. "You must both agree to not talk about work."

"Deal," I said.

"Deal," Benny said smiling.

He held up his hand, and I took it in mine. Despite the obvious pain and his weakened state, his hand felt strong and vital. He was alive and was not giving up.

"Jack, I'm so sorry we can't go fishing this weekend," Benny said. "How about a rain check?"

"That sounds great," I said. "You tell me when, and we'll go. I'll drive." My driving had not quite adapted to the winding Virginia curves. Benny had been a passenger in my car on Virginia roads only once before.

"I tell you what, Jack," Benny said. "I'll drive—it'll be safer."

We all laughed. Benny started to cough again. As Ann reached over to lift him up higher on his pillow I saw the love the two shared. I immediately thought of Tina.

The nurse came into the room and asked if we could step out for a moment. Ann and I stepped toward the end of the hospital corridor.

"Jack, I can't tell you how much you have meant to Benny," Ann said. "He thinks of you just like a part of our family. You're just like a son to us."

"I think of Benny just like a father," I said, trying to keep my tears at bay. "And you just like a mother."

"I don't know how much longer Benny has," Ann said. "He

wants to go to the cabin again. As soon as he is up to it, I think it would be a good idea if you could drive him there—just the two of you. He would really like that."

"I will," I said. "You let me know when, and I'll take him."

• • •

Two weeks passed. Benny was released from the hospital and was ready to go to the lake. I drove to Benny's house early, so we could have as much daylight as possible. As we were getting into my car, he looked back at Ann and said with a smile, "Now for the dangerous part—survive Jack's driving."

I laughed as I settled into the driver's seat. "Ann, I promise I will drive my best today."

"Just bring him back in one piece," she said, laughing. "You two have a great day."

In late winter, Roanoke's weather could produce all four seasons in a single day. But on this day, the temperature was expected to climb to almost fifty degrees. As we made our way out of Salem into the morning traffic, the sun began to intermittently poke through the cloud cover. "Not bad weather for a trip to the lake," Benny said as we drove southward toward Smith Mountain Lake. Most of the talk centered on work. I gave Benny a quick progress report to catch him up.

"You're in charge, Jack," he said. "I trust you. The only thing you must do is never forget where you came from."

I told Benny about Carol, my assistant at PT&G, and the time she said that to me.

"She's a smart lady," Benny said.

We arrived at the lake, and I carried the lunch Ann had packed into the kitchen. Benny sat down in the rocker on the porch. As I emerged from inside, I heard him say, "Let's go out on the boat." Even though he was extremely weak, I knew this was something he wanted to do. *This may be his last time at the lake,* I thought to myself.

We walked to the dock and I prepared the boat. I was now what Benny termed a "semi-accomplished fisherman." At least I was not falling off the dock, and I knew how to bait a hook. I guided the boat into the main channel. Benny looked happy.

After completing a lengthy circle of the lake area, we returned to the dock. Benny had said very little while on the boat. We walked back up the hill to the cabin, stopping several times so he could catch his breath. "This isn't one of the most pleasant things about getting old," he said. "I used to race Ben from the dock to the house. But that was a long time ago." He stood looking toward the cabin and turned to look back at the dock. "Do you want to race?" he said, trying to smile.

I put my hand on his shoulder and said, "You'd still win."

After we reached the cabin, Benny sat down in the rocker facing the lake. I asked him if he wanted me to bring out the sandwiches Ann had prepared. "That would be great, Jack," he said. "If you don't mind, I'm going to sit out here while you get the grub ready."

I took my time. I knew he wanted time alone with his memories.

"Jack, when are you going to bring out those sandwiches?" Benny asked. "You didn't eat them all did you?" I walked onto the porch with the sandwiches. After another trip into the kitchen, I brought the iced tea and apple pie to the porch. The breeze coming from the lake was calm. The sun was shining bright, warming the day to the predicted higher-than-normal temperature.

"I think I told you about Ben and how he always seemed to smile when he ran," Benny said after a few moments. "I don't think I told you why."

I remembered hearing about Ben on this porch. Everything in my life had changed since that day.

"There was a reason. When he was first starting to run, he would get upset when someone would pass him. I never saw a youngster so competitive. He thought losing was going to mark him as something less than human. We wanted to see him enjoy something he was so natural at doing, whether he won or not. I struggled with how I could help. Then I shared with him something I learned in Vietnam. While he didn't understand the conditions I was in as a POW, he took it to heart. In the POW camp, I created my own little ritual. Every morning when I saw the sun rise through the bamboo cage, I would make sure I conjured up a smile on my face. Smiling wasn't the smartest thing to do."

"I remember, you said they beat you if they saw you smile," I said.

"Yes, they thought it was a sign of contempt. But a half-smile was my way to exert my right to choose—not just what I was thinking, but what I was doing." Benny reached over and took a sip of tea. "I told Ben every time someone passed him or he was feeling the burn in his legs to give the world a smile. It was not a sign of contempt or arrogance. What the smile said was 'I'm all right. Everything is okay in my world.' He never had the issues he struggled with when someone would pass him or he felt weary. He remembered that he was responsible for what he did—not someone else."

"When you're in control, you're happy," I said, agreeing with what I thought he was saying.

"No, not control, but being aware of the reality you're in and responding to it from the inside out." He paused and turned to look at me. "Now I'm facing the inevitable. I'm going to die. I told you how Ben taught me how to live. He's now giving me the courage to die." He paused and looked up the road where I remember he said he saw Ben the last time alive. "Death is not an end—it's a beginning. I believe it, Jack. How do I know? When I found Ben that morning along the road, my heart and soul were crushed. I ran to his side, and he was already gone. But he let me know he was all right. He had experienced a new beginning. He had found his way home." Benny paused. "He had a smile on his face. That's why I know I'll be all right, just like him. The pain may pull me down, I may not be able to be like I was, but you'll see me do everything I can to give my smile to the world."

Just like every other moment with Benny, I was learning. I did not want to see Benny leave, even if death was inevitable. I needed him.

"The past year has been a joy for Ann and me. You have meant so much to us. Not just because you can carry on at Citizens after I'm gone, but also because you filled a void. You're so much like a son."

Tears swelled in my eyes. "You have been like a father," I said. "I can never thank you enough."

"Are you happy?" Benny asked.

I thought for a moment. My life had changed. I was living a better life. But something remained missing. He knew me. "I want to be with my family," I said. "I have changed and would give anything to show them I'm different."

"Where there's life, there's hope," Benny said. "Never give up, Jack."

"I'm afraid I'll never be able to show them," I said.

"Remember our hike up the mountain?" Benny said. "You said you were afraid of heights, but really you were afraid of falling."

"Yes, I remember."

"Have you gone back to the cliff and looked over the edge?"

I had ventured on that same trail twice, both times with the intent of overcoming my fear and looking down into the gorge. Both times I failed. I told Benny I had not succeeded yet.

"If you allow fear to control your thoughts, you'll find yourself attached to it," Benny said. "There's no one else or anything to blame. It's a prison you've constructed. Letting go of that fear will give you freedom. Letting go is the key. Your family is in your life—it's just not how you want it to be—now. Let go of the fear and live, Jack. Fate will have its way."

We sat on the porch for several hours talking. I could see Benny was getting tired. "If you don't mind, Jack, let's just sit for a while and listen." We sat and listened to the sounds around us. Then Benny said, "Let's go."

I drove Benny back to his home—safely. Ann met us in the driveway.

"So you brought him back in one piece," she said, hugging Benny as he stood up after getting out of the car.

"Jack has finally learned to drive," Benny said.

I walked around the car and hugged Ann.

"Thank you, son," she said in a low voice. "You made Benny's journey complete."

"Thank you for everything," I said.

I walked to the door and carried the basket of empty containers from our lunch. Ann carried it inside, leaving Benny and me standing at the door.

"Benny, I have a question. How do you thank a person for

saving your life?" I asked. "Because that's what you did. You saved my life."

Benny looked at me and put his right hand on my shoulder. "All I did was ask some questions. The rest was up to you. You know what to do with your life. Never waste a moment—we are never promised another."

We hugged. I saw Benny drape his arm around Ann for support as he walked into their home.

It was the last time I saw Benny alive.

{

*Where there's life
there's hope.*

}

—BENJAMIN FRANKLIN PRICE

42. Why Me?

"WHY ME?" I asked myself.

At work the next day I received a phone call all parents fear. Tina called and said Joshua had been in a car wreck in the early morning rush hour traffic. Joshua and three of his friends had been sideswiped by a tractor trailer while driving to school. His condition was "serious but stable." He had suffered a broken leg and arm and numerous cuts and bruises. One of the boys in the car, the driver, was killed instantly. He was the only one not wearing a safety belt. Even though the car had been crumpled, the other three had survived. I told Tina I was on my way.

I called Ann from my cell phone and told her what had happened. She said they would be praying for Joshua. She said Benny was very tired but happy that he had gotten to visit the lake. "Thank you, Jack, for everything," she said. "Take care of yourself and your son. Let us know if there is anything we can do."

I was fortunate to find a connecting flight from Roanoke to Pittsburgh on US Air and then a shuttle to Philadelphia. I went straight to the hospital. Tina was standing on one side of Joshua's bed and Jessica was on the other. Jessica moved quickly around the bed and hugged me. I walked toward Joshua's bed with Jessica under my right arm. Tina stepped back.

"Hey, Joshua, it's your dad," I said, rubbing his rumpled hair with my left hand, tears falling off my cheeks.

Joshua, still sedated and barely awake, looked up and smiled, speaking in a whisper, "Hey, Dad."

"I'm always here for you, Jessica, and your mom," I said through my tears. I stood at the bed and looked at my son. After standing by his bed until he fell asleep, I stepped into the hall with Tina.

"Thanks for coming, Jack," Tina said. "It means a lot to Joshua. Believe it or not, he looks up to you. He may not ever admit it, but he's proud of his father."

I did not know what to say.

"How is life in the mountains of Virginia?" Tina asked.

I told her about Benny and his condition.

"You really think a lot of Benny, don't you?" Tina asked.

"He's like a father to me," I said.

"Well, I'm glad you have found a friend," she said.

I stayed at the hospital without leaving for the next three days. Joshua was making a strong recovery. The broken leg and arm were healing. The concern over a slight puncture in one of his lungs was dismissed. The hospital released him, and we took him back home.

Joshua was now suffering a different kind of pain, the death of one of his friends. Even though his injuries kept him in a wheelchair, he wanted to attend the funeral service that afternoon. The attention from his friends seemed to help him in his grief. After we returned home and got Joshua in the downstairs guest bedroom, I asked if he wanted to talk. He did.

"Dad, I feel guilty for Brad's death," Joshua said, allowing the first outward expression of loss that I had witnessed since the accident. "Brad never wore a seat belt and always drove too fast. But I got in the car with him and didn't say anything. I could have made things different."

"Joshua, you could have tried, but you never know what would have happened," I said. "He might have listened, or he might have chosen to drive even faster to prove a point. It's not your fault. You can't second-guess something. I thank God you're alive."

Joshua was crying. I had not seen him cry since he was a toddler. I leaned over and hugged him. "You seem good, Dad," he said.

"I am," I said. "I did things before that I'm not proud of. I am trying my best to change."

"I can tell," he said. "You look less stressed. Did you need to leave us to feel that way?"

"It wasn't because of any of you," I said. "I want you, Jessica, and your mother in my life some way and somehow. I miss you all."

"We miss you, Dad," Joshua said.

Joshua had hardly ever called me "Dad." He had even gotten to the point of calling me "Jack" as if I were an acquaintance. Hearing "Dad" gave me a surge of happiness. I left the room so he could sleep.

Tina was in the kitchen making spaghetti. I offered to help, but she said she didn't need any. I couldn't tell if the coldness and harshness in her tone was from near-exhaustion or the anger of having me in her life again, even for a brief time.

"Is it all right if I stay in here and talk?" I asked.

"Yeah, that's fine," Tina said.

"You look great," I said. "Jessica said you were running in a marathon next month."

"Yes, I'm getting myself back into shape. It's been tough. You're looking much fitter, Jack," Tina added. "What's your secret? A young girlfriend?"

"No, nothing that expensive. I quit drinking. I haven't touched a drop in over a year. Along with that, I eat much healthier food. And I have been taking yoga classes to help stretch and relax."

"Jack Oliver in a yoga class! I would pay to see that!" Tina said, laughing.

"You don't have to pay—just come and visit me," I said. "Then you can watch me in the downward dog position."

"I don't think I will ever come to Virginia, Jack," Tina said with her back turned, working on putting the pasta in the boiling water. "Our time has come and gone."

"Why?" I asked.

"Because you wanted it that way," she said. "You left."

I was not going to debate the past. I loved Tina with all my heart. I was here with her again, and that gave me hope. I was not going to give up. "If I could have anything in my life, it would be that you would give me one more chance to prove I'm different," I said. "I love you Tina."

Tina turned quickly toward me.

"I love you, Jack. But I love me more. You taught me that! You almost ruined me with your career and obsession to get to the top. I can't handle that anymore. It would kill me trying to go through that again."

"You would never have to," I said. "I promise."

In our entire marriage I had rarely used the words "I promise," so my using it surprised her.

"You promise?" she asked sarcastically. "That's easier said than done. I don't trust you, Jack. You have a lifetime of lies to overcome."

I wanted to beg, but then I thought back to what Benny had told me. "Let go of the fear," he had said. It was time to let go of the fear and trust time would heal.

"You're right," I said. "I have lived a selfish life, but I have changed. Only time will prove that I'm a better person, a person you can trust. The only thing I ask of you, Tina, is to open your mind to the slim chance that I am telling you the truth."

"We'll see," she said.

That night I slept on the couch in the den, and the inner demons that toyed with me in the middle of the night came to visit. Why had I excused myself from my family? Was it for my career, or was there more? I started to think about my mother. The anniversary of her death was a week away. I sat up on the couch staring into the darkness, looking for an answer. I turned on the light and saw my reflection on the darkened television screen. I had changed in appearance. I had changed as a person. But how could Tina see that? I walked into the kitchen to get a drink of water. I saw the calendar on the refrigerator and peered at it. *Time was flying by,* I thought. Then I saw the name on the calendar I had heard the kids bring up. Charles was his name, Tina's boyfriend. Evidently she had been planning to go to a concert with him the next evening. I felt like I was prying and opened the door to get a bottle of water. As I shut the door, I saw Tina was in the kitchen.

"Still can't sleep?" she said.

"I was thirsty," I said.

"I couldn't sleep," she said. She ran her hand through her hair to pull it back from her face. She leaned back against the counter and folded her arms. "Are you serious about what you said? Do you really love me?"

"With all of my heart," I said.

"And you've changed?" she asked.

"Yes," I said.

"I want you to go downtown with me tomorrow, so I can show you something," she said.

"What is it?" I asked.

"You can wait," she said, smiling.

"Yes, I can wait," I said. "And I'll buy you lunch?"

"Okay, Jack. Goodnight," she said and turned to go back upstairs.

● ● ●

"So what's at the museum you want me to see?" I asked, as we walked up the steps into the large entry hall.

"Your mother's Philadelphia quilt. When was the last time you looked at it?"

"I've only seen it once. I was barely a teenager," I said with shame. We walked without speaking through the exhibition halls. I was following Tina's lead. We entered a large room with paintings of Philly in the Revolutionary War era. Walking through the exhibit hall, we entered a long, narrow walkway. As we turned a corner there on one entire wall was the Philadelphia Bicentennial Quilt.

"Your mother was incredible. She was an artist, Jack," Tina said.

My focus on the quilt went to Town Hall and the Liberty Bell filling the centerpiece. I felt Tina sliding close to me.

"Jack, do you remember what you told me your mother put on the baby quilts she made?"

"Yeah, the baby's name. She never put her name. It was her way of gifting her work. That was my mom," I said, still surveying the mammoth work.

Tina grabbed my arm and repositioned me toward the lower right-hand corner of the quilt. "Do you see anything? Look closely."

I stared closely at the corner of the gigantic tapestry. The scene was a neighborhood with a gaslit street light. I bent over and looked closer. There in the right-hand corner of Philadelphia's Bicentennial Quilt were the initials JDO—my initials. Below the bold letters, written in a cursive style were the words, "With love, Mom." I stood straight and looked at Tina. Tears were streaming down her face. My own tears poured unashamedly down. We both took a step forward and held each other tightly.

"She loved you so much, Jack. You were her life. She was proud of you. I'm sorry I never showed you before now."

I kept holding Tina. Out of the corner of my eyes I saw the quilted scene. I recognized the homes. It was my old neighborhood with our small house in the middle. A boy was sitting on the porch.

It was me.

• • •

We walked out of the museum to our favorite downtown restaurant. It was where we'd had our first official date, but I couldn't remember the last time we had eaten there. "It's been a while," I said as we walked inside. The restaurant had not changed much. As the hostess walked us through the large main dining area, I realized we were being taken to the same table where we had eaten our first meal together.

"You didn't . . ." I started to say, but before I could finish I could see Tina shaking her head.

"That's luck," she said.

"No, fate," I said.

It was a relaxed lunch. We talked without the weight of the past hanging over us. I was telling Tina about how I had learned to fish. She was telling me about her involvement with Habitat for Humanity. They were the lives we had hoped to live when we had first met.

My cell phone began to ring. As I flipped open the phone and said "Hello" I heard Ann's voice. I instantly knew what had happened.

Benny had died.

. . .

"Will you speak at his funeral?" Ann asked after giving me the terrible news. She spoke in her usual calm voice. I hoped that I could retain that same strength. I was devastated. "He asked if you would say a few words—but to keep it short."

I could hear her smile over the phone. I was certain that's what he had said. "It would be my honor," I said, still in a state of shock. I pictured Benny telling Ann—for me to "keep it brief." I smiled. I told her I would return tomorrow afternoon and come by her home.

"One of the last things Benny asked was how your son was doing," Ann said. "We prayed together for him and for you and your family. We talked about Ben and the foundation. Then he laid back down and died in his sleep very peacefully."

"I'm so sorry," I said.

"He was in so much pain. He's better off now. When I saw he was gone, I knew he was at a better place."

"He was smiling," I said without thinking.

"Yes, you knew it would be like that, didn't you?"

"Yes, he had told me."

I held myself together until the conversation ended. I looked across the table at Tina.

"I'm sorry, Jack," she said, understanding what had happened. I excused myself and walked to the bathroom. I splashed water on my face. Looking into the mirror, I saw the eyes of a person I had battled my entire life. The war had taken a toll on everyone involved. I had won the most recent battles, but life was not any easier. Benny had told me it would be that way and to never give up. I understood what he was saying.

On the drive back to Tina's she said, "I wish I could have met him."

"I wish you could have," I said. "There will never be another Benny Price."

We spent a quiet evening together, Tina, Jessica, Joshua, and me. Before I went to the couch to try to find a way to sleep, I walked in and sat down on the edge of the bed beside Joshua. He was already asleep. As I looked at him, I brushed his hair from his forehead. I couldn't remember the last time I had any physical contact with my son. Other than holding his hand briefly at the hospital, the Oliver family tradition of removing emotions and being detached had remained unchanged. And then a memory from the past exploded in my thoughts. When I was very young, I had a severe fever. I was almost delirious from the high body temperature. But I remembered my father staying up with me all night, sitting by my bed. *My father cared*, I thought, but he had difficulties expressing himself. "Just like me," I said in a hushed tone. Hearing me speak, Joshua turned his head and opened his eyes, still somewhere between sleep and awake.

"What did you say?" he asked.

"I didn't mean to wake you up," I said. "Son, I love you."

"I love you, Dad," he said as he turned his head to fall back into a deep sleep. Whether it was exhaustion or a sense that I needed the rest, my demons stayed away that night.

I slept in peace.

• • •

The next morning Tina drove me to the airport. As she pulled up in front of the departure gates I asked her to keep an open mind about me.

"I'm doing my best," Tina said. "I'm sorry about your friend. Call me if you need anything."

I looked in her eyes and leaned over and kissed her on her forehead. "I love you, Tina," I said. Stepping back from the car, I continued to look at her, waiting for eye contact. Without looking at me she turned and quickly drove away.

As the plane traveled in a partial circle over Philly turning to the south, I saw the city I had called home for almost all of my life. *There were many memories there, both good and bad*, I thought as the powerful engines thrust the plane upward, leaving Philly behind. I was going to my new home to witness my best friend being laid to rest. Ann had asked me to eulogize Benny. How could I ever "keep it short?" I wondered as I looked out the window.

• • •

I left the Roanoke airport and drove to Benny and Ann's home. Several of Ann's friends were there. She introduced me to each of them. I had met two of them when I attended church with Benny and Ann on occasion. One of her friends looked out of place. She was much younger, probably my age I guessed. Her name was Rebecca.

After talking with Ann for a few minutes about Joshua, I was ready to leave, so I wouldn't intrude on her time with her friends. But she asked me to stay. She said she wanted to talk to me for a few minutes alone.

Thirty minutes later her friends were leaving. Rebecca was the last to go. She seemed somewhat distant but clearly saddened and in pain. After they left, Ann and I sat down in the living room of their modest home.

"Benny wanted me to ask you if you would help me with Ben's foundation," she said. "Everything we own will be finding its way into the foundation after I'm gone."

The foundation was the Benjamin Franklin Price Jr. Foundation. Benny had started it and had raised over two million dollars over the years to help fund a trauma center for head injuries at Roanoke Memorial Hospital. A large portion of the money had come directly from Benny and Ann. The foundation sponsored one of the Roanoke Valley's largest golf tournaments to raise awareness for the cause and to gather more contributions. It was hard to count how many lives had been saved by the special trauma center. I told Ann it would be my honor to help.

"There's one more item, Jack. Benny wanted me to give you this letter. He wrote it hours before he died." Ann handed me the two-page folded letter. I opened it and read:

Dear Jack,

I write this with a smile on my face. My time here is coming to a close.

I am thinking of you and your family. My one last hope and prayer is that Joshua recovers fully and your family can find common ground to begin a new life together.

We have shared many things over the past year. I have told you many times that my life was very similar to yours. I know you thought I was just saying that to help you overcome the guilt you had locked inside of you. But it was not a deception. It is the truth.

I lived a greedy, selfish life. I hurt my family. I spent too much time at work. I ignored the friends and people in my life who mattered most just to gain power and feed my ego. My life was much more despicable than you can imagine.

You would have thought years in a bamboo cell had taught me to appreciate life. But it took the loss of my son and a war inside me to change me. Finally, I let go. I began to be honest with the man in the mirror. I began to question my life.

I learned from experience, experiences I tried my best to share with you. No one is perfect in this world, but we can learn from and help everyone we meet in our life's journey. That is one of the lessons I pass on to you.

You have changed. I am so proud of you. I am sure your family is proud of you. The journey we shared was brief but held tremendous value for me. I hope it has for you.

I wish you a long, happy life. I will pray in my final moments of consciousness here on this Earth that you and your family will be together again. Never give up hope, Jack.

Do not be sad. This is not an end, but a beginning. I am the happiest man alive in my final hours. I am getting ready to see my son. I'll see you again someday, Jack. Bank on it!

Your friend,
Benny

The tears had been pouring down my cheeks from the first words. Ann had moved beside me on the couch and had her arm over my shoulder.

"He loved you, Jack, like a son," Ann said. "So do I. Benny

worried that you had put him on a pedestal; he wanted to make sure you understand that he was no different than you—just older and more experienced," Ann said. "People can forgive. When we lost Ben, we both lost touch with our lives. Benny blamed himself for Ben's death. It brought back all of the pain he had from Vietnam and the loss of his parents, especially his father. Earlier you met a person who shared much of the turmoil and pain from that time, Rebecca."

After a pause she said, "Rebecca was Benny's mistress. Benny thought he was in love with her. Benny was lost. I was lost. We lost each other. But we never gave up."

I couldn't imagine having the strength to have Rebecca in her life right now. How could she be so forgiving at a time like this?

"Rebecca had not seen Benny for twenty years, but she still loved him. I couldn't change that. She called and asked to see me. She apologized. I had already forgiven her but had never told her. She left when the affair was exposed."

"That's incredible—the way you're handling something like that from the past," I said.

"The past is the past. We both made mistakes. But love finds a way. Love is unquestionable."

I thanked Ann and told her to call me if she needed anything. The memorial service was tomorrow evening, and the funeral would follow the next morning.

"Life may not work out exactly like you think, but it has a way of rewarding us when we are doing our best," she said, pausing and reaching out to grip my hands. "Jack, never give up hope."

"I won't," I said, clutching the letter Benny had written. "I promise I won't."

43. How Are You Doing?

"HOW ARE YOU DOING?" Hearing the voice of my old friend John, I turned away from the open coffin at the end of the long line of waiting mourners. I had been expecting him and his wife earlier, but their flight from Arkansas had been a crossword puzzle of takeoffs and landings. We shook hands and in the same motion leaned forward and hugged each other. We'd been through a lot together. "You're getting too thin, Jack ole boy," he said as he looked at me with a sadness I had never seen in his eyes before. Despite failed marriages and many career challenges John had been a beacon of light for me. His humor couldn't hide the pain. He was struggling just like me.

"It's all of this Southern cookin'," I said in my deep drawl, trying to force a smile. "There ain't no Philly cheesesteak sandwiches 'round here."

He smiled and said, "See, I knew you could turn into a redneck with a little work." We both laughed. After pausing he said, "I'm sorry, Jack. I know how close he was to you. He was my friend too, and I don't know how to deal with all of this."

"He thought the world of you. You helped me leave Philly and put the two of us together here. You've helped me so much, John," I said. We both sidestepped to allow a couple to pass. "I don't know how I can ever express how much I appreciate you putting up with the old Jack Oliver—he was an ugly, despicable guy."

"Well, Jack Oliver is still ugly," he said trying to laugh. "It wasn't easy, but I have great patience. Speaking of patience, there's someone you haven't met I want to introduce you to." He turned sideways giving way to allow a beautiful brunette room to step forward in the cramped space. "This is Vivian." While I had spoken to her on the phone, I had never met her.

"It's my pleasure to finally meet you," I said. "I wish it was under different circumstances."

"I know Benny was special to both of you," she said.

"Vivian is everything I told you about and more," John said, proudly putting his arm around her waist and pulling her close. "She's the person who keeps your boy in tow."

"And that's a tough job," I said.

"Yes, it is," she said, "but I can't complain. He's the best."

Looking toward the open casket ahead John said, "Thanks sweetie, but the best man I've ever met is right up there."

• • •

We slowly made our way forward in the line.

As we stepped closer to the casket, my anxiety grew. I had avoided looking at him earlier, even though I had escorted Ann and Benny's sister and several other family members to the funeral home well before the doors opened to the public. Sensing my dread, Vivian stepped between John and me and held both of our hands.

Looking down at the remains of my best friend, I experienced a different emotion than I expected. While the pain of his passing was very real, seeing him at peace after the pain of the disease made me feel some comfort. *That's why Ann is so strong*, I thought. She had said to me, "He's at a better place—he's with Ben."

I believed it now.

• • •

The next morning I was standing at Benny's grave site. All of the memories of the life I had lived and how Benny had helped me were flowing through my mind.

The minister had finished. The music director for Benny and Ann's church had finished singing.

It was my turn to speak.

"Standing here today we mourn the passing of a great man. While we all struggle with the loss of a fellow traveler on life's journey, one who gave so much of himself to all of us here, I now understand something he said to me and perhaps many of you. 'Death is not an end but a beginning.' I mourn my loss and our loss but cherish his life of giving.

"I find myself in this moment, now, searching for the proper words to celebrate Benny's life. I want to take a moment and speak for what he did for me.

"Benny saved my life. His kindness and generosity were as real as if he had dove into a river and fought a raging current to rescue me. In many ways, that is what happened. He gave of himself and shared his life to teach me how to learn from experience, both good and bad. He taught me to honor the life of every other person and to respect their place in the world as much as my own. For Benny, this was our responsibility as humans. As he said to me, 'We're in this world both alone and together—it's up to each of us to share our lives to make the world a better place.' I know he did his part.

"He told me, 'Life is for living—enjoy every moment.' Benny's enthusiasm for life, living every moment like it was his last, was an inspiration to all of us. I know we can all say that spending even a few moments with Benny was time well spent. I will cherish all of my moments with him.

"One of the last things Benny said to his wife Ann was for me to 'keep it short.' So in closing, I will do my best to say what is in my heart.

"Somewhere right now, Benny is smiling, the reward for a life of giving. He is with Ben, probably planning on a jog or a hike through the woods and then some fishing.

"He said, 'Death can be our greatest teacher.' I now realize he was so right. When the sum total of what we have given in this life is examined, a life lived to its fullest never dies. What Benny gave to us will never die.

"He promised me I would see him again. I believe him. Until that day, I will do my best to give to others and to live the best life I possibly can, every moment of every day. I know you can hear these words, Benny. While life should be lived by questions, there is an answer evidenced here today. Why are we here? We're here to thank you. We thank you for the life you shared. We miss you Benjamin Franklin Price. We all take comfort knowing that you will greet us when we begin again. I look forward to seeing you in that new beginning, my friend."

As I turned to step back, the vocalist began singing "Amazing Grace" accompanied by a single violin. Ann hugged me and held me for a moment.

She whispered, "This is a new beginning, Jack. Your family is here."

I looked up and saw Tina standing behind Joshua's wheelchair. They were wiping away tears. Jessica was looking at me and as we made eye contact I could read her lips as she said, "I love you, Daddy."

· · ·

That night my family visited my condo for the first time. Tina told me why she had decided to come to Virginia. She handed me a folded piece of paper. It was a letter Benny had sent to Tina. It was dated the day he died.

Dear Tina,

I apologize for never having the pleasure of meeting you. Jack has talked about you, Jessica, and Joshua so much I truly feel like I know all of you.

With great hopefulness I pray Joshua is recovering from the injuries he suffered in the car wreck. Ann and I have prayed constantly for his speedy and healthy recovery.

Writing this letter is something I would not normally do, but given the circumstances, I feel compelled to impose.

I am now but a short time from passing away from this world. In the past year I have shared my life with Jack, a person I have seen change and grow.

Jack is a good person. He was very much like me, working too much and spending the precious time we are given in life at a job instead of with his family. He has realized his errors, as I did, and learned from his experiences. He has made himself into a much different and more giving person. I am proud of him and think of him as if he was my son.

As one of my last acts on this planet I ask with all humility that you would give Jack an opportunity to show you how he has changed. I do this not to attempt to manipulate or push you into something you may not feel comfortable doing, but with a more selfish purpose. I would enjoy meeting you and the children before I leave. What happens after that will be up to you and Jack.

Since my time is limited, I hope you forgive me for my urgent plea. I am enclosing airline tickets for you, Jessica, and Joshua.

I look forward to meeting you, if not now, some other time.

Sincerely,
Benny

"I didn't know," I said. "Cause and effect." I leaned forward and cupped my hands over my eyes. It was true. Even though he was gone he still had an effect. As we sat in silence on the couch together I felt Tina's hand touch me on my back. I dropped my hands and turned my head to look at her.

"Benny said in his letter 'To live is to learn,' and I've learned a lot," she said, lifting her head upward and slowly turning to face me. Our eyes met.

"So have I," I said, reaching down and taking her hands in mine. "I've changed. Can I prove it to you?"

"You don't have to—I know it."

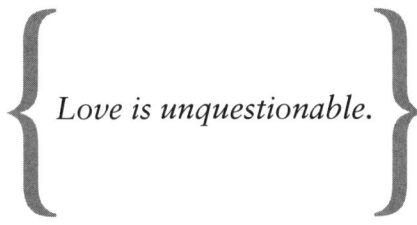

Love is unquestionable.

—BENJAMIN FRANKLIN PRICE AND
ELIZABETH ANN PRICE

EPILOGUE:

What Is Love?

I T ' S   N O W   J U L Y . O V E R a year has passed since Benny began a new journey.

Tina and the kids love the Roanoke Valley. Jessica will begin graduate school at Virginia Tech next month. She is planning to be a psychologist. Joshua was accepted at Roanoke College and will begin his freshman year in a few weeks. He wants to be a banker.

They're both happy.

Tina is teaching kindergarten at South Salem Grade School. She has run two marathons and is preparing for the Boston Marathon.

She is happy.

Tina and I exchanged marriage vows for the second time a year ago tomorrow. We are now a happy family.

What about me? I am first a husband and a father. I also happen to be a banker, trying my best to keep my promise to Benny to keep Citizens Bank thriving and part of the community. Ann and I continue to work together on the Benjamin Franklin Price Jr. Foundation. Tina, Jessica, and Joshua are also very involved with the foundation.

Not that it matters much, but Merchants Bank was sold. Andrew Ledger abruptly retired and remains under indictments for several purported crimes, including fraudulently misleading investors by reporting overstated earnings. Additional indictments were handed out to three of the corporation's top executives. "Cause and effect" as I can almost hear Benny say it.

Where am I? I now stand at the edge of the gorge looking down on the river far below. The trek up the mountain is something I now do often to remind myself of what fear can do. I've shared the hike with Tina, Jessica, and Joshua and told them about Benny. Benny was right, it wasn't a fear of heights that held me back; it was a fear of falling. I'm not afraid of falling, now.

"The view is incredible, but you have to look over the edge to appreciate it," Benny had said to me. As I stand looking down into the gorge, another memory resurfaces. I remember rafting with Benny in the wild white water far below.

One of the rafts near us had capsized. Since I was not a good swimmer, I was in a panic. Benny leaned over and yelled so I could hear him over the rapids, "Don't be afraid! The safest thing is to lean out and row—or we will all get wet!"

I listened and responded. I quit hanging on and began to row, leaning out of the boat to reach the water. We never capsized.

As I start my hike back down the mountain, I look past the heavy summer foliage into the bright blue sky knowing my friend is aware that I finally let go and began living. It took a lot of time and practice to quit hanging on, but I did it—with his help. I live *now*. The world that surrounds me may be turbulent, but just like navigating the white water, I have learned to row and do my part. Not just for me, but for everyone.

I'm happy.

While I continue to question my life to keep me on course, being with my family reminds me of something Benny and Ann had both said to me.

"*Love is unquestionable.*"

They were right.